Psychology: The Key Concepts is a comprehensive overview of 200 concepts central to any understanding of modern Psychology. Addressing both academic and practical uses of Psychology in settings such as the clinic, the classroom and human resources, topics covered include:

- Learning
- Memory
- Psychometrics
- Motivation and emotion
- Perception
- Gender

Fully cross-referenced with ideas for further reading and links to the most useful Psychology sites on the web, this is an excellent guide for students on introductory courses at all levels as well as anyone interested in the workings of the human mind.

Graham Richards was recently Director of the British Psychological Society's History of Psychology Centre and Professor of History of Psychology at Staffordshire University. His previous publications include *Putting Psychology in its Place* (2nd edition 1992), *'Race', Racism and Psychology: Towards a Reflexive History* (2001) and *On Psychological Language* (1989), all published by Psychology Press.

ALSO AVAILABLE FROM ROUTLEDGE

Fifty Key Thinkers in Psychology
Noel Sheehy

Sport and Exercise Psychology
The Key Concepts (2nd edition)
Ellis Cashmore

Psycholinguistics
The Key Concepts
John Field

PSYCHOLOGY

The Key Concepts

Graham Richards

LONDON AND NEW YORK

First published 2009
by Routledge
2 Park Square, Milton Park, Oxon OX14 4RN

Simultaneously published in the USA and Canada
by Routledge
270 Madison Avenue, New York NY10016

Routledge is an imprint of the Taylor & Francis Group, an informa business

© 2009 Graham Richards

Typeset in Bembo by
Taylor & Francis Books
Printed and bound in Great Britain by
TJ International Ltd, Padstow, Cornwall

British Library Cataloguing in Publication Data
A catalogue record for this book is available from the British Library

Library of Congress Cataloging in Publication Data
Richards, Graham.
Psychology : the key concepts / Graham Richards.
p. cm.
Includes bibliographical references and index.
1. Psychology–Dictionaries. I. Title.
BF31.R53 2008
150.3–dc22

ISBN 978-0-415-43200-9 (hbk)
ISBN 978-0-415-43201-6 (pbk)
ISBN 978-0-203-89293-0 (ebk)

For my grandchildren Reuben and Eva
for whom this book will be an historical curiosity by the
time they are old enough to be interested.

CONTENTS

LIST OF CONCEPTS

Deconstruction
Degenerationism
Dementia praecox
Depression
Development
Discourse analysis
Displacement activity
Dissociation
Divergent thinking
Double bind
Drive
DSM
Dualism
Dyslexia
Dyspraxia
Ecological Psychology
EEG (electroenecephalograph)
Emotion
Empathy
Empiricism
Encounter groups
Epiphenomenalism
Ergonomics
ESP (extrasensory perception)
Ethnocentrism
Ethology
Eugenics
Evolutionary Psychology
Existentialism
Experimenter effect(s)
Extraversion/introversion
Extrinsic vs intrinsic
Factor analysis
Faculty Psychology
False consciousness
False memory syndrome
Family therapy
Fatigue
Fear of failure
Fear of strangers
Feeling
Field dependency

Flicker fusion
Folk Psychology
Frustration
Functionalism
Game theory
Gestalt Psychology
Group therapy/psychotherapy
Growth movement
Halo effect
Handedness
Hedonic tone
Hormic psychology
Humanistic Psychology
Hypnagogia
Hypnosis
Hypothetical construct
Hysteria
Idealism
Identification
Identity
Idiographic and nomothetic
Imagery
Implicit personality theory (IPT)
Individual Psychology
   (Adlerian)
Information processing
Inhibition
Inspection time
Instinct
Intelligence
Intentionality and intensionality
Interpersonal attraction
Intervening variable
Just world belief/hypothesis
Kin selection
Kinesics
Language acquisition device
Lateralisation of function
Leadership
Learning and learning theory
Learning difficulties
Level of aspiration (LoA)

Psychophysics
Psychosis
Psychosomatic
Psychotherapy
Psychotropic
Q-sort
Qualia
Qualitative methods
Racism
Reaction time (RT)
Recency effect
Redintegration
Reductionism
Reflexivity
Reification
Reliability
Religion, psychology of
REM (rapid eye movement)
Repetition compulsion
Representationalism
Restricted vs elaborated code
Reticular activating system (RAS)
Reversal theory
Rhetoric
Role/role theory
Rorschach test
Scaling
Schema
Schizogenic
Schizophrenia
Schizothymic
Schools of Psychology
Self
Semantics
Sensory deprivation
Sexuality and gender
Sibling rivalry
Signal detection theory (SDT)
Situationism

Sleeper effect
Social cognition
Social constructionism
Social Darwinism
Social facilitation
Social identity theory
Social representations
Sociobiology
Somatisation
Somatotypes
Stereotyping
Stress
Stroop effect
Structuralism
Subliminal perception
Suggestion, suggestibility
Synaesthesia
Synapse
Tachistoscope
Telekinesis
Temperament
Thematic apperception test (TAT)
Theory of mind (TOM)
Theriomorphism
Top-down and bottom-up
Topological Psychology
Trait
Unconscious
Validity
Vigilance
Visual illusions
Visual search
Whorfian hypothesis
Will
Word association
Zeigarnik effect
Zone of proximal development (ZPD)

PREFACE

This book is intended for Psychology students at Advanced GCSE and undergraduate degree course levels who need a quick guide to the meanings of the main (and occasionally the not-so-main) psychological concepts and an indication of where they can pursue them further. Hopefully it may also be useful for anyone else venturing into Psychology for the first time. Given the sometimes controversial nature of psychological concepts, it would be misleading to pretend that entirely objective or neutral expositions of their meanings and significance can always be provided. While striving to be as fair and balanced as possible, I have also on occasion felt it necessary to indicate my own position. But if Psychology tells us anything, it is that the notion that *anyone* can be purely 'objective' about such matters is an illusion, so it is better to be upfront than to pretend that what one is saying is totally impartial. I have also continued the practice adopted in my other writings (and now being occasionally adopted by others) of differentiating Psychology/Psychological (capitalised) from psychology/psychological (uncapitalised). The former refer to the discipline and the latter to its subject matter. This is not entirely unproblematic but simplifies discussion of the relationship between the two and also helps avoid ambiguity.

Identifying the key concepts in Psychology presents numerous difficulties. In the first place, psychologists use many words common in everyday language, while frequently giving these a technical spin (e.g. 'personality') and, conversely, many psychological terms have entered everyday language and to some extent lost their technical character (e.g. 'ego'). A second problem is that Psychology overlaps with a number of other disciplines such as physiology, sociology and linguistics. Concepts drawn from these can thus become common in some specialist fields of Psychology too (e.g. 'reticular activating system'). In the present work, such terms have been omitted as far as possible but a few necessarily remain. More seriously perhaps, Psychology is, unlike most physical sciences, extremely diverse not only in what it studies but also theoretically. It has thus never achieved a discipline-wide consensus on even its core technical vocabulary. Consequently, many concepts are controversial and we often encounter technical terms with very similar meanings. Meanings and connotations can also shift over time in a way which is uncommon in the physical sciences, so it has sometimes been necessary to note these. Finally, it should be stressed that the relative lengths of entries does not necessarily reflect their importance as concepts. Explaining some major concepts is fairly straightforward, some less commonly used ones require more extended unravelling. Also of course it is impossible to claim an Olympian grasp of all fields of Psychology, and those regarding which the author is more knowledgeable may inevitably receive greater, or more expert, coverage than others.

A note on references

Most, if not all, entries are followed by references. These are of two main kinds. First are all those cited in the entry, second, I have tried to identify the most recent reliable academic works on the topic in question and occasionally more popular introductions which can serve as initial further reading. In addition, I have also noted (sometimes in the entry itself) relevant websites. It should not, however, be assumed that only recently published works are valuable, and regarding topics which are no longer flourishing as once they did, older books are often the best initial sources for further reading. In some cases, the reference lists could be expanded many times over and, to a greater or lesser degree, most are necessarily selective. Where no references are provided, this is usually because (1) they are included in a cross-referenced main entry or (2) the entry is of a kind which does not warrant them, such as a simple exposition of the meaning of a word. Locating accessible references can also be difficult for topics which have not received book-length treatment, in these cases, journal papers are cited.

A note on web resources

Quality of resources and ease of locating relevant sites vary tremendously when dealing with Psychology. It has to be conceded that as far as Psychological topics are concerned (as opposed to living politicians!), Wikipedia is often very useful and reliable, but as a general principle one should never rely on a single site alone if possible. One good point of departure is www.psychology.org which provides links to Psychology-relevant sites of all kinds. There are a number of on-line Psychology dictionaries but many of these are confined to two- or three-line entries, unreferenced, and quite useless. The better ones include allpsych.com/dictionary/, psychology.about. com and webref.org/psychology. Academically, the best site for many topics is plato.stanford.edu., and if an entry from this occurs in a Google search list, it is probably the most advisable first port of call. High Beam Encyclopedia (on www.encyclopedia.com) can be useful once you get the hang of it and includes references to recent relevant publications on topics. Another route to take is via the British Psychological Society (www.bps.org.uk) and the American Psychological Association (www. apa.org) sites which can send you directly to the sites of their internal Divisions and Sections (via the Member Networks option on the BPS home page), these in turn often provide links to others relevant to specific topics which they consider reliable – this may be a little tortuous but does offer a certain level of assurance. Society and organisation sites may commonly be found related to particular theories, psychotherapies and schools and can similarly serve as good points of departure. There are also many sites devoted to particular eminent individuals which can be more extensive, if more partisan, than the Wikipedia entries on them. At the end of the day, hard copy texts remain more convenient and reliable (or at least easier to evaluate) than websites, and web-based research can at present still only serve as a complementary supplement to these.

A note on the text

In the main entries, upper case words in **bold** signify concepts which have main entries, lower case words in *italics* are either sub-entry headers or additional concepts listed in the Index.

ACKNOWLEDGEMENTS

I would particularly like to thank Geoff Bunn, Alan Collins and Elizabeth Valentine for their feedback on initial drafts of this work. Without their help I fear the incidence of howlers would have been quite embarrassing, while their suggestions regarding references and entry content have been quite invaluable. And, of course, Maura has provided her usual unstinting support.

PSYCHOLOGY

The Key Concepts

ACHIEVEMENT MOTIVATION (N-ACH)

American personality theorist Henry Murray, writing in the late 1930s, identified a large number of 'needs', among them *need for achievement* usually referred to as *N-Ach*. This particular 'need' soon attracted more attention than most of the others, leading to an extensive literature on 'Achievement Motivation' from the late 1950s into the early 1960s and including the creation of methods of assessing or measuring 'N-Ach' ('n.Ach' and 'N.ach' being occasional slight variations) beyond Murray's own **thematic apperception test** method. This research genre became, for a while, a significant strand in US Social Psychology with attempts made to apply it to ancient and non-European cultures, using e.g. decorative design motifs as indices of level of N-Ach on the basis that certain design features such as strong ascending lines signified higher levels than others, such as circles or descending lines. This particular project was highly speculative and short-lived. A more enduring consequence was the devising of a number of **psychometric** techniques for assessing not only N-Ach itself but related issues such as **fear of failure** and, indeed, fear of success. These tests often took the form of tests of *Level of Aspiration (LoA)*, requiring those taking them to estimate, for example, the number of simple faces they would be able to draw in a minute (filling in a sheet of circles). This led to the identification of phenomena such as *under-achievement*. A series, *Advances in Motivation and Achievement*, continued to be issued into the 1990s (see Urdan, 1999).

References and further reading

Atkinson, J.W. and Feather, N.T. (eds) (1966) *A Theory of Achievement Motivation*, New York: John Wiley & Sons, Ltd.

Eccles, J. (2002) *Development of Achievement Motivation*, New York: Elsevier.

McClelland, D.C. (1955) *Studies in Motivation*, New York: Appleton Century-Crofts.

Smith, C.P. (ed.) (1992) *Motivation and Personality: Handbook of Thematic Content Analysis*, Cambridge: Cambridge University Press.

Urdan, T.C. (ed.) (1999) *The Role of Context, Advances in Motivation and Achievement*, New York: Elsevier.

ACQUIESCENCE RESPONSE SET (OR ACQUIESCENCE BIAS)

The tendency of people to answer in the affirmative or agree with statements presented in questionnaires. Thus someone might agree with both 'Sexual immorality is very widespread these days' and 'The level of sexual immorality today is often greatly exaggerated'. This means that questionnaire items should be carefully counterbalanced in the direction in which they are scored. Hence, in a questionnaire about attitudes towards green issues, items such as 'I always try to buy organic food' (agree scoring positive) and 'Global warming has been greatly exaggerated' (disagree scoring positive) should be equally represented. The problem began receiving wide attention in the early 1960s in critiques of the *F-scale* devised to assess **authoritarianism**, such as N.H. Berkowitz and G.H. Wolkon (1964). In the 1970s and 1980s, it was the focus of an extensive research programme by Australian psychologist J.J. Ray (see jonjayray.fortunecity.com/acquies.html) and continues to concern psychometricians.

Reference

Berkowitz, N.H. and Wolkon, G.H. (1964) 'A Forced Choice Form of the "F" Scale-free of Acquiescent Response Set', *Sociometry*, 27: 54–65.

ADHD (ATTENTION DEFICIT HYPERACTIVITY DISORDER)

Syndrome characterised by inability to sustain attention, high levels of impulsive physical activity and difficulty in remaining seated or still for any length of time. The term *ADD* (Attention Deficit Disorder) is used in cases where hyperactivity is absent. Usually diagnosed in young children, since it affects school performance and can be disruptive in the classroom, it may persist into adulthood. The term only became widely used during the 1980s but case descriptions corresponding to the condition can be found in psychiatric, educational and other writings since the ancient Greeks. Previous, apparently synonymous, terms included 'hyperkinetic reaction of childhood' and 'hyperactive child syndrome'. In the past two decades, diagnosis of ADHD has risen dramatically, but how far this signifies a real increase in prevalence is unclear. The most popular treatment is the drug Ritalin, with Dexedrine sometimes being used as an alternative. ADHD is a controversial category. The respective roles of genetic causes, social environment and diet remain unclear, and it is widely considered to refer to the extreme end of the normal range of temperamental variability rather than to a genuinely distinct medical condition. Diagnosis can also be affected by other factors, such as being used by mental health professionals in borderline cases to ensure family access to child and family mental health services when this is felt desirable on broader grounds. Levels of caretaker and teacher tolerance of, and skill in dealing with, ADHD symptoms also vary widely and will affect the likelihood of the ADHD label being bestowed. There are indeed parents who, believing Ritalin to be a panacea for their child-management difficulties, pressurise professionals into diagnosing their child as ADHD. Some critics argue that the apparent rise in ADHD partly at least reflects the highly arousing and fast-moving entertainment stimuli (such as TV cartoons and computer games) to which children now have high exposure levels, while dietary factors, in particular, food additives, have also been blamed. While ADHD symptoms can clearly reach genuinely pathological levels, the ever-widening use of the label may be an instance of 'medicalisation' or 'pathologising' of behaviour hitherto considered unremarkable – a kind of technical-sounding way of describing children who fidget and will not concentrate on the adult-determined matter at hand.

References and further reading

Gill, M., Bellgrove, M. and Fitzgerald, M. (2007) *Handbook of Attention Deficit Hyperactivity Disorder*, Chichester: John Wiley & Sons, Ltd.
Stead, J., Cohen, D. and Lloyd, G. (2006) *Critical New Perspectives on ADHD*, London: Routledge.

ADOLESCENCE

The period between the onset of puberty and attainment of adulthood, i.e. approximately 13–19 years of age. The word itself is surprisingly old, dating to the fifteenth century. While this now seems to us a natural period of both physiological and psychological transition, rarely endured without some anxiety and confusion, its psychological importance only began receiving serious attention in the late nineteenth century with the general extension of education into the early teens. Previous discourse on the topic (which was extensive) usually refered to 'youth'. The term 'teenage' was coined in the USA in 1921 and 'teenager' as late as 1941. It was only in the late twentieth century that adolescent sub-cultures emerged and acquired their current commercial significance. There is a clear sense then in which, as currently understood, adolescence could be considered to be a socially constructed (**social constructionism**) phenomenon. The literature on the role of adolescence in psychological development and associated psychological problems is now huge. For Erik H. Erikson (1950, 1964) it was the sixth of eight developmental stages, marked by ego-confusion, the felt need to become socially competent and general emotional upheaval. Adolescents obviously experience considerable *role conflict* (see **role theory**) being required to act as both adults and children, or be both independent and dependent, in ways which can seem quite arbitrary. The upper age-limit for adolescence has, for some sociological purposes, risen to 21 or even 25 due to the growth of higher education. This would have greatly baffled our ancestors, for whom adolescence, or 'youth', was probably over by 17 despite 21 being the legal age of maturity. For a recent overview of the topic, see Lerner and Steinberg (2004).

References

Erikson, E.H. ([1950] 1965) *Childhood and Society*, Harmondsworth: Penguin.
—— (1968) *Identity, Youth and Crisis*, New York: W. W. Norton.
Lerner, R.M. and Steinberg, L.D. (2004) *Handbook of Adolescence*, 2nd edn, Chichester: John Wiley & Sons, Ltd.

AFFECT

Basically a more neutral and objective sounding synonym for '**emotion**'. Hence 'an affective response' refers to an emotional response and 'absence of affect' to lack of emotion. Its relationship to the word 'affectionate' is obvious. Unfortunately, due to their similarity, 'affect' and 'effect' are among the regularly confused words in undergraduate Psychology essays. Remember, 'affect' is how you are 'affected' *by* something, an 'effect' is something you bring about (as in 'put into effect') or the result of something ('cause and effect'). So displaying an 'affect' may be the 'effect' which someone's behaviour has on you. 'Affect' is in a sense passive, 'effect' active.

AGENCY

The power to intentionally initiate events (see also **intentionality**). It is, however, a peculiarly complex concept since the need for it is closely bound up with the need in human affairs to ascribe responsibility and accountability. It also appears logically necessary that agents, those exercising agency, should be conscious. The question then arises whether 'agency' is really an 'objective' or 'empirical' property, or if its conceptual function is not rather the moral one of serving the management of human social life. Naturally, then, it is closely connected to the 'free will' debate. One area where it has become especially contentious is **AI (artificial intelligence)**. Computing and robotic engineering has now reached a level where human artefacts do indeed display many capabilities once considered uniquely human. At what point can we legitimately ascribe 'agency' or, which amounts to much the same thing, 'personhood' and 'consciousness' to such artefacts? Where, in short, does the agency for their actions lie? And how can it be empirically demonstrated (if at all)? Sceptics can argue that, however long and convoluted the link between humans who create machines and the behaviour of these machines, agency still rests with humans. It is they who are doing things *with* the machines, and the machines' status is no different, logically, from e.g. a hand-pushed lawn-mower. Their opponents will argue that one has to decide operationally and that if a point is reached where the output of a machine and a human become indistinguishable, then we can rightly ascribe agency (and all that goes with it) to the machine. The criterion often invoked for this is the *Turing Test*, proposed by Alan Turing in 1950. A computer has 'passed' the Turing Test if a person using some kind of interactive terminal cannot differentiate its output from that of a human linked to a similar terminal. There are, however, a host of logical and philosophical problems with this which we cannot explore here. One very important critique of the Turing Test, a common point of reference for subsequent debate, was made by J. R. Searle (Searle, 1980), who put forward what is known as 'the Chinese Room Argument'. The present author is, for the record, in the sceptical camp, but it is perhaps worth noting that were a 'robot' or 'android' created which displayed the full range of human characteristics – including emotions, social relationships and personal opinions – one would really be back at square one. Yes, one would have created a 'person' by non-biological means, but their psychological functioning would be just as unique and opaque as anyone else's.

References

Searle, J. R. (1980) 'Mind, Brains and Programs', *Behavioral and Brain Sciences*, 3(3): 417–57.

Turing A.M. (1950) 'Computing Machinery and Intelligence', *Mind*, 49: 433–60.

AGGRESSION

Aggression has long been high on Psychology's agenda for obvious reasons, and most Psychological theories have offered their distinct explanations of it. There is a serious conceptual or linguistic problem with 'aggression' in that it is used to describe behaviours of widely differing kinds, having in common only that they involve some form of actual or threatened violence, ranging from a heated argument and a drunken pub brawl, to a door kicked in frustration and a high altitude bombing raid. One well-known Psychological suggestion was the *'frustration-aggression hypothesis'* (Dollard *et al.*, 1939) – aggression was caused by frustration. This is undoubtedly true in many cases, but in others frustration is not obviously involved at all. In **ethology**, animal aggression is understood as variously related to territorial defence, establishing and maintaining social hierarchies, competition for mates and disciplining of young as well as predation. Equivalents of all these may be found in human behaviour. In addition, the most dangerous mode of human aggression is what might be termed 'instrumental' aggression. Unlike one-on-one physical fights, which involve unsustainably high levels of arousal and can usually be terminated by one party submitting, modern wars are largely fought with 'instrumental' methods such as firing missiles from a great distance. These require quite the opposite psychological states in those deploying them – low arousal, calm attention, high self-discipline and sustained engagement, and if opponents wish to submit they may be hard put to let their attackers know! A second way in which the term can be misleading is that, when used as a noun, it gives the impression of referring to a thing-like entity or principle, such as an 'aggression instinct' perhaps. More correctly it should be understood as 'adjectival' or 'adverbial', referring to a style or mode of behaving. Some people have an aggressive personality style, for example, we may do anything from pruning a tree to driving to ordering meals in restaurants *aggressively*. Psychology and ethology have undoubtedly illuminated many facets of how, when and why aggressive behaviour occurs, but the notion of aggression as a unitary psychological phenomenon has been hard to shake off. A final cautionary point is that psychologists may be tempted to offer Psychological explanations for aggression which is more appropriately accounted for at a sociological level. This can let those with socio-political power off the hook. And sometimes to engage in aggression is simply to be conforming to a social norm. Again, if faced with the choice of fighting and maybe surviving or not fighting and certainly being shot for cowardice, 'aggression' as such plays no obvious psychological role in someone's deciding to take the first option. Recent research has focused mainly on aggression in girls, adolescent aggression, aggression in sport and inter-group aggression.

References and further reading

Dollard, J., Doob, L., Miller, N., Mowrer, D. and Sears, R. (1939) 'Symposium on the Frustration-Aggression Hypothesis', *Psychological Review*, 38: 337–66.
Flannery, D. (ed.) (2007) *The Cambridge Handbook of Violent Behaviour and Aggression*, Cambridge: Cambridge University Press.
Lorenz, K. (1966) *On Aggression*, London: Methuen.
Morgan, J.P. (2006) *Perspectives on the Psychology of Aggression*, New York: Nova Science.

AGNOSIA

From the Greek word meaning 'not knowing'. A general term for a number of conditions resulting from brain damage in which sufferers are unable to understand the meaning of objects and events in their surroundings. These typically involve visual perception – hence someone may be unable to understand complete scenes although they can identify individual elements ('simultanagnosia'), may know the function of an object (such as a table knife) if asked but be unable to recognise one ('associative agnosia') – or conversely be able to recognise an object but not know what it is for. Sufferers from 'mirror agnosia' are impaired in one half only of their visual field, while 'finger agnosia' refers to inability to differentiate between one's fingers, and 'prosopagnosia' is a functionally specific inability to recognise faces. Most agnosias seem to involve either a disruption in the connections between semantic memory and sensory input or disruption of sensory (usually visual) processing itself ('apperceptive agnosia'). For a fascinating account of agnosia, see Sacks (1985), now many times reprinted.

References and further reading

Farah, M.J. (2004) *Visual Agnosia*, Cambridge, MA: MIT Press.
Sacks, O. (1985) *The Man who Mistook his Wife for a Hat and Other Clinical Tales*, New York: Summit Books.

AI (ARTIFICIAL INTELLIGENCE)

General term for the computer simulation of intelligent human performance and the development of programmes which achieve this. Modern AI arguably began with Newell, Shaw and Simon (1958) and it has formed a central strand in **Cognitive Psychology** ever since. The range of human abilities and psychological traits which it is now possible to simulate is huge: from neurosis to language comprehension, creativity to 'scientific discovery'. And of course in many respects computers can far exceed human capacities, especially where reasoning, logic and mathematical calculations are concerned. The literature on this is vast, much of it more properly classified as 'computer science' than Psychology. Two major traditions have arisen in AI, 'Computationism' and **connectionism**, including **parallel distributed processing (PDP)**. In interpreting the broader significance of these developments, a number of deeper conceptual issues have surfaced, or resurfaced, notably relating to the cluster of inter-woven concepts of **agency,** free will, creativity, consciousness and 'personhood'. For a recent overview, see Boden (2006b).

References and further reading

Boden, M.A. (2006a) *Computational Models of Mind: Computational Approaches in Theoretical Psychology*, Cambridge: Cambridge University Press.
—— (2006b) *Mind as Machine*, Oxford: Oxford University Press.
Newell, A., Shaw, J.C. and Simon, H.A. (1958) ' Elements of a Theory of Human Problem Solving', *Psychological Review*, 65(3): 151–66.

ALEXANDER TECHNIQUE

Devised by F.M. Alexander (1869–1955), the Alexander Technique is a fusion of psychological and behavioural physiological methods into a holistic educational system. Alexander, originally an actor, had laid the foundations of this by around 1900 and achieved increasing success during the 1920s and 1930s. It is now well established and widely respected as an approach within physiotherapy and psychotherapy, although has always operated more in parallel with mainstream psychotherapy and counselling than as a school within it. The technique focuses very much on how bodily movement and posture interact with thinking and feeling, usually taking the form of a one-on-one educational programme, although group work is also used. It has been most applied in the performing arts, sport and music as a way of enhancing the efficiency and simplicity of bodily movement, increasing stamina and overcoming creative blocks. More generally, it apparently works well as a method of eliminating bad behavioural habits and re-educating the motor co-ordination system. Medically, it is widely accepted to have an important role as a complementary technique for pain relief, mobility problems and recovery from physical injury, although its efficacy in some of these contexts has been contested. While, like most psychotherapeutic systems, it has had a few over-evangelical exponents, by and large, the Alexander Technique has avoided a controversial high public profile. This is partly due to its early origins and partly to the character of Alexander's own numerous writings. Alexander (1931) was one of the most influential of several works he published during the 1920s and 1930s. Alexander was, except for a few years in the early 1940s, based in London. Among his greatest fans was the American philosopher, John Dewey.

References and further reading

Alexander, F.M. (1931) *The Use of the Self*, London: Methuen.
Bowden, G.C. (1965) *F. Matthias Alexander and the Creative Advance of the Individual*, London: L.N. Fowler.
Drake, J. (1993) *Thorson's Introductory Guide to the Alexander Technique*, New York: HarperCollins.
Langford, E. (2004) *Only Connect: Reflections on Teaching the Alexander Technique*, Louvain: Alexandertechnik Centrum.

Useful website

The website for the international 'Alexander Technique Centre' is: www.alexandertechniquecentre.be/engels/index.htm

ALIENATION

This term was originally introduced in Karl Marx's early work, but only became widely used during the mid-twentieth century. It refers primarily to a form of psychological **dissociation** in which the individual's life-style cannot satisfy or serve their central psychological needs, due in part to their lack of autonomous control over it leading to a feeling of disconnection from their social world. A classic example is the effects of monotonous routinised assembly-line factory work, but it may also apply more generally to circumstances in which the individual feels socially powerless. Those in such situations become unable to identify with the concerns and interests of society at large, resulting in profound psychological isolation. In the post-Second World War period, the concept was widely used by existentialist thinkers (see **existentialism**) as well as those on the left, and also enjoyed a vogue in more mainstream Social Psychology and Sociology. While it has entered everyday language in expressions such as 'feeling alienated', one's impression is that it is now less commonly used in a technical sense. It is closely related to **anomie**, although this has a more distinctly sociological meaning.

References and further reading

Meszaros, I. (1986) *Marx's Theory of Alienation*, London: Merlin Press.
Parker, I. (2007) *Revolution in Psychology: Alienation to Emancipation*, London: Pluto Press.
Price-Laporte, R.S. and Claudewell, S.Y. (eds) (1976) *Alienation in Contemporary Society*, New York: Praeger.

ALTRUISM

Helping others with no expectation of personal reward or benefit. During the 1980s, the topic became a central bone of contention in the wider controversy over the applicability of **sociobiology** to human behaviour. For sociobiologists and proponents of **Evolutionary Psychology**, altruism appeared paradoxical since it seemed to involve behaving in a way which had no benefit to the altruist and could even risk their survival or reproductive chances. The American sociobiologist Robert Trivers (1971) had previously produced a theory related to earlier work on *inclusive fitness* by W.D. Hamilton (see also sociobiology), in which he argued that altruism was actually of covert benefit to the altruist and that hence true selfless altruism was a myth (Trivers, 1971). He introduced the phrase 'reciprocal altruism' to describe this evolutionarily beneficial version, which many would consider oxymoronic, the essence of altruism as usually understood being precisely that it is not reciprocal. There were, however, a substantial number of difficulties with Trivers's analysis suggesting that while perhaps valid for apparent altruism in non-human species, its applicability to humans was highly problematic. Some of these were conceptual. For example, by defining altruism in terms of the consequences of the act, rather than the individual's motivation, its identification became in effect impossible,

because these consequences could extend and oscillate between beneficial and damaging throughout a person's subsequent life-span. Others
were theoretical, for example, a conflation between behaviour in which
there was evident intrinsic cost to the altruist (self-sacrifice in battle being
a favourite and long-standing example) and behaviour in which cost
only occurred if the altruistic act failed (e.g. drowning while attempting
to save another swimmer in difficulties). More empirically, much
common, almost routine, altruistic behaviour such as giving a small sum
of money to a busker or helping somebody up stairs with a heavy
suitcase, involves neither significant overt cost nor identifiable covert
personal benefit. Social psychologists could also oppose the sociobiological account on the grounds that human altruism is governed by
a multitude of factors unrelated to genetics. While it is almost true by
definition that humans must have a genetic capacity for altruism and
that this has been advantageous for the species, this is probably best
viewed as a necessary but insufficient condition for explaining any specific altruistic act. It is also plausible that its evolutionary roots lie most
specifically in child-rearing behaviour. In addressing the difficulties with
Trivers's original theory, later writers such as Lumsden and Wilson
(1981) rather back-tracked, hypothesising the existence of 'altruism
systems' and reincorporating motivational factors, but the upshot was
that this progressively reduced the direct role of genes themselves by
comparison with environmental, social and biographical factors. The
topic continues to figure prominently in debates regarding sociobiology
and Evolutionary Psychology. See Richards (1987: Chap. 5, Part B) for
a more extended discussion. For a recent review of the issue, see Barber
(2004), which, while remaining committed to the evolutionary
approach, has abandoned the earlier 'altruism is a myth' line.

References and further reading

Barber, N. (2004) *Kindness in a Cruel World: The Evolution of Altruism*, New
York: Prometheus Books.
Lumsden, C. J. and Wilson, E.O. (1981) *Genes, Minds, and Culture*, Cambridge,
MA: Harvard University Press.
Richards, G. (1987) *Human Evolution: An Introduction to the Behavioural
Sciences*, London: Routledge.
Ridley, M. (1996) *The Origins of Virtue: Human Instincts and the Evolution of
Cooperation*, London: Penguin Books.
Sober, E. and Wilson, D.S. (1998) *Unto Others: The Evolution and Psychology
of Unselfish Behavior*, Cambridge, MA: Harvard University Press.
Trivers, R.L. (1971) 'The Evolution of Reciprocal Altruism', *Quarterly Review
of Biology*, 46: 35–57.

ANALYSIS OF VARIANCE (ANOVA)

Statistical method for analysing the respective contributions of variables (usually 2 or 3) to the variance in the data. Given two sets of scores, e.g. (a) 10, 10, 10, 10, 10, 10 and (b) 12, 12, 12, 12, 12, 12, it is intuitively obvious that all the variance is due to the sets (of which there may of course be more than two), if they were: 10, 12, 10, 12, 10, 12 and 10, 12, 10, 12, 10, 12, it equally obvious that it is all 'internal', if they were 10, 11, 10, 11, 10, 11 and 11, 12, 11, 12, 11, 12, then half is obviously due to the sets and half internal. More subtly, if they were 10, 11, 10, 11, 10, 11 and 12, 15, 11, 14, 12, 10, there would be an additional 'interaction' effect since the amount of internal variance itself also differs. In real life, however, it is invariably more complicated than that, requiring statistical analysis to calculate. This would involve a '2-way' ANOVA, '3-way' ANOVA being used when there is an additional variable (e.g. you might be comparing male and female performance in two or more conditions). The ANOVA enables one to unravel the various sources of variance and determine which are statistically significant. In cases where the number of variables exceeds 3, it is usually more appropriate to use **factor analysis**.

References and further reading

Roberts, M. and Russo, R. (1999) *A Student's Guide to Analysis of Variance*, London: Routledge.

Shupe, D.R. (1995) *Inferential Statistics: An Introduction to the Analysis of Variance*, McGraw-Hill.

ANALYTICAL (OR JUNGIAN) PSYCHOLOGY

C.G. Jung, after breaking with Sigmund Freud in 1912, developed his own distinct theory which he called Analytical Psychology to differentiate it from Freud's **psychoanalysis**. Although they share many concepts, several are distinctively Jungian. Among these are **extraversion** and **introversion** which have become widely used in **personality** theory generally and are given a separate entry. The most important of the others are discussed below. Although Jung's reputation in academic Psychology slumped during the second half of the twentieth century, his wider popularity remained strong. However, see Shamdasani (2003) for a well-received recent re-evaluation of his significance which restores his central role in Psychology's twentieth-century development.

There is a substantial genre of introductory works, mostly from the 1950s to 1970s, of which Hall and Nordby (1973) is among the most reliable. See also Storr (1997) for an anthology of Jung's writings and Storr and Bishop (1999) for a collection of essays by others. Jung's multi-volume *Collected Works* was published by Routledge and Kegan Paul during the 1950s and 1960s, but most of his important books remain in print individually.

The best-known of Jung's concepts are as follows:

- *anima*. The *archetype* of the unconscious feminine principle in the male *psyche*.
- *animus*. The *archetype* of the unconscious masculine principle in the female *psyche*.
- *archetype*. Perhaps the best-known Jungian concept. Existing in the *collective unconscious* (see below), archetypes may be understood as inherited forms of psychological wisdom denoting specific universal situations, developmental tasks, problems etc. They cannot be known directly, however, and in order to become accessible to consciousness, they have to assume symbolic forms which are to a considerable degree culture-specific, although all representations of an archetype may share a similar structure, appearing, as it were, as variations on a theme. During individual analysis, they typically manifest themselves in dreams, but also constitute the core repertoire of religious and artistic symbolism. No specific archetypal symbol can itself exhaust or fully capture the 'meaning' of the archetype itself, hence they can possess a quality of *numinosity* (see below) and new symbolic forms can emerge.
- *collective unconscious* (see also **unconscious)**. The level of the unconscious which all people have in common. Jung's introduction of this concept marked a central divergence from Freud's psychoanalysis (see **psychoanalytic concepts**: *unconscious*). In contrast to the negative character of the Freudian unconscious, in Analytical Psychology, the collective unconscious is seen as a repository of *archetypal* ancestral wisdom and the core resource for psychological healing. The contents of the collective unconscious are not, as in Psychoanalysis, *repressed*, although as in Psychoanalysis they cannot be accessed directly (see *archetype*). Jung's formulations of the concept somewhat varied over time and there is a definite suggestion that there are various less universal levels of the collective unconscious shared by people of different ethnic groups or cultures. Many have argued that the concept depends on the notion of inheritance of acquired characteristics, which is genetically now

known to be impossible, although a closer reading of Jungian theory suggests otherwise. Shamdasani (2003) and, for example, Progoff (1953) should be consulted before drawing any firm conclusions on the issue.

- *complex* (see also psychoanalysis: *complex*). Although Jung's usage of the term does not differ significantly from Freud's, it is somewhat more widely used in Analytical Psychology. Jung's earliest published work was on the use of a word-association technique to identify the presence of unconscious complexes.

- *individuation*. The process by which a person achieves a full integration of the various *psychological functions*, transcending psychological conflicts. This is marked by the emergence of the **Self**. This does not mean that everything in the unconscious has become conscious, but only that conscious and unconscious processes are working in harmony – that, in a man, the tensions between conscious *animus* and unconscious *anima*, for example, have been reconciled. Nor does it imply that an endpoint in psychological development has been reached, on the contrary, it renders further development easier. Individuation is generally only achieved during or after middle age.

- *mandala*. A typical symbol of the *Self* or 'wholeness' *archetype*, often emerging in dreams during the later stages of the *individuation* process. Mandalas are invariably variations on symmetrical circles, squares, crosses or polygons, with or without figurative content, as a way of representing the integration of opposites into a unity. The term was adopted from the Sanskrit word for 'disc'. Mandalas are common in all religious symbolism, including the Christian cross.

- *numinosity*. This term was adopted from theology by Jung to refer to the quality of 'holiness' or seemingly 'supernatural' presence, typically characteristic of powerful religious symbols and situations, evoking complex feelings of awe, dread, wonder, etc. For Jung, this signified the activation and raising to consciousness of *archetypal* forces. See Casement and Tacey (2006) for a recent treatment of the topic.

- *persona*. From the Greek work originally meaning 'mask'. The 'face' one presents to the world. While everyone has a persona, problems can arise if this becomes too rigid and/or disconnected from the rest of the *psyche*. This can happen if the persona becomes a way of overprotecting the individual from others and masking their true feelings.

- *psyche*. The term 'psyche' is Jung's preferred word for denoting the mind and the mental in its totality. While not unique to Jungian thought, and long predating it, in his writings 'psyche' assumes a distinctive, if somewhat indefinable, almost metaphysical quality, as something of cosmic significance and presence. See Jung (1969) for the complexities of this concept.

- *psychological functions*. In *Psychological Types* (1923), Jung proposed that there were four basic psychological functions: thinking, *feeling* (both 'rational'), sensation and intuition (both 'irrational'). This permitted the generation of eight personality types using the rule that a dominant conscious function was complemented by a dominant unconscious one, these being opposite in terms of their 'rationality'/'irrationality', and each was accompanied by a sub-ordinate function. Since, however, people were also consciously either *extraverted* or *introverted* (and the opposite unconsciously), the full number of types is 16. It should though be stressed that Jung did not intend this classification as a straitjacket constraining the variety of individual personalities, which are each unique, but as an aid to their analysis. The degree to which a dominant function dominates its subordinate is also variable. This typology was later used as the basis for the widely used *Myers-Briggs Type Indicator* or *MBTI* questionnaire. See also **cognitive style**.
- *shadow*. An *archetype* denoting the consciously denied, negative, rejected or evil side of the individual's personality. Confrontation, reconciliation with, and mastery over the Shadow are an essential aspect of *individuation* (see above).
- *transcendent function*. The underlying drive towards *individuation*, considered as a universal motivational force driving the quest for the **Self**.

References and further reading

Casey, A. and Tacey, D. (2006) *The Idea of the Numinous. Contemporary Jungian and Psychoanalytic Perspectives*, London: Routledge.

Hall, C.S. and Nordby, V.J. (1973) *A Primer of Jungian Psychology*, New York: Mentor.

Jung, C.G. (1923) *Psychological Types, or the Psychology of Individuation*, London: Kegan Paul, Trench & Trübner.

—— (1969) *The Structure and Dynamics of the Psyche. (Collected Works*, vol. 8, London: Routledge & Kegan Paul.

Papadopoulos, R.K. (2006) *The Handbook of Jungian Psychology: Theory, Practice and Applications*, London: Routledge.

Progoff, I. (1953) *Jung's Psychology and Its Social Meaning*, London: Routledge & Kegan Paul.

Shamdasani, S. (2003) *Jung and the Making of Modern Psychology: The Dream of a Science*, Cambridge: Cambridge University Press.

Storr, A. (ed.) (1997) *The Essential Jung*, New York: Barnes & Noble.
Storr, A. and Bishop, P. (eds) (1999) *Jung in Contexts. A Reader*, London: Routledge.

ANOMIE

Tends to be a sociological rather than Psychological term. Psychologically it is very similar to **alienation**, without the latter's Marxist connotations. A feeling of life being devoid of purpose and interest due to a felt lack of viable ideals and moral standards. Unlike alienation, anomie is defined in terms of deficiencies in the social or cultural context rather than as a consequence of personal disempowerment by the production system and socio-economic order. The term may also be used to refer to conditions of social instability and unrest generally resulting from lack of values, etc. Introduced in 1895 by the French sociologist Emile Durkheim (who borrowed it from the philosopher J.-M. Guyau) in his classic study of suicide, and later taken up in the USA by sociologist R.K. Merton. Considered characteristic of periods of rapid social change and fragmentation, and symptomatised by delinquency and suicide. Incidentally, the www.answers.com entry has useful introductory coverage of the topic, including several alternative definitions, which are not entirely consistent. One equates it to 'anarchy', which is very misleading.

ANOREXIA (ANOREXIA NERVOSA)

Eating disorder marked by refusal or extreme reluctance to eat, leading to loss of body weight and potentially fatal self-starvation. Typically, if not exclusively, anorexia occurs in adolescent females and is usually related to obsession about body size and shape. The condition has attracted widespread attention and publicity over recent decades as its incidence appears to have dramatically increased in this section of the population. Most disturbingly, the rise of the internet has seen the emergence of something verging on an anorexia subculture with the posting of pro-anorexia websites. The psychological causes of anorexia are complex and still not fully understood but a number of factors are commonly implicated, ranging from family dynamics to the fashion industry's stress on slimness as an aesthetic ideal and relentless pressure from the dieting industry. Both individual psychological and cultural factors are clearly involved. Anorexia is sometimes associated with **bulimia**. There is now a huge literature on anorexia of which the references below are but a sample. A recent history of the topic is Brumberg (2000).

References and further reading

Aronson, J.K. (2001) *Understanding and Treating Anorexia and Bulimia*, Lanham, MD: Jason Aronson Publishers.
Brumberg, J.J. (2000) *Fasting Girls: The History of Anorexia Nervosa*, New York: Vintage.
Craggs-Hinton, C. (2006) *Coping with Eating Disorders and Body Image*, London: Sheldon Press.
Leone, D.A. (2001) *Anorexia*, San Diego: Greenwood Press.
Logue, A. W. (2004) *The Psychology of Eating and Drinking*, London: Taylor & Francis.
Robert-McComb, J.J. (2000) *Eating Disorders in Women and Children: Prevention, Stress Management, and Treatment*, London: Taylor & Francis.

ANTHROPOMORPHISM

Generally refers to the erroneous ascription to animals of uniquely human psychological characteristics. The classic condemnation of this is '*Lloyd Morgan's Canon*', named after C. Lloyd Morgan (1852–1936) who wrote in 1903 that, 'In no case is an animal activity to be interpreted in terms of higher psychological processes, if it can be fairly interpreted in terms which stand lower in the scale of psychological evolution and development' (Lloyd Morgan, 1930, is the most mature statement of his position). This is not quite as clear-cut as it sounds because it seems to assume that we know in advance what this 'scale' is and where various animal activities lie on it, which are often precisely what comparative psychologists are trying to discover. (And there is also surely something odd in saying that it is anthropomorphic to say a sheep is being sheepish.) Precisely what Lloyd Morgan's intentions were has also been debated in recent years. Certainly, however, he was, among other things, striving to mark a clear break from an earlier tradition of animal studies in which criminality, jealousy, shyness, cunning and pride were ascribed to magpies, cats, deer, foxes and peacocks, typically exemplified in W. Lauder Lindsay's *Mind in the Lower Animals* (1879). Although it is necessary to avoid the error, the logic underlying how we ascribe 'personhood' to non-humans is actually too complex to be adequately dealt with simply by condemning 'anthropomorphism'. It is not to be confused with *anthropocentrism* which refers to viewing the world from a human-centred perspective. Indeed, they are in some senses opposites, for a world full of other person-like but non-human creatures is incompatible with anthropocentrism. Few book-length discussions of the concept have appeared in recent decades. The term is also, one should note, used in a different technical sense by archaeologists and anthropologists to refer to animal-shaped artefacts.

References

Lauder Lindsay, W. (1879) *Mind in the Lower Animals in Health and Disease* (2 vols), London: Kegan Paul & Trench.
Lloyd Morgan, C. (1930) *The Animal Mind*, London: Edward Arnold.

ANTI-PSYCHIATRY

From the mid–1960s till the mid–1970s, a number of psychiatrists, psychotherapists and psychologists became radically hostile to orthodox medical psychiatry. The grounds for their hostility were a mixture of theoretical, philosophical and political. They argued that psychiatry was dehumanising, served the interests of the economic and political establishment and was based on a profound misunderstanding of the conditions it sought to treat, particularly **schizophrenia**. The rapidly expanding use of drugs, electroconvulsive therapy (ECT), and other physical methods obscured the social and psychological origins of 'mental illness' and, while suppressing symptoms, prevented their genuine 'cure'. The most famous figure in this movement was the Scottish psychiatrist R.D. ('Ronnie') Laing, with Laing (1959) acquiring almost a founding text status. Others included David Cooper (1971) and Joe Berke (1977, with Barnes, 1971). The American psychiatrist Thomas Szasz, author of *The Myth of Mental Illness* (1962), might also loosely be included in this group but his philosophical and ideological position, as it later emerged, was rather different from the broadly left-wing character of the British. The late Anthony Clare's balanced, if ultimately negative, critique (Clare, 1976) should also be noted. While anti-psychiatric sentiments were widespread in Europe and the USA at this time, the anti-psychiatry 'movement' as such was a largely British phenomenon. Although it faded out by the end of the 1970s, anti-psychiatry left a legacy of genuine insights and, to use the politician's cliché, 'important lessons were learned'.

References and further reading

Barnes, M. and Berke, J. (1971) *Mary Barnes: Two Accounts of a Journey through Madness*, New York: Harcourt, Brace & Jovanovich.

Berke, J.H. (1977) *Butterfly Man: Madness, Degradation and Redemption*, London: Hutchinson.

Clare, A. (1976) *Psychiatry in Dissent: Controversial Issues in Thought and Practice*, London: Tavistock.

Cooper, D. (1971) *The Death of the Family*, London: Allen Lane.

Laing, R.D. (1959) *The Divided Self: An Existential Study of Sanity and Madness*, London: Tavistock.

Szasz, T. (1962) *The Myth of Mental Illness*, London: Secker & Warburg.

ANXIETY

A general term roughly meaning worry and concern of a fairly intense kind. Although in popular usage we talk of being anxious *about* specific things, in Psychology it more commonly refers to *free-floating anxiety*, i.e. anxiety lacking a specific object. It has been a topic of interest from a wide range of angles, figuring prominently in **psychoanalysis** (in which the German term *Angst* is often used) as well as in the work of personality theorists such as H.J. Eysenck. High anxiety typically signifies **neurosis** – hence the phrase *neurotic anxiety*, and there has been much work in Clinical Psychology on how to manage it. '*Separation anxiety*' refers to children's fears of separation from a parent (see **attachment theory**). 'Anxiety' can be used both to refer to a personality **trait** of people prone to anxiety states, and to a **mood** or **emotion** which anyone can experience. Grammatically it is also interesting in that while the substantive form 'anxiety' suggests something thing-like – a kind of negative energy – the qualifying usages 'anxious' and 'anxiously' suggest that it is a property or quality of behaviour or personality.

References and further reading

Crozier, W. R. (2001) *International Handbook of Social Anxiety: Concepts, Research and Interventions Relating to the Self and Shyness*, Chichester: John Wiley & Son, Ltd.

Griez, E.J.L., Faravelli, C. and Nutt, D. (2001) *Anxiety Disorders: An Introduction to Clinical Management and Research*, Chichester: John Wiley & Sons, Ltd.

Saleci, R. (2004) *On Anxiety*, London: Routledge.

Sanders, D. and Wills, F. (2003) *Counselling for Anxiety Problems*, London: Sage.

APHASIA

Speech disorder resulting from brain damage to either **Broca's area** or Wernicke's area. Broca's aphasia is marked by difficulties in speaking, articulation, word ordering and access to words (depending on the exact nature of the damage). Wernicke's aphasia, by contrast, involves problems with comprehension, spoken word recognition and word meanings. Not all speech disorders are considered as aphasia since they may also result from deafness and other forms of neurological damage.

References and further reading

Berthier, M.L. (2001) *Transcortical Aphasias*, Hove: Psychology Press.
Boller, F. (ed.) (2001) *Handbook of Neuropsychology*, vol. 3, *Language and Aphasia*, New York: Elsevier.
Parr, S. (2003) *Aphasia Inside Out*, Milton Keynes: Open University Press.
Spreen, O. and Risser, A.H. (2003) *Assessment of Aphasia*, Oxford: Oxford University Press.

APPERCEPTION

Now little used but once very common in Psychology texts. It is a problematic concept with a long philosophical history and underwent various subtle shifts in meaning. Broadly speaking, it means the totality of one's conscious awareness at any given time, but it often has a connotation of active 'grasping' rather than simply being passive. The great German philosopher Immanuel Kant used the expression 'The Transcendental Unity of Apperception' Kant (1781/1787) to refer to the fact, as he held, that, however varied the contents of conscious awareness, they were, at the highest level, an indissoluble unity. Later, nineteenth-century and early twentieth-century psychologists used it in a less metaphysical sense. The German psychologist-philosopher J.F. Herbart adopted the term for the totality of what was in consciousness at any given moment, calling this the 'apperceptive mass' (Herbart, 1850). It fell into disuse in English writing after about 1910, but still occasionally crops up. Lange (1907) probably remains the best review of the concept.

References

Herbart, J.F. ([1850] 1968) *Psychologie als Wissenschaft*, Amsterdam: E.J. Bonset.
Kant, I. ([1781] 1787) *The Critique of Pure Reason*, Basingstoke: Palgrave Macmillan.

Lange, K. (1907) *Apperception: A Monograph on Psychology and Pedagogy*, Boston, MA: D.C. Heath.

AROUSAL

Broad term covering states of alertness, high emotional states, action-readiness, and excitement, etc. Often used with a qualifying term such as 'sexual arousal' or 'arousal of interest'. The **hedonic tone** of arousal ranges from ecstasy to terror (see also **reversal theory**). Often used in **motivation** literature. The Psychological use of the term is not clearly distinct from its everyday use. Although it can often give the impression of being more technical, its breadth of meaning prevents it doing much genuine scientific work on its own. Most books currently in print with 'arousal' in the title are about sex, Pfaff (2005) appears to be the only recent heavyweight monograph on the topic but coverage is pervasive in the general **emotion** literature.

Reference

Pfaff, D. (2005) *Brain Arousal and Information Theory: Neural and Genetic Mechanisms*, Cambridge, MA: Harvard University Press.

ASPERGER'S SYNDROME

First identified in 1944 by the eponymous Viennese doctor Hans Asperger. Currently classified as an 'autistic spectrum disorder' (see **autism**), the nature and status of Asperger's syndrome are somewhat controversial, and becoming more so. Like autism, it is characterised by poor social skills and communication difficulties, obsessional interests, love of routine, poor imagination, and difficulty with abstract concepts and figurative uses of language. This last results in 'over-literal' understanding of language and inability to understand word-play and jokes. Despite the similarities, however, children with Asperger's typically have average or superior intelligence, and if considered a bit odd by their peers, nevertheless often function or even flourish in academic settings and at certain kinds of task. What is now complicating the picture is that Asperger 'sufferers' are increasingly getting themselves organised as a lobby, asserting their own rights and proclaiming their normality or even superiority. The internet has greatly facilitated this since computer skills are widely appealing to them. Retrospective diagnoses of Socrates, Michaelangelo, Jane Austen and Isaac Newton as possible 'sufferers' have also begun changing the public image of the Asperger's sufferer as a dysfunctional and emotionally empty iso-late. In the present climate, I am wary of offering any statements about Asperger's syndrome that might give the impression there is anything like an authoritative consensus on any aspect of it. For an entry into the topic readers might skip Wikipedia and go straight to: www.assupportgrouponline.co.uk

References and further reading

Attwood, T. (2003) *Asperger's Syndrome*, London: Jessica Kingsley.
Baker, L.J. (2004) *Asperger's Syndrome: Intervening in Schools, Clinics and Communities*, London: Taylor & Francis.
Rhode, M. (2004) *The Many Faces of Asperger's Syndrome*, London: Karnac Books.

ASSOCIATIONISM

The concept of 'association' in Philosophy and Psychology originates in the British **empiricist** school from the work of J. Locke onwards (although there are hints of it in T. Hobbes, and even Aristotle). Oversimplifying somewhat, they saw all our ideas, concepts and complex behaviour as originating in the 'association' between ele-mentary 'sensations', or between actions and 'sensations'. In the last version of classical associationism, James Mill (1829) reduced a small number of types of 'association' such as 'succession' and 'simultaneity' to the single principle of 'contiguity' (proximity in space or time). It was argued that all higher concepts and 'general ideas', such as 'cau-sation', were acquired and built up from elementary associations of this kind. In the mid-nineteenth century, the associationist framework was adopted by early British Psychological writers such as A. Bain and H. Spencer and eventually provided the underlying basis for **beha-viourism** and American **learning theory**. Thus *conditioned responses* are acquired when *conditioned stimuli* are associated with *unconditioned stimuli*. Its latest incarnation is **connectionism** in **AI**. '*Associative learning*' often refers specifically to experimental tasks such as learning word pairs, but can be used more broadly for learning based on forming associations between stimuli or, in the case of behaviour, stimuli and specific behaviours. By its nature, associationism is an environmentalist and '**bottom up**' theoretical approach. From the eighteenth century onwards, the sufficiency of association to account for all our concepts and learned behaviour has been challenged as it raises numerous philosophical difficulties. In modern Psychology, it may be contrasted with, first **Gestalt Psychology** and **instinct**-based theories and then with **Cognitive Psychology**. Warren (1921) remains the most useful general historical account.

References and further reading

Mandler, J.M. and Mandler, G. (1964) *Thinking from Association to Gestalt*, New York: John Wiley & Sons, Ltd.
Mill, J. (1829) *Analysis of the Phenomena of the Human Mind*, London: Longmans, Green, Reader & Dyer.
Warren, H.C. (1921) *A History of the Association Psychology*, London: Constable.

ATAXIA

A family of neurological disorders, usually of genetic origin, affecting muscular co-ordination and resulting in various kinds of clumsiness or unsteadiness. Speech, vision and hearing can also be affected. In some cases the condition is progressive, leading, for instance, to an eventual inability to walk. Speech ataxia is thus distinct from Broca's **aphasia**. Ataxic conditions may also arise in adulthood following substance abuse, multiple sclerosis or damage to the cerebellum. Genetically caused ataxias of numerous kinds are now identified. The major reference source is Klockgether (2000).

Reference

Klockgether, T. (2000) *Handbook of Ataxia Disorders: Neurological Disease and Therapy Series Vol.50*, Monticello, NY: Marcel Dekker.

ATTACHMENT/ATTACHMENT THEORY

In psychology this has nothing to do with e-mails. Attachment is the natural mutual bonding between mother or initial primary care-taker and new-born baby, which, ideally, subsequently extends to other care-takers. More arguably this provides the template for all later close personal relationships. The idea was introduced by the British child psychologist and **neo-Freudian** psychoanalyst John Bowlby in 1951 and expounded at length in his three-volume *Attachment and Loss* (Bowlby, 1969, 1973, 1980). It was, in many respects, an application in the human context of the concept of *imprinting* which ethologists (see **ethology**) such as Konrad Lorenz had introduced in the 1940s in studying animal behaviour. 'Attachment theory' continues to be developed, particularly in relation to psychotherapy and counselling. Both failure of the attachment mechanism and over-attachment persisting into adulthood can, attachment theorists claim, have psychopathological consequences of numerous kinds. Under normal circumstances, the strength of the attachment bond weakens after early childhood as the individual matures into an autonomous adult. This is known as 'separation' and its achievement is invariably accompanied by some degree of '*separation anxiety*' in either or both parties. If this anxiety is too high, it may prevent or inhibit separation. Bowlby's initial work had an immense impact with great attention being paid to what he had called *maternal deprivation*, i.e. the mother's absence in early infancy. Bowlby and others identified numerous negative effects of prolonged maternal deprivation, especially from research on orphaned children reared in institutions. Subsequently, their exclusive focus on the mother was contested, it being argued that loving caretaking was the key factor and that neither caretaker's gender nor biological relationship to the child were necessarily important. Some feminists also pointed out that, intentionally or not, Bowlby had reinforced a post-Second World War cultural wish to return women from paid work, supported by work-site crèches, to the domestic environment in order to provide jobs for ex-servicemen. Whatever the varieties of interpretation it has received, the concept of attachment itself is now very widely accepted, particularly among child psychologists and psychotherapists.

References and further reading

Bowlby, J. (1969, 1973, 1980) *Attachment and Loss*, vol. 1.: *Attachment;* vol. 2: *Separation;* vol. 3: *Loss, Sadness and Depression*, London: Hogarth Press.
—— (2004) *Fifty Years of Attachment Theory*, London: Karnac Books.
Cassidy, J. (2002) *Handbook of Attachment: Theory, Research, and Clinical Applications*, New York: Guildford.
Holmes, J. (1993) *John Bowlby and Attachment Theory*, London: Routledge.
Van Dijken, S. (1998) *John Bowlby: His Early Life – A Journey to the Roots of Attachment Theory*, London: Free Association Books.

ATTENTION

Although having a deep history as a topic of Psychological interest, attention has become a major theme in **Cognitive Psychology**. It is conceived as the process enabling us to select a specific stimulus from the total array of sensory input. For cognitivists, it has become highly relevant as a component of the total information processing system and use of attention-related tasks can shed light on the levels at which sensory information is being coded and the structure of the system itself. One early topic of interest was the so-called 'cocktail party phenomenon' (which perhaps tells us something about the lives being led by 1950s psychologists!), our ability to concentrate on a single conversation when others are going on all around us. Research showed that virtually no information at all was being processed from other sources beyond some very basic filter which automatically rejected them on the basis of their physical characteristics. This was not undisputed, however. If our name is mentioned in the background hubbub, we are likely to notice it, suggesting that some level of semantic analysis is also going on. Attention is not only a matter of selection, it is closely bound up with the processes by which we control our behaviour, which in turn links it to **motivation**. Few psychologists now therefore consider attention to be a single process. It clearly becomes less important as behaviour becomes automated – we do not closely attend to individual letters when reading as we did when learning to read. Given the comprehensive range of inter-related sensory modalities in which attention operates, and the variety of phenomena it relates to, its complexity presents researchers with a number of challenges. Unravelling them may though prove rewarding and some believe it is the *cognitivist* route for understanding consciousness itself. More traditional aspects of attention tackled by psychologists include *attention span* and **vigilance** (which became a whole sub-field of research especially during the 1940s and 1950s). Pathologically it also figures prominently in **aphasia** and, to some extent, **agnosia**, as well as **ADHD**.

References and further reading

Cohen, R.A. (2007) *The Neuropsychology of Attention*, Berlin: Springer-Verlag.
Johnson, A. and Proctor, R.W. (2003) *Attention: Theory and Practice*, London: Sage.
Muller, H. and Krummenacher, J. (eds) (2006) *Visual Search and Attention. Special Issue*, London: Taylor & Francis.

ATTITUDE

A now notoriously problematic concept which often dominated North American Social Psychology from the 1930s into the 1970s. Interestingly, 'attitude' originally referred to physical posture or orientation (as in 'she struck an attitude of intense concentration'), only acquiring its psychological meaning in the early twentieth century. One reason it became so popular was that it lent itself so easily to measurement by questionnaire methods. Thus, by the late 1930s, attitude measurement questionnaires had been devised for everything from political attitudes and attitudes towards foreigners and religion to topics such as art and morality, at the same time as being taken up by market researchers to measure attitudes towards consumer products, advertisements, physical appearance and anything else their clients required. The attitude literature expanded dramatically during the 1940s–1960s, with analyses of attitude 'components' (typically 'cognitive', 'evaluative' and 'behavioural'), and numerous theories of attitude structure and attitude change being proposed. The underlying problem, however, was defining what kind of psychological phenomenon the term really referred to, which became more acute as the sheer number of things towards which people were said to have 'attitudes' expanded. A second difficulty which forced itself on researchers was the relationship between measured 'attitudes' and actual behaviour. Sometimes, it was clear, behaviour was governed more by social context, such as pressure to conform, or other aspects of personality, such as shyness, rather than the individual's attitude itself. On other occasions, it was unclear what behavioural consequences logically followed from possessing a particular attitude. I might have a positive attitude towards the 'Big Bang' theory of the origins of the universe as opposed to the 'Steady State' theory, but aside from answering the question accordingly when asked, it is hardly obvious what else I can do about it! Third, on closer scrutiny it was becoming clear that the nature of the questions being asked in attitude questionnaires was far more problematic than was originally assumed (a point also applicable to many personality-assessment questionnaires). The nub of this was how to differentiate between individual's *beliefs*, which, whether true or false, were sincerely held to refer to facts, and *attitudes* which were assumed to be simply about liking and disliking the 'attitude object'. If I genuinely believe, on the basis of what I have been taught or the information available to me, that black people have smaller brains than white people this does not, in itself, count as a racist *attitude*. These difficulties began to erode the 'cognitive', 'evaluative', 'behavioural' component analysis, leaving only the 'evaluative' one standing. But this dramatically weakened the very value of measuring attitudes as a route for predicting behaviour, its major source of appeal to market researchers and opinion pollsters. Things got worse. How far, critics began to ask, can attitudes really be said to exist prior to the individual being asked for them? Is it not rather that, since people are generally disposed to assume a question is meaningful, when asked what they feel about, e.g. how punctual Danes are (to cite an example from the author's own market research experience), they will happily rate them on a five-point scale, even though the question has never occurred to them before? Attitudes also clearly varied in terms of whether they were embedded in elaborate belief or value systems (like a religion) or were quite discrete, such as one's attitude to avocado pears. Among other things this affected how easy they were to change. By the mid-1970s, it was unclear quite what scientific work the concept of 'attitude' was doing any more. More sophisticated efforts were made to measure attitudes by overt behaviour, but in a sense the concept itself now became redundant, since attitudes were supposed to be psychological entities of some sort, not behavioural tendencies. The measurement techniques, such as questionnaires, created in pursuit of attitude measurement, continue to have a major place in Psychological research and are valid if the user is clear regarding their limitations and relevance to the matter at hand, while the word 'attitude' itself is now so well established that it is unlikely to disappear soon. As a meaningful scientific concept possessing explanatory value, on the other hand, 'attitude' has probably had its day. The kinds of things it was used to explore, from the formation and changeability of public opinion to how attractive people find an item of cosmetic packaging, can continue to be investigated without it. The topic is extensively covered in all pre-1980 Social Psychology textbooks (such as Brown, 1965), and continued to receive some attention in more recent ones (e.g. Hewstone *et al.*, 1996). See Aizen (2006) and Blair *et al.* (2005) for the current state of play.

References

Aizen, I. (2006) *Attitudes, Personality and Behaviour*, Milton Keynes: Open University Press.

Blair, D.A., Johnson, T. and Zanna, M.P. (2005) *The Handbook of Attitudes* Mahwah, NJ: Erlbaum.

Brown, R. (1965) *Social Psychology*, New York: Free Press.

Hewstone, M., Stroebe, W. and Stephenson, G.M. (1996) *Introduction to Social Psychology*, Oxford: Blackwell.

ATTRIBUTION THEORY

A field of Social Psychology which, although rooted in the earlier work of F. Heider, came to prominence from the late 1960s and dominated much social psychological research thereafter. In some respects, it filled the gap left by the declining fortunes of classical **attitude** theory as well as reflecting the wider rise of Cognitive Psychology. The key foundational text is usually taken to be Kelley (1967). Attribution theory centres on the question of how people 'attribute' the causes of behaviour (either others' or their own). To take a fundamental distinction, do they attribute it to the individual or to the situation? Kelley proposed that we act as intuitive statisticians applying a kind of **analysis of variance (ANOVA)** procedure to judge which factors co-vary with behaviour. An early conclusion was that people often committed what was termed the *fundamental attribution error*, attributing behaviour to the individual rather than the situation. As research continued, a host of new questions arose regarding such points as the differences between 'reasons' and 'causes' or between 'excuses' and 'justifications', while exceptions to early generalisations were soon spotted. For example, it had been assumed that unusual behaviour was most likely to be ascribed to the individual while 'normal' behaviour was situationally explained. But what was seen (rightly or wrongly) as normal behaviour could, when displayed by a member of a minority group, be seen as confirming a stereotype about what such people were like. Even the assumption that internal attributions were only elicited by intentional behaviour was torpedoed by the realisation that unintended behaviour could be internally explained by attributing a trait of 'clumsiness' to the actor. A central theme has always been the respective roles of 'motivational' and 'cognitive' factors in determining the kinds of attribution people choose. During the 1970s, attribution theory research rapidly began to impact on, and overlap with, other topics of research such as **locus of control, achievement motivation**, and *learned helplessness* (see under **learning and learning theory**), as well as proving relevant in clinical and other applied areas. Kelley's original ANOVA model has been severely mauled over the years and while attribution theory has generated a number of technical expressions (such as 'correspondence bias', 'attributional style' and the 'covariation principle'), it can hardly be said to possess a single, rigorous theoretical structure. 'Attribution theorising' might be a more accurate expression. It has nevertheless proved enlightening in at least one basic respect – the numerous ways in which it has unmasked the irrational and biased character of our explanations of much of the behaviour of both others and ourselves. There is, one might comment, a reflexive sense in which the entire discipline of Psychology is itself largely an exercise in attribution, but this seems to have been unnoticed. Social psychology textbooks will usually devote at least a chapter to the topic, and Forsterling (2001) provides a fairly recent and widely used overview. An earlier work of some interest in indicating quite how widely the impact of attribution theory had spread is Jaspars *et al.* (1983).

References

Forsterling, F. (2001) *Attribution: An Introduction to Theories, Research and Applications*, Philadelphia, PA: Psychology Press.

Jaspars, J., Fincham, F.D. and Hewstone, M (eds) (1983) *Attribution Theory and Research: Conceptual, Developmental and Social Dimensions*, London: Academic Press.

Kelley, H.H. (1967) 'Attribution Theory in Social Psychology' in D. Levine (ed.) *Nebraska Symposium on Motivation,* vol. 15, Lincoln, NE: University of Nebraska Press, pp. 192–238.

AUTHORITARIANISM

While anticipated in earlier work undertaken in Germany by Erich Fromm, the concept of 'authoritarianism' came to the attention of English-speaking Psychology in 1950, with the publication of *The Authoritarian Personality*, co-authored by T.W. Adorno *et al.* (Two of the authors, Adorno and E. Frenkl-Brunswik, were exiles working in the tradition of the German *Frankfurt School*, see **Schools of Psychology** sub-entry.) This immediately attracted widespread attention not only among psychologists but among the North American and British intelligentsia generally, 'authoritarian' rapidly entering everyday language. The term refers to a particular combination of traits including a favouring of simple hierarchical power structures, over-obedience to authority, intolerance of ambiguity and complexity, closed-mindedness, rigidity of thought, and a tendency to project (see *projection* under **psychoanalytic concepts**) negative characteristics onto others, particularly members of minority groups or other 'races'. The original exposition of this drew heavily on Psychoanalytic concepts, postulating that it was a typical outcome of patterns of child-rearing in which the father was so feared that Oedipal hostility towards him could not be resolved (see psychoanalytic concepts sub-entry *Oedipus Complex*). This resulted in extreme adulation of the father and consequent projection onto others of the individual's own negative attitudes towards him and Oedipal desires for the mother. This facilitated a 'scapegoating' process in which both collective and individual misfortunes could be blamed on others, as well as a weakening of willingness to take personal moral responsibility for one's actions. The historical context in which this idea emerged is important, for it was seen as a way of explaining how many Germans behaved as they did under Nazism in Germany, and the nature of the psychological appeal of Nazi and fascist ideologies. While the Psychoanalytic theory underlying the concept has largely fallen into disregard, the existence of the authoritarian personality type itself remains widely accepted. One modification of the original account, however, was to claim that there were left-wing as well as right-wing forms of authoritarianism, a view advanced by British psychologist H.J. Eysenck (1960), who saw 'radical' vs 'conservative' (left vs right) as a personality dimension **orthogonal** to 'tough' versus 'tender' mindedness in characterising political attitudes, 'authoritarian' equating to 'tough-mindedness' in either direction. This is now generally rejected as the attitudes characteristic of 'tough-mindedness' do not correspond clearly to those typical of 'authoritarianism' as originally conceived. How far the concept of authoritarianism is a social construct (see **social constructionism**) of a specific socio-historical period remains an open question. It is worth noting that it provided a receptive context for S. Milgram's famous **obedience** experiment.

References

Adorno, T.W., Frenkel-Brunswik, E., Levinson, D.J. and Sanford, R.N. (1950) *The Authoritarian Personality* (2 vols), New York: Harper & Brothers.
Christie, R. and Jahoda, M. (eds) (1954) *Studies in the Scope and Method of 'The Authoritarian Personality': Continuities in Social Research*, Glencoe, IL: Free Press.
Eysenck, H.J. (1960) *The Psychology of Politics*, London: Routledge & Kegan Paul.

AUTISM

Prior to the 1960s 'autism' nearly always referred to 'autistic thinking'. This was considered typical of **schizophrenia** and meant self-absorbed, cut off from reality, 'living in a world of their own'. 'The autistic child' only seems to have emerged as a concept in the 1960s, and this condition is marked by far more than traditionally conceived autistic thinking. First manifesting itself in infancy or early childhood, it is symptomatised by severe difficulties in managing social interaction, difficulties in communicating both verbally and non-verbally, apparent lack of empathy or ability to understand others' viewpoints, obsessional and repetitive behaviour, episodic violence, learning difficulties and other signs of psychological dysfunction. Not all autistic children display all of these symptoms, however, and in practice a wide range of behavioural disorders are swept into the 'autistic' diagnostic net. It is now common to refer to 'autistic spectrum disorders', which, at the 'upper' end, controversially include **Asperger's syndrome**. The reported incidence of autism has increased enormously over recent decades, and public concern correspondingly intensified. As so often with such trends, it is not entirely easy to disentangle genuine increases from increases in diagnosis. Both the causes and treatment of autism remain matters of debate. While some genetic and/or neurological factor or factors are probably involved, the roles of developmental environment and biology in the aetiology of autism remain obscure. Intense and prolonged individual psychotherapy can be successful, as in the famous case of 'Dibs' (Axline, 1966), which did much to put the condition on the map, but this is impractical on a large scale and unpredictable in outcome. Pharmacological treatment may have beneficial effects in alleviating some symptoms but progress on this front is as yet very limited. It is fair to say that at present confusion continues to reign regarding most aspects of childhood autism. Some sufferers do though exhibit decreasingly severe symptoms as they enter adulthood and may eventually lead 'normal lives' (whatever they are!). The literature on autism is now vast, much of it popularly pitched towards parents and others coping with the condition. The references below include only a selection of recent serious works. B.M. Myles, it should be noted, has published several other works on the topic.

References and further reading

Axline, V. (1969) *Dibs: In Search of Self*, London: Gollancz.
Casanova, M.F. (ed.) (2005) *Recent Developments in Autism Research*, London: Nova Science.
Frith, U. (2004) *Autism: Mind and Brain*, London: Oxford University Press.
Hollander, E. and Wong, C.M. (2003) *Autistic Spectrum Disorders*, Monticello, NY: Marcel Dekker.
Myles, B.M., Swanson, T.C., Holverstott, J. and Duncan, M.M. (eds) (2007) *Autistic Spectrum Disorders: A Handbook for Parents and Professionals*, Westport, CT: Greenwood.
Volkmar, F.R. (2005) *Handbook of Autism and Pervasive Developmental Disorders*, New York: Wiley.
Zager, D. (2004) *Autistic Spectrum Disorders: Identification, Education and Treatment*, London: Taylor & Francis.

AVERSION THERAPY

Based on **learning theory** principles, aversion therapy was introduced during the 1960s, as a psychiatric procedure for *deconditioning* undesirable behaviour (Rachman and Teasdale, 1969). Most notoriously it was adopted in the 'treatment' of male homosexuals to whom electric shocks were administered while they were presented with erotic pictures of males. Less controversially it has also been explored in relation to smoking, gambling and alcoholism, for example. In the case of alcoholism, the aversive stimulus has typically been provided by prescribing the patient a drug, usually disulfiram (Antabuse), which induces nausea in reaction to alcohol intake. The efficacy of aversion therapy proved far more limited than its pioneers expected but it continues to be widely used as one technique among many, having been incorporated into **cognitive–behavioural therapy** (CBT). With the growing acceptance of homosexuality in western cultures after 1970, and the removal of homosexuality from the *DMSI*, it has long ceased to be used in that context. Ironically the bad public image aversion therapy acquired was in no small part due to its early use in attempting to 'cure' gay men, leading many people to become averse to aversion therapy (see Sansweet, 1975, for an early attack). Aversion therapy is a particular version of the more general approach known as **behaviour therapy** (Eysenck and Rachman, 1964).

References

Eysenck, H.J. and Rachman, S. (1964) *Behaviour Therapy and the Neuroses*, London: Oxford University Press.

Hadley, N.H. (1985) *Foundations of Aversion Therapy*, SP Medical and Scientific Books.

Rachman, S. and Teasdale, J. (1969) *Aversion Therapy and Behaviour Disorders – An Analysis*, London: Routledge & Kegan Paul.

Sansweet, S.J. (1975) *The Punishment Cure: How Aversion Therapy Is Being Used to Eliminate Smoking, Drinking, Obesity, Homosexuality ... and Practically Anything Else*, New York: Mason/Charter.

BEHAVIOUR

This term is now so common that it is worth noting that its use for referring to all activity in a general way actually dates back little over a century, its adoption by C. Lloyd Morgan (1900) really marking its debut. It was then taken up by J.B. Watson when he launched

behaviourism. Prior to this, it primarily referred to: (1) correct conduct, as it still does in phrases such as 'behave yourself' and 'she didn't know how to behave'; or (2) how inanimate materials responded under different conditions, which again persists in phrases like 'the behaviour of steel at high temperatures'. In the former of these, its use was generally restricted to human conduct.

Reference

Lloyd Morgan, C. (1900) *Animal Behaviour*, London: Edward Arnold.

BEHAVIOURISM

Generally considered to have been introduced by the US psychologist J.B. Watson (1878–1958) in a 1913 paper (although there were some precursors), behaviourism was an attempt to avoid the difficulties of trying to study consciousness by restricting scientific attention to overt behaviour. This was coupled with a central ambition to introduce more rigorous approaches to experimental research and report writing. The task of Psychology thus became the identification of the laws governing the relationship between environmental stimuli and behavioural responses, and Psychology was cast as an adjunct to physiology. This would, Watson believed, produce knowledge which could be applied to the prediction and control of behaviour. Behaviourism thus possessed a number of distinct features: it was extremely environmentalist, its technical vocabulary was restricted to a few non-mentalistic terms, its explanations were highly reductionist, and it was greatly concerned with experimental methodology. By the 1920s, it had assimilated the ideas of the Russian physiologist Ivan Pavlov (1849–1936) and incorporated his notions of *conditioning* and *reinforcement* as central theoretical concepts (see **learning** sub-entries). Watson's version of behaviourism (often termed 'classical behaviourism') was soon considered too crude and he himself quit academia following a divorce scandal, but in his wake a number of 'neo-behaviorists' took the doctrine in a variety of directions. These included many of the 'big names' in mid-twentieth-century US psychology: E.C. Tolman, Clark L. Hull, B.F. Skinner, E.R. Guthrie and Ernest R. Hilgard. In retrospect, it is clear that behaviourism was not so much a theory as a conceptual framework of a rather broader kind *within* which theorising could be conducted. Neo-behaviorists' theories were, in fact, quite varied in kind. During the 1950s and early 1960s, behaviourism was steadily ousted by **Cognitive Psychology** from the dominant position it had held in US Psychology for about three decades (although the extent of this dominance is often exaggerated). It did, however, leave a legacy of practical expertise in behavioural control by reinforcement and conditioning which continues to be used by behaviour therapists (see **behaviour therapy**). Two further points need to be made. First, that the term is now often used in a fairly broad way to refer to the study of behaviour regardless of theoretical viewpoint – this is to be discouraged; second, that despite acquiring a bad public image, especially during the 1960s, as a technology of behavioural control being deployed in the service of 'the system', most leading neo-behaviourists, such as Tolman, Hull and Hilgard, were on the political left and also saw their findings as providing routes for individual liberation (as did Watson himself). Whether, at the end of the day, behaviourism achieved more than the rigorous refinement of traditional folk-wisdom about the relationships between reward, punishment and behaviour is a moot point, but historically its initially extreme environmentalism acted as a brake on then rampant nativist **eugenics**, and its concern with scientific rigour and method also had a much wider influence than its specific doctrines. In Britain, behaviourism's impact was largely muffled until after the Second World War, the famous and controversial H.J. Eysenck (1916–97) keenly adopting it, but by the 1960s, as in North America, its influence was waning with the advent of cognitivism. B.F. Skinner (1904–90) was the last really influential behaviourist. O'Donnell (1985) is the best general historical account, covering more than Behaviourism itself. Watson (1924) is his most accessible full position statement and Buckley (1989) the best biography. Mackenzie (1977) and Smith (1986) are both excellent on the deeper theoretical issues. Skinner (1976), the entertaining first volume of his autobiography, is essential for anyone wishing to get to grips with this enigmatic character.

See also: **learning and learning theory**.

References

Buckley, K. (1989) *Mechanical Man. John Broadus Watson and the Beginnings of Behavioursm*, New York: Guilford Press.

Mackenzie, B.D. (1977) *Behaviourism and the Limits of Scientific Method*, London: Routledge & Kegan Paul.

O'Donnell, J.M. (1985) *The Origins of Behaviorism: American Psychology, 1870–1920*, New York: New York University Press.

Skinner, B.F. (1976) *Particulars of My Life*, London: Jonathan Cape.

Smith, L.D. (1986) *Behaviorism and Logical Positivism: A Reassessment of the Alliance*, Stanford, CA: Stanford University Press.

Watson, J.B. (1913) 'Psychology as the Behaviorist Views It', *Psychological Review*, 20: 158–77.

—— ([1924] 1970) *Behaviorism*, New York: W. W. Norton.

BEHAVIOUR THERAPY

The use of **learning theory** principles in the treatment of behaviour which is either pathological or otherwise felt undesirable. Introduced by B. Wolman in the 1950s and promoted by H.J. Eysenck, it was seen as a hard-line, practical, scientifically-based approach which would have greater success than **psychoanalysis** and other forms of **psychotherapy**. As usually happens with such innovations, they prove over time to vary widely in the kinds of condition for which they are suitable. Behaviour therapy proved quite good at treating **phobias** but less so for more serious neuroses or conditions which were not in themselves overtly behavioural in character. Behaviour therapy has now been integrated into **cognitive behavioural therapy**. Hersen and Rosqvist (2005) should be sufficient to tell you all you wish to know.

See also: **aversion therapy**.

References and further reading

Eysenck, H.J. and Rachman, S. (1964) *Behaviour Therapy and the Neuroses*, London: Oxford University Press.

Hersen, M. and Rosqvist, J. (eds) (2005) *Encyclopedia of Behavior Modification*, 3 vols, London: Sage.

BIORHYTHM

A general term for the cyclical nature of many biological processes. 'Jet-lag', for example, refers to a disruption of the sleep rhythm caused by rapid air-travel across time-zones. There are numerous different biorhythms occurring at varying rates. Psychologically these are significant because they can affect many psychologically related phenomena such as alertness, **fatigue**, hunger and **mood**. Most book-length works on the topic tend to be either 'self-help' (and, interestingly, astrological), or highly technical physiological texts, but Bentley (1999) is a reliable academic introduction.

Reference

Bentley, E. (1999) *Awareness: Biorhythms, Sleep and Dreaming*, London: Routledge.

BIPOLAR DISORDER (MANIC DEPRESSION)

Characterised by oscillation between the extremes of elated or enthusiastic hyperactivity and **depression**. The term 'manic depression' has now been generally replaced by the less dramatic sounding 'bipolar disorder'. Not uncommon, nor incompatible with high levels of creativity, but can wreak havoc with personal lives of both sufferers and those around them. Treatment tends to be pharmacological since the condition appears to be organically based rather than arising for purely psychological reasons.

References and further reading

Fuller, T.E. (2005) *Surviving Manic Depression*, New York: Basic Books.
Goodwin, F.K. (2007) *Manic-Depressive Illness: Bipolar and Recurrent Depression*, New York: Oxford University Press.
Maj, M., Akiskal, H., Lopez-Ibor, J.J. and Sartorius, N. (eds) *Bipolar Disorder*, Chichester: Wiley.
Siegfried, K. (ed.) (2005) *Handbook of Bipolar Disorder*, London: Taylor & Francis.
Soares, J.C. (2007) *Bipolar Disorder*, London: Taylor & Francis.
Soares, J.C. and Gershon, S. (eds) (2000) *Bipolar Disorders: Basic Mechanisms and Therapeutic Implications*, Monticello NY: Marcel Dekker.

BLINDSIGHT

Caused by damage to the visual cortex resulting in a 'scotoma' or 'blind spot', blindsight is a curious phenomenon in which, despite absence of conscious awareness, an individual's behaviour (such as grasping) is nevertheless guided by visual stimuli presented to this region of the visual field. The literature on blindsight is generally in the form of either journal papers or embedded in more general texts concerned with perception and psychoneurology, but Weiskrantz (1986) is the most accessible introduction to the topic and often described as a 'classic'.

Reference

Weiskrantz, L. (1986) *Blindsight: A Case Study and Implications*, Oxford: Clarendon Press.

BORDERLINE PERSONALITY DISORDER (BPD)

A technical-sounding expression introduced to refer to people who, as **DSM** IV puts it, display 'a pervasive pattern of instability of inter-personal relationships, self-image, and affects, and marked impulsivity that begins by early adulthood and is present in a variety of contexts'. Nine criteria are listed, which, if five or more are present, justify the diagnosis (I note that I meet three of these!). This is deceptive, '*any* pervasive' rather than '*a* pervasive' would be more accurate given the variegated nature of the list. A case could be made that this is a typical example of a phrase which, while conveying an air of expert author-ity, is in reality a confession of ignorance. Its function is primarily to impose a false image of bureaucratic order on multi-dimensional chaos. However, putting this label on someone also makes everyone else feel a lot better (including perhaps the sufferer themselves). 'Oh, they've got BPD, that's okay then.'

References and further reading

Judd, P.H. and McGlashan, T.H. (2002) *Developmental Model of Borderline Personality Disorder. Understanding Variations in Course and Outcome*, New York: American Psychiatric Press.

Linehan, M.M. (1995) *Understanding Borderline Personality Disorder*, New York: Guilford.

Zanarini, M.C. (2005) *Borderline Personality Disorder*, London: Taylor & Francis.

BRAINWASHING

Popular term for any intensive programme designed to change someone's ideas and instil those of the brainwasher. It became widely used in the 1950s following the Korean War in which some US prisoners (very few, in fact) apparently switched allegiance having been subjected to pressure of this kind. This was publicised in Hunter (1951). Lifton (1961) remains the classic Social Psychology text, while eminent British psychiatrist William Sargant's magisterial *Battle for the Mind* (Sargant 1957) became a Cold War best-seller.

References

Hunter, E. (1951) *Brain-Washing in Red China: The Calculated Destruction of Men's Minds*, New York: Vanguard Press.

Lifton, R.J. (1961) *Thought Reform and the Psychology of Totalism: A Study of 'Brainwashing' in China*, New York: W. W. Norton.
Sargant, W. (1957) *Battle for the Mind: A Physiology of Conversion and Brain-Washing*, London: Heinemann.

BROCA'S AREA

An area of the left frontal lobe (in the inferior frontal gyrus) of the brain cortex controlling speech and language production. Named after the French physiologist P.P. Broca, who discovered it in 1861. To grossly oversimplify, it is subdivided into sections controlling speech programming and speech itself. Language comprehension, however, is controlled by *Wernicke's area* located further back in the superior temporal lobe. Damage to these areas causes different kinds of **aphasia**, and, in the case of Broca's area, 'verbal apraxia' (inability to speak) or 'verbal dyspraxia' (difficulty in speaking). For a translation of the original Broca paper and others, see von Bonin (1960), for Wernicke's (1874) paper, Eggert (1977).

See under aphasia for current references.

References

Bonin, G. von (ed.) (1960) *Some Papers on the Cerebral Cortex Translated from the French and German*, Springfield, IL: Charles C. Thomas.
Eggert, G.H. (ed.) (1977) *Wernicke's Works on Aphasia: A Sourcebook and a Review*, The Hague: Mouton.

BULIMIA

An eating disorder characterized by 'binge-eating'. Often associated with **anorexia** in a cyclical fashion but less predominantly an adolescent phenomenon, although again occurring most commonly among women. There is now a large popular literature on the topic, the references below are among the more academically oriented now available.

References and further reading

Aronson, J.K. (2001) *Understanding and Treating Anorexia and Bulimia*, Lanham, MD: Jason Aronson Publishers.
Craggs-Hinton, C. (2006) *Coping with Eating Disorders and Body Image*, London: Sheld Press.

Logue, A.W. (2004) *The Psychology of Eating and Drinking*, London: Taylor & Francis.

Robert-McComb, J.J. (2000) *Eating Disorders in Women and Children: Prevention, Stress Management, and Treatment*, London: Taylor & Francis.

BULLYING

The topic of school and workplace bullying has acquired a high public profile in recent years and psychologists have naturally begun paying attention. Although not a technical term, there are close links with a number of established Psychological ideas and topics. In the case of one-on-one bullying, connections can obviously be drawn with *authoritarian personality* (see **authoritarianism**), concepts from **ethology** (such as *dominance hierarchy* establishment and *pecking order* as well as displaced **aggression**). In the case of group bullying, there are links with *scapegoating*, and **social identity theory**. Issues such as what kinds of people bully or become victims of bullying and the types of social situation which facilitate it are all now being studied. (The rise of the topic is indicated by the fact that I was unable to identify any book-length works on bullying prior to the early 1990s.)

References and further reading

Hanfling, O., Cooper, H. and Einarsen, S. (2002) *Bullying and Emotional Abuse in the Workplace: International Perspectives in Research and Practice*, London: Chapman & Hall.

Macklem, G.L. (2003) *Bullying and Teasing: Social Power in Children's Groups*, Amsterdam: Kluwer.

Randall, P. (2001) *Bullying in Adulthood: Assessing the Bullies and their Victims*, London: Routledge.

Sanders, C.F. (2004) *Bullying: Implications for the Classroom*, New York: Academic Press.

BYSTANDER EFFECT/BYSTANDER APATHY

Reluctance of bystanders to intervene and help when someone is obviously in difficulties, for example, when being subjected to violent assault or apparently drunk. This phenomenon became widely known after the 1964 New York case of Kitty Genovese whose murder was allegedly witnessed by 38 people watching from apartment blocks surrounding the small park where it, again allegedly, took place, none of whom, yet again allegedly, contacted the police. This version was based on a *New York Times* article by Martin Gansberg two weeks after the event. Virtually every detail of this story, regularly, and ritually, given in Social Psychology textbooks, has now been shown to be false (Manning *et al.*, 2007): her death occurred in the obscure entrance to a building, police were contacted by at least one witness early on, the night-time visibility of the scene was poor and, to cap it all, *Kitty Genovese* was widely known to be related to a top Mafia don, hence further inhibiting bystander involvement. In fact, the real social psychological significance of the event lies more in the light it sheds on social processes of mythologisation and rumour than on bystander indifference. Nevertheless the bystander effect itself is real enough, and is to some extent a function of the number of witnesses. It is, however, a complex phenomenon which can result from a variety of factors, and figures prominently in experimental studies of **altruism**.

References and further reading

Latané, B. (1981) 'The Psychology of Social Impact', *American Psychologist* 36: 343–56.

Manning, R., Levine, M. and Collins, A. (2007) 'The Kitty Genovese Murder and the Social Psychology of Helping: The Parable of the 38 Witnesses' *American Psychologist* 62: 555–62.

Rosenthal, A.M. (1964). *Thirty-Eight Witnesses: The Kitty Genovese Case*, Berkeley, CA: University of California Press.

CATEGORY MISTAKE

A useful expression introduced by mid-twentieth-century linguistic philosophers such as Gilbert Ryle (Ryle, 1949). A category mistake occurs when we ascribe the wrong 'ontological' status to the referent of a word or expression. Ryle's classic example was of a visitor to Oxford having been shown the various colleges, the Bodleian library and the Sheldonian Theatre, then asking where the university was. To spell it out, the visitor had failed to understand that Oxford University did not exist as a separate thing aside from the various physically housed institutions they had just toured. For Ryle, this was the key to understanding the **mind–body problem** itself, but we need not go there now. A common form of category mistake, especially in Psychology, is **reification.** In short, things can exist in numerous different ways – as physical entities, as properties and qualities (like speed or colour), as abstract concepts (such as numbers –

you will never find the number 77 as such in the physical world, only objects such as buses so numbered), as social or economic concepts (the balance of trade, democracy, marriage), as ways of behaving (jolly, stubborn), and so on. Category mistakes occur when the status of something in this respect becomes muddled.

Reference

Ryle, G. (1949) *The Concept of Mind*, London: Hutchinson.

CENTRAL EXECUTIVE

Hypothesised component of *working memory* (see **memory**) responsible for a variety of functions related to the regulation and integration of information flow and the implementation of goal-directed behaviour. It is difficult to avoid the conclusion that in some respects this is the *cognitivist* equivalent of the *Ego* (see **psychoanalysis**). One recent technical definition, however, describes it as a 'modality-independent, flexible, but limited capacity processing resource that also serves as an interface between two slave-systems, the phonological loop … and the visuo-spatial scratch pad' (Davey, 2005: 131). So there. First proposed by A.D. Baddeley and G. Hitch in 1974 and further developed in Baddeley (1986).

References

Baddeley, A.D. (1986) *Working Memory* Oxford: Oxford University Press.
—— (1998) 'The Central Executive: A Concept and Some Misconceptions', *Journal of the International Neuropsychological Society* 4: 523–26.
Baddeley, A.D. and Hitch, G. (1974) 'Working Memory' in G.A. Bower (ed.) *Recent Advances in Learning and Motivation, Vol.8*, New York: Academic Press.
Davey, G. (ed.) (2005) *Encyclopedic Dictionary of Psychology*, London: Hodder Arnold.

COGNITION

'Cognition' is really almost synonymous with 'reasoning' and 'logical thinking' (which may not be conscious). It is by using 'cognitive processing' that we convert sensory input into knowledge about the external world. Prior to the 1950s, the terms 'reasoning' and 'thinking' were widely used by psychologists interested in this aspect of psychological functioning, but from the late 1950s the term 'cognition' came to dominate with the rise of **Cognitive Psychology**.

COGNITIVE BEHAVIOURAL THERAPY (CBT)

CBT emerged in the 1990s as a modification or renaming of A. Ellis's Rational-Emotive Therapy, developed in the 1960s. Ellis had become highly dissatisfied with the practical effectiveness of **psychoanalysis** and similar forms of therapy. The key features of CBT are, first, its focus on the present and the behavioural changes the client wishes to make and, second, that the therapist specifies behavioural exercises and tasks for the client to undertake between therapy sessions. There is little doubt that CBT has developed some highly workable techniques and proven very suitable for certain kinds of problem, becoming extremely popular in **counselling** and **psychotherapy** especially in the context of short-term therapy. Practitioners of other approaches are, however, increasingly concerned that, with official backing, CBT is becoming seen as a universal panacea for psychological distress, and something of a bandwagon. Numerous books on CBT are currently available, some of the more popular 'self-help' kind and others on its use with specific conditions. If web-searching, remember that the US spelling is 'behavioral' not 'behavioural'.

References and further reading

Dobson, K.S. (2000) *Handbook of Cognitive-Behavioral Therapies*, 2nd edn, New York: Guilford.

Mulhern, R., Grant, A., Short, M. and Mills, J. (2004) *Cognitive Behavioural Therapy in Mental Health Care*, London: Sage.

Tarrier, N. (2007) *Cognitive-Behavioural Therapy*, Chichester: John Wiley & Sons, Ltd.

Whitfield, G. and Davidson, A. (2007) *Cognitive Behavioural Therapy Explained*, Oxford: Radcliffe.

COGNITIVE DISSONANCE

Cognitive dissonance theory was founded by US social psychologist Leon Festinger (1959). It is concerned with exploring how we deal with situations where we are experiencing two (or more) contradictory 'cognitions' – I am an expert mountain climber and have just fallen off a short ladder; I have just bought a new car and am not as happy with it as I thought I would be; I want my daughter to be independent but am anxious because she has not rung me for two days; I am financially very smart but have just fallen for an e-mail scam involving a bank in Burkina Faso ... One of the most famous cases contributing to Festinger's theory was of a sect which, believing the end of the world was due on a specific date, holed themselves up awaiting the event, from which their pious faith would save them. The failure of the prediction naturally resulted in great cognitive dissonance in sect members. Their strategies for dealing with this were reported in Festinger *et al.* (1956). In many respects, cognitive dissonance theory amounts to a mapping of all the rationalisation strategies we use in these circumstances, of which there are many. To mention just three, we tend to read advertisements for a particular brand of expensive goods more after purchasing them than before (to reassure ourselves it was a good buy), we find an alternative reason why expending much time and energy on a failed task was a good thing ('well, the exercise did me good anyway'), we find reasons why our behaviour was reasonable under the circumstances – perhaps we were acting on advice from someone we presumed trustworthy (thus dissonance is higher if you lose a bet on the horses having been tipped by a complete stranger than if tipped by a jockey friend). (And of course, the end of the world was postponed because God was so impressed by our faith.) A good source of examples of efforts at reducing cognitive dissonance is politicians' pronouncements in the face of policy failures, 'we were acting in good faith on the best available evidence at the time' being classic (even if the policy was being highly opposed). Dissonance theory basically predicts that we will strive to avoid dissonance by ignoring dissonance-producing information and exposing ourselves to its opposite, 'consonance'-producing information. Thus we respond to dissonance-inducing events by seeking out information that can justify our behaviour. Although this can generate good behavioural predictions about how people will respond in certain situations the variety of actual strategies can render this difficult. One may, after all, genuinely change one of the conflicting 'elements' – admitting one was not so smart after all and had indeed been genuinely stupid. Cognitive dissonance remains an active research topic in Social Psychology.

References

Brehm, J.W. and Cohen, A.R. (1962) *Explorations in Cognitive Dissonance* New York: John Wiley & Sons, Ltd.

Festinger, L. (1957) *A Theory of Cognitive Dissonance*, Stanford, CA: Stanford University Press.

Festinger, L., Riecken, H.R. Jr. and Schachter, S. (1956) *When Prophecy Fails*, Minneapolis: University of Minnesota Press.

Harmon-Jones, E. and Mills, J. (1999). *Cognitive Dissonance: Progress on a Pivotal Theory in Social Psychology*. Washington, DC: American Psychological Association.

COGNITIVE MAP

Phrase introduced by American behaviourist E.C. Tolman (1948) to explain *latent learning* (see **learning**). It has since become a standard term in **Cognitive Psychology** and Environmental Psychology to refer to a hypothesized internal representation of the layout of an environmental feature. Thus we have cognitive maps of our town, house, the world and workplace, etc.

Reference

Tolman, E.C. (1948) 'Cognitive Maps in Rats and Men', *Psychological Review* 55(4): 189–208.

COGNITIVE PSYCHOLOGY

Inspired by developments in computing and information theory during the 1940s, a number of psychologists began exploring their applicability to psychological processes. While Cambridge-based British psychologist Kenneth Craik (1943) was perhaps the earliest to attempt this, it was in the United States that a movement calling itself Cognitive Psychology first stirred in the early 1950s and had, by the end of the 1960s, largely replaced **behaviourism** and other theoretical orientations in experimental Psychology. Leading figures in this shift were G. A. Miller, J. Bruner and H. Simon, although the overlap with mathematicians such as J. von Neumann plus a variety of engineers and physiologists, including W. McCulloch, C. Shannon and the founder of cybernetics, N. Weiner, was considerable. In the UK, D. Broadbent, W. Grey Walter and R. Ashby were pursuing a somewhat independent course which converged with the US one during the 1960s. The fortunes of Cognitive Psychology have never significantly waned since, while links with physiology have become firmly established in what is now commonly called 'cognitive neuroscience'. In some quarters, especially in the USA, this has resulted in an effective split from the rest of Psychology, reinforced by its essentially multidisciplinary character.

But why 'cognitive'? The answer is primarily because to its advocates in the USA, it marked a recentring of experimental Psychology on *thinking* as opposed to *learning*. Psychological research on thinking was not new, it was a prominent topic in **Gestalt Psychology**, for example, as well as the focus of **Piagetian theory**. These were rebaptised as 'proto-cognitivist' by the new sub-discipline, while N. Chomsky's structural linguistics was also co-opted into the camp. It was not so much the subject-matter that was new but the adoption of the revolutionary concepts emerging in information theory, cybernetics and computing (such as 'programming'). Cognitivism rapidly affected other fields of Psychology, so that by the end of the last century 'cognitive approaches' were represented in most sub-disciplines, **attribution theory** in Social Psychology, **cognitive behavioural therapy** (CBT) in counselling, studies of **cognitive style** in **personality**, and an ongoing fusion of Piagetian and US cognitivism in Child Psychology. (J. Bruner played a major role in this after spending time in Geneva with Piaget.) For the origins of Cognitive Psychology, see Hirst (1988) and Murray (1995). There are currently a large number of textbooks available on the topic, those listed below being among the most notable.

References and further reading

Balota, D.A. (2004) *Cognitive Psychology: Key Readings*, London: Taylor & Francis.
Craik, K. (1943) *The Nature of Explanation*, Cambridge: Cambridge University Press.
Eysenck, M.W. (2005) *Cognitive Psychology*, London: Taylor & Francis.
Galotti, K.M. (2007) *Cognitive Psychology In and Out of the Laboratory*, Belmont, CA: Wadsworth.
Hirst, W. (ed.) (1988) *The Making of Cognitive Science: Essays in Honor of G.A. Miller*, Cambridge: Cambridge University Press.
Murray, D.J. (1995) *Gestalt Psychology and the Cognitive Revolution*, New York: Harvester Wheatsheaf.
Sternberg, R.J. (2005) *Cognitive Psychology*, Belmont, CA: Wadsworth.

COGNITIVE STYLE

Since people tend to approach **problem-solving** tasks in different ways, it is unsurprising that psychologists have attempted to bring some order to this by identifying basic types or dimensions of thinking. These are considered to be unrelated to **intelligence** as such. The majority of this work has been done since the 1950s in the contexts of **Cognitive**

Psychology and **personality** research. Prior to this C.G. Jung's *psychological functions* model (see **Analytical Psychology**) had provided a typology of what are now called 'cognitive styles', since each personality type was characterised by, among much else, a different way of approaching problems. Later used as a basis for the *Myers-Briggs type indicator* this has remained influential. Although appearing in several guises, one common classification is into **divergent** and **convergent thinking**. Somewhat similar are the holistic *vs* analytic and holistic *vs* serialist polarities. Other distinctions which have been made are: reflective *vs* impulsive, verbal *vs* imagery-based, adaptors *vs* innovators, level of **field dependency**, **locus of control** preferences, and, associated with **authoritarianism**, high intolerance of ambiguity. Most of these are self-explanatory. More recently, it has been suggested that there are distinct cultural cognitive styles. The early cognitivist classic, *A Study of Thinking* (Bruner *et al.*, 1956), although not directly concerned with cognitive style, is also relevant as opening up the study of cognitive strategies. The concept does have applied relevance, since educational performance is enhanced by congruence between the cognitive styles of teacher and learner. It is also evident that in a few cases (such as intolerance of ambiguity) certain cognitive styles may be less effective than others in a general way, rather than only in relation to specific types of task. Given the centrality of 'how people think' to so many areas of Psychology, the borders of the topic are actually somewhat fuzzy, one might include **personal construct theory**, for example, as concerned with similar issues and, at a popular level, the numerous works of Edward de Bono.

References and further reading

Bruner, J.S., Goodnow, J. and Austin, G. (1956) *A Study of Thinking*, New York: Wiley.

Riding, R.J. (2000) *International Perspectives on Individual Differences Vol. 1: Cognitive Styles*, Westport, CT: Greenwood Press.

—— (2002) *School Learning and Cognitive Styles*, London: Taylor & Francis.

Sternberg, R.J. and Zhang, Li-Fang (eds) (2001) *Perspectives on Thinking, Learning and Cognitive Styles*, Mahwah, NJ: Lawrence Erlbaum.

Witkin, H.A. (1978) *Cognitive Styles in Personal and Cultural Adaptation*, Worcester, MA: Clark University Press.

CONFORMITY

Adherence to the behavioural norms, tastes, opinions, dress, etc. of the group to which one assumes one belongs. The topic became especially high on the Social Psychology agenda during the 1950s, reflecting a much broader concern among US intellectuals, almost amounting to a moral panic. The cultural conditions for this were a complex combination of the economic explosion of consumerism (involving advertising at unprecedented levels of intensity and pressure to 'keep up with the Jones's') and the virulently anti-left ideological climate of the early Cold War. For psychologists, anxieties were reinforced by the claim of a correlation between conformity and **authoritarianism**, while science fiction writers commonly produced dystopian visions of utterly conformist futures and folk-singer Pete Seeger sang of people all living in identical 'Little Boxes'. There was also a widespread belief that Nazism and Communism alike were rooted in unthinking mass conformity. The famous 'Asch experiment' of 1951 in which many subjects agreed that the longest of two lines was the shortest under pressure from others, who were in fact confederates of the experimenter, became iconic of Social Psychology's work on the topic at this period. (See Asch, 1952, for a full and amusing account.) Concern about conformity also spread to Britain and Western Europe, but somewhat less intensely. This initial phase of Psychological interest in conformity faded during the 1960s, although in a sense the 'alternative culture' and protest movements of that era were in some part reactions against conformity. It does, however, remain a topic of some interest, since psychological pressures to conform have never disappeared, and are in some respects necessary for social cohesion. Of most concern now is the way in which young people, particularly those in marginalised communities, feel bound to conform to sub-cultural norms of which society at large disapproves. At a wider level, however, with the advent of the internet and anonymity of urban life, the cultural trend has shifted in the opposite direction and 'normality' becomes ever harder to identify. As a topic in Social Psychology, conformity has now largely become subsumed under broader areas such as 'group influence'. Sternberg and Lubart (1995) is one of the few post-1990 book-length treatments in Psychology, although general Social Psychology textbooks continue to give it some coverage.

References

Asch, S.E. (1952) *Social Psychology*, Englewood Cliffs, NJ: Prentice-Hall.
Sternberg, R.J. and Lubart, T.I. (1995) *Defying the Crowd. Cultivating Creativity in a Culture of Conformity*, Old Tappan, NJ: Free Press.

CONNECTIONISM

Approach to modelling used in **AI (artifical intelligence)**, based on the broadly **associationist** principle of linear circuitry. Rooted in classical **learning theory**, in which learning involved the elaboration of *S-R* connections, it provided AI modellers with a relatively simple starting point for designing or hypothesising circuitry which emulated this principle. In doing so, they broke away from the notion that the brain operated like a computer processing a symbolic language, for by incorporating a differential weighting of the postulated synapses linking their virtual 'neurons' they were able to develop what is known as 'neural networks' capable of analoging more complex psychological processes. The central advantage of this was that the system could 'learn' and did not require, nor was constrained by, preset programming, connections developing in the light of feedback. Few connectionists, however, now believe the opposition between Connectionist and Computational approaches is clear–cut, and some believe them to be complementary. Historically, Connectionism thus represents the 'analog' theoretical strand in AI. Neural network theory provides a model of how representation (see **representationalism**) may be neurally implemented in a distributed fashion, such that my idea of a 'tree' does not have a single corresponding site in my brain. As with AI as a whole, a number of philosophical issues have surfaced over recent decades in relation to the sufficiency of neural network models to account adequately for all psychological phenomena, with some of its exponents such as Churchland (1986) and Churchland (1988) and Stich (1983) adopting radically reductionist positions, especially in relation to **Folk Psychology**. These debates are too complex for summary here. **Parallel distributed processing** (PDP) represented a major advance in connectionist theorising.

See also: **AI**.

References and further reading

Churchland, P.S. (1986) *Neurophilosophy. Toward a Unified Science of the Mind/Brain*, Cambridge, MA: MIT Press.

Churchland, P.M. (1988) *Matter and Consciousness*, rev. edn, Cambridge, MA: MIT Press.

McClelland, J.L. and Rumelhart, D.E. (1986) *Parallel Distributed Processing: Explorations in the Microstructure of Cognition: Psychological and Biological Models (Computational Models of Cognition)*, Cambridge, MA: MIT Press.

Quinlan, P.T. (1991) *Connectionism and Psychology: A Psychological Perspective on New Connectionist Research*, Chicago, IL: The University of Chicago Press.

Stich, S. (1983) *From Folk Psychology to Cognitive Science*, Cambridge, MA: MIT Press.

Useful website

http://plato.stanford.edu/entries/connectionism/

CONTENT ANALYSIS

A technique for analysing the content of written texts, particularly those elicited in response to **thematic apperception tests** and open-ended questionnaires, but also adapted for the analysis of dreams (Hall and Van De Castle, 1966). Developed initially in the 1950s, there was some overlap in earlier uses with **discourse analysis**, in that the material analysed often included transcripts of spoken responses. A variant form of content analysis was occasionally used for analysing visual material such as decorative motifs, notably by some researchers on **achievement motivation**. There appears to have been relatively little work done in the area over the last decade, Discourse Analysis having largely taken its place.

References and further reading

Hall, C.S. and Van De Castle, R.L. (1966) *The Content Analysis of Dreams*, New York: Appleton-Century-Crofts.
Smith, C.P. (1992) *Motivation and Personality: Handbook of Thematic Content Analysis*, Cambridge: Cambridge University Press.

CONVERGENT THINKING

Introduced by Liam Hudson in his *Contrary Imaginations* (Hudson 1966), convergent thinking refers to a **cognitive style** which is pre-dominantly analytical and logical, oriented towards logical problem-solving in a focused fashion. This he opposed to **divergent thinking**. In making this distinction, Hudson was concerned to differentiate between two sorts of creativity. Earlier Psychological studies of crea-tivity tended to concentrate on divergent thinking, but Hudson felt it was absurd to claim that a schoolboy (these being the subjects of his research) who could build a radio or complex machine from scratch should be considered less creative than one who excelled at writing imaginative stories or painting original pictures.

Reference

Hudson, L. (1966) *Contrary Imaginations*, London: Methuen.

COUNSELLING

The current use of the term counselling originated in the religious context of 'pastoral counselling', in which religious professionals such as church ministers advised lay members of their faith on their psychological problems. During the 1920s and 1930s, many such people began to look sympathetically towards the new **psychotherapy** techniques being developed by **psychoanalysis** and other schools. Relations between these and some religious counsellors, such as the Methodist Leslie Weatherhead in Britain, became very close. Up until around 1960 there was, nevertheless, felt to be a fairly clear boundary between 'counselling' and 'psychotherapy', the former being a less medical, less theoretically technical, way of dealing with psychological distress, such as grief, which was not actually pathological. With the advent of the **Humanistic Psychology** associated with Carl Rogers and Abraham Maslow in the late 1950s, the ensuing broader rise of the **growth movement** and demands from counsellors for professional recognition the situation became increasingly blurred. By the 1970s, the feeling became widespread that there was actually little difference between the two, or at least a huge area of overlap. The main advantage of the term 'counselling' was that it carried no medical connotations of 'mental illness', and thus did not deter those afraid of being stigmatised for seeking professional Psychological help. Conversely, 'psychotherapy', which could be cast as a branch of medicine, had the advantage of being more readily accepted in official public health systems and hospitals. After 1980, counselling grew very rapidly in Britain and North America, with expanded numbers of training courses and increased recognition by professional associations such as the British Psychological Society. The original religious connection, best represented in Britain by the Westminster Pastoral Foundation, still remains as one strand in the counselling tradition but diminished greatly during the late 1970s and most now think of it as an entirely secular field. From the outset, counselling was marked by pragmatic eclecticism, and although many theoretical concepts and theoretically-rooted procedures are in play, it is basically up to the counsellor to decide which approaches they are most comfortable with. On the other hand, there are quite strict ethical rules laid down by the British Association of Counsellors, including a mandatory requirement for qualified supervision, as well as guidelines on professional conduct. The market is flooded with Counselling books, the publisher Sage in particular having an extended series, but those listed are among the most recent British academic titles.

References and further reading

Feltham, C. and Horton, I. (eds) (2006) *The Sage Book of Counselling and Psychotherapy*, London: Sage.
Nelson-Jones, R. (2006) *Theory and Practice of Counselling and Therapy*, London: Sage.
Rowan, J. (2006) *Transpersonal: Spirituality in Psychotherapy and Counselling*, London: Taylor & Francis.
Woolfe, R., Dryden, W. and Strawbridge, S. (2003) *Handbook of Counselling Psychology*, London: Sage.

Useful websites

www.bacp.co.uk/ (British Association of Counselling)
www.bps.org.uk/dcop/dcop_home.cfm (British Psychological Society, Division of Counselling Psychology)

CULTURE

The concept of 'culture' has always proved problematic for those in the human sciences, notably anthropology, even if the term itself seems indispensable. The difficulties lie primarily in the question of whether: (1) 'culture' is understood as something superordinate to the individual members of society as a kind of independent factor separable from e.g. individual interests and motivations; (2) it is a hypothetical abstraction imposing a false unity on the miscellaneous totality of social practises, beliefs; (3) similar to (1), but an expression of the deep collective psychological character of the members of the society. The relationship between 'culture' and 'psychology' has thus been a perennial bone of contention and must be considered something of a 'chicken and egg' problem. In Psychology, this became a prominent topic during the 1930s–c.1960 with the work of the *Columbia 'Culture and Personality' School* (see **Schools of Psychology**). Another kind of difficulty, becoming more evident, is the validity of the continued use of the term in so-called 'multi-cultural' twenty-first-century societies. While each of the various communities has particular customs of dress, domestic life, religious practice, etc., there are also huge areas of everyday life in which no such differences exist as well as major generational differences. Do the ancestral cultural features which communities preserve any longer amount to their having a distinct 'culture' in the traditional sense? If everyone is using the same money, driving the same cars, using the same public transport, using mobile phones and computers, living in the same kind of houses and cooking on the same kind of stoves, then a point is reached at which the term 'culture' must become misleading. For an introduction to the topic, T. Ingold's entry 'Introduction to Culture' in Ingold (1994) should suffice.

Reference

Ingold, T. (ed.) (1994) *Companion Encyclopedia of Anthropology: Humanity, Culture and Social Life*, London: Taylor & Francis.

CYCLOTHYMIA

Term introduced by German psychiatrist Emil Kraepelin as a label for one of four types of personality disorder he identified (the others being depression, **mania** and irritability). He proposed that in the cyclothymic personality depressive and manic states alternate. It is now considered a variety of **bipolar disorder**. Current descriptions of the condition stress that cyclical oscillations of a variety of kinds can occur – between sociability and reclusiveness, high activity and lethargy, hedonistic sexual excess and guilt, and so on. There is also a suggestion that the condition typifies a certain kind of artistic personality, Ernest Hemingway being commonly cited as exemplifying this. There is a particularly useful summary on the *Encyclopedia of Mental Disorders* site.

Useful website

www.enotes.com/mental-disorders-encyclopedia/cyclothymic-disorder

DECONSTRUCTION

The term is generally ascribed to Jacques Derrida and is commonly encountered in *Critical Psychology* and postmodernist writing, especially as influenced by the French historian Michel Foucault, but has become more widely used. 'Deconstruction' refers to the analysis of texts in a way which discloses underlying hidden agendas, 'subtexts', author motivations, assumptions about the readership and rhetorical methods. It can also be used in relation to single concepts to reveal their underlying complexity, implicit assumptions and the like. Derrida's initial use of it was narrower, the exposure of hidden 'binary' or oppositional assumptions in texts. Thus, one might deconstruct the concept of **schizophrenia**, looking at how it has been used, why it emerged, the implicit imagery of 'splitting' it evokes and what effects that has on how it is popularly understood, etc. The references list some applications of the approach to Psychological topics.

References and further reading

Burman, E. (2007) *Deconstructing Developmental Psychology*, 2nd edn, London: Routledge.

Forrester, M.A. (1996) *Psychology of Language: A Critical Introduction*, Thousand Oaks, CA: Sage.

Parker, I., Georgaca, E., Harper, D., McLaughlin, T. and Stowell-Smith, M. (1995) *Deconstructing Psychopathology*, London: Sage.

Parker, I. and Shotter, J. (1990) *Deconstructing Social Psychology*, London: Routledge.

DEGENERATIONISM

A central, if not strictly essential, doctrine of **eugenics**, 'degenerationism' was the belief that certain hereditary lineages were on a downward spiral of decline and reversion to more primitive characteristics. While coined somewhat earlier, this gained great momentum in the late nineteenth century when there was a virtual panic about degeneration across Europe, the most powerful statement of this being the German Max Nordau's book *Degeneration* (Nordau, 1895), while the Italian C. Lombroso's work on crime and genius gave it firmer 'scientific' credentials (e.g. Lombroso, 1891; Lombroso and Ferrero, 1895). Until about 1920, the concept, although highly contested, played a major role in framing Psychological thought and social policy regarding 'idiocy', crime and mental illness, all being cast as resulting from an increase in the prevalence of degeneracy due to the suspension of 'natural selection' and misplaced philanthropy. In the United States, evidence of degenerating lineages was sought, the two most famous cases being the Jukes family (Dugdale 1877) and, more influentially, the Kallikaks (Goddard 1912). The best overview of the topic is Pick (1989).

References

Dugdale, R.L. (1877) *"The Jukes". A Study in Crime, Pauperism, Disease and Heredity*, New York: Putnams.
Goddard, H.H. (1912) *The Kallikak Family: A Study in the Heredity of Feeble-Mindedness*, New York: Macmillan.
Lombroso, C. (1891) *The Man of Genius*, London: Walter Scott.
Lombroso, C. and Ferrero, W. (1895) *The Female Offender*, London: Fisher Unwin.
Nordau, Max (1895) *Degeneration*, London: Heinemann.
Pick, D. (1989) *Faces of Degeneration: A European Disorder, c.1848–c.1919*, Cambridge: Cambridge University Press.

DEMENTIA PRAECOX

Obsolete term, gradually abandoned after 1911, for **schizophrenia** (coined by E. Bleuler). The term roughly meant 'premature dementia' (as opposed to senile dementia) and did not entirely vanish from psychiatric usage until the 1950s.

DEPRESSION

Perhaps the single most widely diagnosed form of mental distress. It is generally stressed that 'clinical depression' is qualitatively different from normal forms of sadness and grief in being resistant to ordinary modes of consolation, and in the utterly debilitating effects it has on the sufferer. Despair, feelings that life is meaningless, suicidal thoughts and the like are its hallmarks. Two broad categories are typically identified. The first, 'endogenous depression', is the most problematic since it seems to be an enduring **personality** trait and the sufferer's depressive episodes are unrelated to external events. 'Exogenous depression' can be attributed to identifiable events or experiences of an extremely negative kind. Grief and traumatic events (see **post-traumatic stress disorder**), if unresolved, are obvious sources of exogenous depression. During the latter half of the twentieth century, treatment of depression, especially endogenous depression, became increasingly reliant on anti-depressant drugs such as Prozac. There is a huge literature on the topic from the popular self-help genre to the psychiatric. Historically it ultimately emerged from the old concept of *melancholia* or 'Melancholy', but the cultural meanings and connotations of the terms differ in some important respects and their relationship is a tangled one. Despite the common insistence on clearly differentiating depression from other forms of 'normal' unhappiness, the boundary remains hard to define. It is significant that, in the past, extreme 'melancholia' was not seen as pathological in all cases, the 'dark night of the soul' being considered a necessary stage in full religious understanding, for example, and when construed in religious terms such as feelings of guilt, worthlessness and rejection by God, melancholia might even be seen as signifying the sufferer's holiness and high spiritual status (which was of little help to the sufferer!). The respective roles of physiological, psychological and cultural factors in determining the nature and meanings of depression remain unclear. The literature, both popular and academic, is vast, but the following recent titles should provide a sound introduction. For a historical perspective, see Jackson (1986).

See also: **bipolar disorder**.

References and further reading

Gilliam, F.G., Sheline, Y.I. and Kanner, A.M. (eds) (2005) *Depression and Brain Dysfunction*, London: Taylor & Francis.

Jackson, S.W. (1986) *Melancholia and Depression: from Hippocratic Times to Modern Times*, New Haven, CT: Yale University Press.

Licinio, J., Ma-Li, Wong (2005) *Biology of Depression: From Novel Insights to Therapeutic Strategies*, 2 vols, Somerset, NJ: Wiley.

Praag, H.M van, Kloet, E.R. de and Os, J. van (2004) *Stress, the Brain and Depression*, Cambridge: Cambridge University Press.

Schwartz, T.L. (ed.) (2006) *Depression*, London: Taylor & Francis.

DEVELOPMENT

'Development' appears, on the face of it, to be a quite innocuous and natural concept. Writers such as Burman (2007) and Morss (1990, 1996) have, however, raised serious questions about its use in the expression 'Developmental Psychology'. Their case, broadly, is that the 'developmental' perspective has serious implications for how the psychology of the child is understood. In particular, it leads to an over-emphasis on the significance of children's behaviour and experience in terms of what it tells us about their maturation, as a way of diag-nosing how well the child is 'progressing'. This has two important, inter-related, consequences. First, a preoccupation with establishing developmental 'norms' and, second, a relative lack of interest in chil-dren's individual personalities and differences except when these are seen as having some developmental significance. More profoundly, the developmental approach leads to (and historically emerged from) a view of childhood as a natural biological process as opposed to a socially embedded phase of the individual's psychological bio-graphy. The alternative to this 'developmentalism', it is argued, is to consider children as fully functioning individual persons living in the present whose experiences, understanding and behaviour should be treated in their own terms, not simply in relation to what they portend about the child's future or say about their position in some kind of linear scale of developmental norms. While extremely valu-able, this critique does not alter the fact that the traditional 'devel-opmental' perspective is also necessary in contexts such as education and general monitoring of the child's psychological maturation (but see also **norm**).

References and further reading

Burman, E. (2007) *Deconstructing Developmental Psychology*, 2nd edn, London: Routledge.

Morss, J.R. (1990) *The Biologising of Childhood. Developmental Psychology and the Darwinian Myth*, Hove: Erlbaum.

Morss, J.R. (1996) *Growing Critical: Alternatives to Developmental Psychology*, London: Routledge.

DISCOURSE ANALYSIS

A technique for analysing the content of spoken and written lan-guage. Greatly developed in the latter twentieth century in research based on recorded interviews, discourse analysis is now one the lead-ing **qualitative methods,** used particularly by social psychologists. The types of 'text' with which it is used span the entire spectrum from books to adverts, TV shows, even scientific papers. It is also used by historians of the human sciences, this being rooted in French historian M. Foucault's 'archaeology of knowledge' which centred on analysing historical discourses related to topics such as madness, sexu-ality and crime. It is in many respects similar to **deconstruction**.

References and further reading

Caldas-Coulthart, C. (1995) *Texts and Practices: Readings in Critical Discourse Analysis*, London: Taylor & Francis.

Hoey, M. (2000) *Textual Interaction: An Introduction to Written Discourse Analysis*, London: Taylor & Francis.

Paltridge, B. (2007) *Discourse Analysis: An Introduction*, London: Continuum.

Wetherell, M., Taylor, S. and Yates, S.J. (2001) *Discourse as Data: A Guide for Analysis*, London: Sage.

Wodak, R. (2000) *Methods of Text and Discourse Analysis*, London: Sage.

DISPLACEMENT ACTIVITY

In **ethology**, displacement activity is behaviour engaged in when the usual behavioural expression of an **instinct** is blocked, thereby providing an outlet for the pent-up energy. The concept is easily deployed with regard to human behaviour as well – the person with an unsatisfactory home life who works obsessionally long hours, or bullies a partner because they cannot express their aggression towards an employer, or finds an outlet for sexual frustration in extreme religious piety might all be considered as examples. Less dramatically it may take such everyday forms as avoiding starting work on a task by deciding to tidy the kitchen. The concept not only occurs in ethological contexts but, in the case of displaced **aggression**, for example, features in the *frustration-aggression hypothesis*. There appear to be no book-length works on the topic, for references, see **ethology**.

DISSOCIATION

Term used since the late nineteenth century to describe conditions in which there appears to be a split between two or more psychological systems which then continue to operate independently and, as it were, unaware of each other. Most widely known in the form of **multiple personality disorder (MPD)/dissociative identity disorder (DID)**. It is, however, used in a number of other contexts.

DIVERGENT THINKING

Introduced by Liam Hudson (Hudson, 1966), this refers to the ability to think 'outside the box' – to come up with novel and imaginative solutions to problems or with new ways of approaching issues which outflank the implicit assumptions and categories within which others are operating. It also refers to 'creative' or 'imaginative' thinking such as required in producing art and literature. See also **convergent thinking**. The term *lateral thinking* (especially as promoted by popular writer Edward de Bono) (De Bono, 1967) is also a virtual synonym though refers more explicitly to problem-solving. (If you try to connect all the dots in a 3 × 3 dot square with four continuous straight lines you will understand why the phrase 'think outside the box' came into use.)

References

De Bono, E. (1967) *The Use of Lateral Thinking*, London: Cape.
Hudson, L. (1966) *Contrary Imaginations*, London: Methuen.

DOUBLE BIND

Coined by anthropologist and psychologist Gregory Bateson (see Ruesch and Bateson, 1951) and taken up by R.D. Laing and others in the **anti-psychiatry** movement of the 1960s. Double binds are situations where one person communicates to another in such a way that they cannot win however they respond. An example would be when a parent verbally tells a child they love him/her dearly but actually behaves in a rejecting fashion, avoiding affectionate physical contact and never paying attention to his/her feelings and concerns. So if the child responds by disputing the verbal assurance of love, the parent reprimands him/her, but if the child tries to be affectionate, he/she is rejected. Another case would be when efforts at independence elicit anxiety and over-protectiveness, but failure to make such efforts elicits accusations of being clinging and over-dependent. The person responsible for double-binding may often not be conscious of doing so. Laing believed that being the target of long-term sustained double-binding was a factor in causing **schizophrenia**. Although few would endorse this view so strongly, there is little doubt that such unconscious double-binding can have deleterious consequences. Conscious, or semi-conscious, double-binding, on the other hand, is a common feature of human interaction.

References and further reading

Laing. R.D. and Esterson, A. (1964) *Sanity, Madness and the Family*, London: Tavistock.

Ruesch, J. and Bateson, G. (1951) *Communication: The Social Matrix*, New York: Norton.

Sluzki, C.E. and Ransom, D.C. (eds) (1976) *Double Bind: The Foundation of the Communicational Approach to the Family*, London: Grune & Stratton.

DRIVE

With the demise of classic **instinct** theories and rise of the concept of **motivation**, the term 'drive' became widely used during the 1930s and remains in wide use in terms such as 'hunger drive' and 'sex drive'. May be loosely defined as energy producing behaviour directed towards a specific kind of goal, usually in order to satisfy a basic **need**. Its status is somewhat fuzzy, however, and it remains a **hypothetical construct** serving a primarily descriptive role rather than an explanatory one.

See also: **motivation**.

DSM (*DIAGNOSTIC AND STATISTICAL MANUAL OF MENTAL DISORDERS*)

An official manual issued by the American Psychiatric Association, but also used in the UK and many other countries, in which all mental disorders are defined and classified. The first edition (DSM I) appeared in 1952. It is now up to DSM IV (1994, but revised in 2000) with DSM V planned for 2012. Successive editions reflect not only a simple growth of psychiatric knowledge but also changes in prevailing theoretical orientation and social attitudes. Thus, **psychoanalysis** greatly influenced DSM I but this had diminished enormously by DSM III, 'homosexuality' was included as a mental disorder until 1974 when, responding to the success of the 'Gay Liberation' movement, it was dropped from a DSM II reprint, replaced by 'sexual orientation disturbance'. Despite its authoritative status, the DSM has never escaped controversy. While apparently indispensable in ensuring some kind of profession-wide consensus and providing a common point of reference, there is a hovering question mark. The DSM enshrines a medical approach in which 'mental disorders' can all be clearly defined, diagnosed and differentiated as distinct pathological conditions. Yet much, if not all, 'mental disorder' cannot in reality be neatly defined so easily, especially if no organic factors are involved. Such 'mental disorders' may involve non-psychological causes such as family dynamics or social deprivation, while in some cases it is a matter of debate whether a specific behaviour or 'symptom' represents a mental disorder or not (e.g. talking to oneself or hearing voices). The DSM represents, in fact, the position against which **anti-psychiatry** rebelled in the 1960s. It will be interesting to see which direction DSM V takes.

DUALISM

Philosophically this refers to all proposed solutions to the **mind-body problem** which involve postulating the existence of two separate (if, in most versions, interacting) entities, substances, forces or whatever. This is now rarely advocated, although the eminent neurologist Sir John Eccles continued to espouse it (Popper and Eccles, 1981).

References and further reading

Popper, K.R and Eccles, J.C. (1981) *The Self and Its Brain: An Argument for Interactionism*, Berlin: Springer.
Valentine, E.R (1992) *Conceptual Issues in Psychology*, London: Routledge.

DYSLEXIA

More correctly, one should talk of 'the dylexias', since this refers to a variety of problems which can arise in relation to processing written language. The term 'strephosymbolia' was apparently suggested at one time (but perhaps nobody could spell it). Dyslexics may have difficulty in differentiating letters of the same topological form (*p*, *d*, *b*, *q* being notorious), in sequencing letters when spelling (writing *ht* instead of *th*), in remembering the different spelling of words which sound the same (homophones) such as *pare* and *pear* (or *rein*, *reign* and *rain*; *vane*, *vain* and *vein*), and in visually tracking printed text. These errors are, then, of several different types. Some are predominantly visual and some to do with deeper levels of information processing, while the sometimes arbitrary nature of the sound–spelling link, especially in English, is implicated, as well as visual memory. It is important to stress that the dyslexias are unrelated to intelligence and that the underlying causes currently appear to be neurological. This is especially so in the case of 'deep dyslexia', in which reading is radically impaired to the extent that presented with a word, the sufferer may respond with a quite different one which has a semantic connection to it (e.g. *fork* eliciting *spoon*). This condition invariably turns out to be associated with **aphasia** and, unlike most other dyslexias, is acquired. The topic remains controversial within Psychology since it is as yet unclear which of a number of competing theoretical explanations is most appropriate (if any), how unitary a phenomenon it is (leaving brain damage aside), and whether it is even a pathology at all, but simply arises because reading is too recent a development in human history for a universal reading ability to have evolved at the neurological level. It is also noteworthy that some forms of dyslexia (such as those involving inability to differentiate between similar letters) do not arise with readers of syllabic scripts, such as Japanese, containing no such characters and less formally tied to pronunciation than alphabetic scripts. Despite the publicity and scientific attention dyslexia has attracted, as well as the emergence of numerous effective practical techniques for helping children overcome it, it is all too often left undiagnosed in the early school years and the child simply labelled stupid or backward, with unhappy consequences. The earliest book-length work on the topic I have located is Hallgren (1950), however, as 'word-blindness' it appears in Hinshelwood (1917), this term being used in medical circles at least from the 1890s as it occurs in an 1892 journal paper title by the great William Osler. (You do not really need to know this but the historian in me won out.)

References and further reading

Colheart, M., Patterson, P. and Marshall, J.C. (1980) *Deep Dyslexia*, London: Routledge & Kegan Paul.

Csepe, V. (2003) *Dyslexia: Different Brain, Different Behavior*, New York: Springer-Verlag.

De Hirsch, K. (1952) *Specific Dyslexia or Strephosymbolia*, Berne: Folia Phoniatrica.

Hallgren, B. (1950) 'Specific Dyslexia ("Congenital Word-Blindness"). A Clinical and Genetic Study', *Acta Psychiatrica et Neurologica*, Supplementum 5.

Hayes, C.B. (2006) *Dyslexia in Children: New Research*, New York: Nova Science.

Hinshelwood, J. (1917) *Congenital Word Blindness*, London: H.K. Lewis.

Hoien, T. and Lundberg, I. (2000) *Dyslexia: From Theory to Intervention*, Amsterdam: Kluwer.

Leong, C.K. (2003) *Developmental and Acquired Dyslexia: Neuropsychological and Neurolinguistic Perspectives*, New York: Springer-Verlag.

Turner, M., Rack, J.P. and Turner, M. (eds) (2005) *The Study of Dyslexia* New York: Springer-Verlag.

DYSPRAXIA

Difficulties in motor co-ordination apparently unrelated to muscular or sensory impairment, and thus caused at the neurological level. Two forms are identified. 'Acquired dyspraxia' is the result of brain-damage, 'developmental dyspraxia' (also called 'developmental coordination disorder') is due to failure in normal neurological development during early years. The term 'apraxia' is sometimes used synonymously with dyspraxia although the 'a-' prefix in medical terms properly denotes complete, or near complete, absence.

References and further reading

Kirby, A. (2002) *Dyspraxia: The Hidden Handicap*, London: Souvenir Press.
Kirby, A., Drew, S. and Kirby, A. (2003) *Guide to Dyspraxia and Developmental Coordination Disorders*, London: David Fulton.
Portwood, M. (2000) *Understanding Developmental Dyspraxia: A Textbook for Students and Professionals*, London: Taylor & Francis.

ECOLOGICAL PSYCHOLOGY

Rooted in the 'ecological' approach to perception of J.J. Gibson, Ecological Psychology emerged in the USA in the early 1980s as an alternative approach to **Cognitive Psychology** and other mainstream schools. Ecological Psychology is characterised by its focus on the dynamically interactive interplay between individuals and their total environmental situation, between 'the knower and the known', and rejects the assumption that behaviour can be understood except in this 'situated' fashion. The term *Environmental Psychology* is in many respects almost synonymous with this. In the UK, Ecological Psychology established a presence at the University of Portsmouth in 1995. Theoretically, it appears to be very similar, if not entirely identical, to **mutualism** and the University of Plymouth Centre for Ecological Psychology is currently headed by leading mutualist Alan Costall. A journal, *Ecological Psychology* was founded in 1989.

References and further reading

Heft, H. (2005) *Ecological Psychology in Context: James Gibson, Roger Barker and the Legacy of William James's Radical Empiricism*, Mahwah, NJ: Erlbaum.
Reed, E.S. (1996) *Encountering the World: Toward an Ecological Psychology*, New York: Oxford University Press.

EEG (ELECTROENECEPHALOGRAPH)

Method of monitoring the electrical activity of the brain using electrodes attached to the scalp. Pioneered from 1929 onwards by the German physiologist Hans Berger (who later committed suicide under Nazi persecution), the technique remained largely ignored until confirmed in 1934 by E.D. Adrian and H.C. Matthews working at the Cambridge Physiological Laboratory. After 1945, it was soon attracting widespread attention, notably in the work of W. Grey Walter, popularised in his *The Living Brain* (Walter, 1953). The EEG identified three basic kinds of electrical rhythm in the brain – Alpha (the most rapid), Beta and Delta (the slowest) – and soon became a major technique in the study of sleep and diagnosis of brain disorders such as epilepsy, the *EEG Journal* being founded in 1949.

References and further reading

Adrian, E.D. and Matthews, H.C. (1934) 'The Berger Rhythm: Potential Changes from the Occipital Lobes in Man', *Brain: A Journal of Neurology*, LVII(4): 355–85.

Shaw, J.C. (ed.) (2003) *The Brain's Alpha Rhythms and the Mind: A Review of Classical and Modern Studies of the Alpha Rhythm Component of the Electroencephalogram with Commentaries on Associated Neuroscience and Neuropsychology*, Amsterdam: Elsevier.

Walter, W.G. (1953) *The Living Brain*, London: Duckworth.

EMOTION

Its sheer importance and almost universal bearing on other aspects of psychology have guaranteed emotion a long-standing and central place in Psychological thought. It is also singularly complex. It is salutary to note that while the major emotions are identified in more or less the same way in virtually all cultures, an equivalent to the category 'emotion' itself is not universal. Historically, it is also noteworthy that the English word only acquired its current meaning from the mid-eighteenth century onwards, in the work of, first, Henry Home, Lord Kames (1762) and then Thomas Brown (1820) (see Dixon, 2006). Prior to that, the word *passions* was usually used, and Home devoted great effort to differentiating between emotion and passion. Etymologically, they are in some senses opposites because 'emotion' originally meant an outwardly directed expression or movement, while a 'passion' was something one *passively* experienced or endured (hence 'Christ's Passion' as referring to the Crucifixion). By the early nineteenth century, 'passion' had assumed its current meaning of unusually intense emotion. When modern psychologists began addressing the topic, they brought to bear a variety of theoretical frameworks, from evolutionary and psychoanalytic to behaviourist and psychophysiological, with the upshot that by the end of the last century there were numerous 'theories of emotion' in play. By and large, however, this work shared two basic features. First, it tended to concentrate on a small number of extreme emotions such as fear, hate, **depression** and love. In real life, these are fairly rare in their extreme forms, but Psychology has had relatively little to say about such everyday emotions as mild boredom, contentment, slight irritation or concern, and feeling a little envious or 'under the weather'. Second, the old philosophical view that emotion and reason were opposite (stated by David Hume in his *A Treatise of Human Nature* (Hume, 1739/1740) and, as he put it, 'reason is the slave of the passions', tended to be accepted, if often only implicitly. Ultimately it is surely true that it is our emotions which give our lives meaning and point, but they are still often treated by Psychology as irrational interruptions or mini-psychopathologies (especially the negative ones). And we are also, surely, always in *some* emotional state or other, if only one of quiet resignation. Even a calculatedly *unemotional* voice or manner seems to communicate that the person is in a coldly repressed state.

Darwin's *Expression of the Emotions in Man and Animals* (Darwin, 1872) marked a major step in formulating an evolutionary theory of emotion. This was further developed in two other early theories:

- *James–Lange theory.* One of the first and most enduringly challenging theories, independently formulated by the American psychologist and philosopher William James (most fully elaborated in Chapter 25 of his *Principles of Psychology,* James, 1890) and the German philosopher Karl Lange. This argued that emotion was a *consequence* of behaving or physiologically reacting in a certain way, not the *cause* of this behaviour or reaction, thus we are afraid because we find ourselves running away, are sad because we are crying and so forth, rather than, as most initially assume, the other way round. If we reflect on our own experience, we may find this to be a little more plausible than it first seems – we might be aware that something has slightly upset us, but it is only when we bump into a friend and promptly collapse in a flood of tears that we realise quite how upset we are, we think we are handling a slight knock to the car quite calmly and then find ourselves shaking and trembling with shock. There was, however, a long-held consensus that during the 1920s animal experiments by Walter Cannon had empirically falsified the James–Lange theory (Cannon, 1929).

- *McDougall's theory.* In his *Introduction to Social Psychology* (1908) – one of the most successful Psychology textbooks ever published – the British psychologist William McDougall put forward an elaborate instinct-based theory. He identifies 11 'primary' instinct-emotion pairs which can combine to yield further complex' emotions. By 1936 this had increased to 16. Moreover, emotions tend to organise into systems centred on particular classes of object, which he calls 'sentiments', adopting fellow psychologist Alexander Shand' term.

A major mid-twentieth-century overview of the field was given by M. Arnold (Arnold, 1960). The interplay between emotion and cognitive factors such as beliefs and memories received detailed attention in *cognitive appraisal theory* (Schachter and Singer, 1962). As far as the classification of emotions is concerned, the number of *basic emotions* is now generally considered to be between six and ten, the cross-cultural work of P. Ekman (e.g. Ekman, 1980) having played a major role in unravelling the extent to which emotions are genuine 'universals'. One should also note J.-P. Sartre's **existentialist** account (Sartre, 1948).

Emotion remains a central topic in Psychology, with perception of emotion in facial expression continuing to receive attention as well as extensive psychophysiological research. The concept of *emotional intelligence* (EI) has come to the fore since the mid-1990s and the emotional development of the child is a perennial topic in Child Psychology. Theoretically, however, there have been few recent attempts to formulate totally comprehensive theories of the McDougall type, although virtually every broader theoretical approach, from **Cognitive Psychology** to **Evolutionary Psychology** has something to say on the matter. For a general current overview, see Strongman (2003), for well-received historical accounts, see Dixon (2006), and, more wide-ranging, Kagan (2007), although there are several others referenced below you may find useful. Further ruminations by the present author are in a chapter in Gouk and Hills (2005, pp. 49–65) entitled 'Emotions into Words – or Words into Emotions?', along with a variety of other interesting monographs. Given the multi-faceted nature of the topic, the reference list is inevitably a little extended.

References and further reading

Arnold, M. (1960) *Emotion and Personality* (2 vols), New York: Columbia University Press.

Brown, T. (1820) *Lectures on the Philosophy of the Human Mind*, Edinburgh: W. & C. Tait.

Cannon, W. (1929) *Bodily Changes in Pain, Hunger, Fear and Rage*, 2nd edn, New York: Appleton.

Darwin, C. (1872) *Expression of the Emotions in Man and Animals*, London: John Murray.

Dixon, T. (2006) *From Passions to Emotions: The Creation of a Secular Psychological Category*, Cambridge: Cambridge University Press.

Ekman, P. (1980) *The Face of Man: Expressions of Universal Emotions in a New Guinea Village*, New York: Garland.

Gouk, P. and Hills, H. (eds) (2005) *Representing Emotions: New Connections in the Histories of Art, Music and Medicine*, Aldershot: Ashgate.

Home, H. (Lord Kames) (1762) *Elements of Criticism*, London: A. Miller and A. Kincaid & J. Bell.

James, W. (1890) *Principles of Psychology*, New York: Holt.

Kagan, J. (2007) *What is Emotion? History, Measures and Meanings*, New Haven, CT: Yale University Press.

McDougall, W. (1908) *An Introduction to Social Psychology*, London: Methuen.

Oatley, K. (2006) *Emotions: A Brief History*, 2nd edn, Oxford: Blackwell.

Sartre, J.-P. (1948) *The Emotions: An Outline*, New York: Philosophical Library. (Later translations are generally titled *Sketch Toward a Theory of the Emotions.*)

Schachter, S. and Singer, J. (1962) 'Cognitive, Social, and Physiological Determinants of Emotional State', *Psychological Review*, 69: 379–99.

Solomon, R.C. (ed.) (2000) *What is an Emotion?* Oxford: Oxford University Press.

Strongman, K.T. (2003) *The Psychology of Emotion: Theories of Emotion in Perspective*, 5th edn, Chichester: Wiley.

Wierzbicka, A. (1999) *Emotions across Languages and Cultures: Diversity and Universals*, Cambridge: Cambridge University Press.

EMPATHY

A term in general use for the phenomenon of being able to put oneself in another's place and believe one is sharing their feelings and emotions. Psychologists have periodically studied this in the contexts of Social Psychology and **personality** since it appears to be a crucial factor in maintaining social relationships and **altruism**, for example.

See also: **identification**.

EMPIRICISM

A very general philosophical term referring to the acquisition of knowledge by experience of the external world as opposed to reasoning or logic alone. Closely identified with **associationism** in the work of the British School of empiricist philosophy from John Locke's *An Essay Concerning Human Understanding* (1690) to James Mill's *Analysis of the Phenomena of the Human Mind* (1829), although one can be an empiricist without being an associationist. Philosophical theories of knowledge, a topic known as *epistemology*, have long been somewhat crudely classified as empiricist or *rationalist*. Science in general is an empirical enterprise but the respective weightings of, as it were, thought or reasoning and 'empirical evidence' has varied. Einstein's theory of relativity was virtually arrived at by mathematical reasoning and 'thought experiments' alone and only subsequently empirically confirmed. In Psychology, the issue arises regarding the roles of subjective experience, reasoning and introspection as opposed to empirical data-gathering in research and theory construction. Strong empiricism also, however, produces primarily environmentalist Psychological theories, such as **behaviourism**. The phrase 'crude empiricism' is commonly encountered in criticisms of approaches in which the role of reasoning or theorising is minimised or rejected.

ENCOUNTER GROUPS

Originating in Carl Rogers's (1902–87) **Humanistic Psychology**, encounter groups were conceived as settings in which individuals could ruthlessly but sensitively explore themselves and their psychological issues in a safe and supportive setting. They were understood as playing both therapeutic and personal development roles, and thus not confined to those diagnosed as requiring psychological 'treatment'. From the late 1960s till the 1970s, encounter groups were very popular. Variants such as T-groups and 'sensitivity training' groups also flourished. From the outset they suited the outgoing social self-disclosing American style more than the British one, although for a while they were as fashionable in the UK as in the USA. For many British people, the notion that reluctance to self-disclose signified a 'hang-up' grated harshly. Inevitably such methods, however open in principle, soon acquire their own ritualised features and generate their own vocabulary. 'Tell the person on your left something you like about them' was an original move the first time an encounter group leader suggested it, but would now only elicit a heavy groan. Few book-length texts on the topic have appeared since 1990. The real effectiveness and genuine long-term legacy of the encounter group movement are ripe for some historical investigation.

References and further reading

Burton, A. (1969) *Encounter: The Theory and Practice of Encounter Groups*, San Francisco: Jossey-Bass.
Coulson, W. (1972) *Groups, Gimmicks and Instant Gurus: An Examination of Encounter Groups and their Distortions*, New York: Harper & Row.
Rogers, C. (1970) *Carl Rogers on Encounter Groups*, New York: Harper & Row.

EPIPHENOMENALISM

A view of the **mind–body problem** which caused huge uproar when proposed by the great Victorian scientist T.H. Huxley and his nearly-as-great friend John Tyndall in the 1870s. Huxley argued that mind and consciousness were simply side-effects ('epiphenomena') of physio-logical processes, like the noise of a steam engine's whistle, having no effect on the body itself. The furore peaked with Tyndall's Presidential 'Belfast Address' to the British Association for the Advancement of Science Annual Meeting of 1874. The most radical **materialist** solution to the problem on offer, but understandably among the least popular. The Stanford website is particularly good on this topic.

References and further reading

Huxley, T.H. (1874) 'On the Hypothesis that Animals are Automata and its History', *The Fortnightly Review*, New Series 16: 555–80, reprinted in T.H. Huxley (1893) *Methods and Results. Essays by*, London: Macmillan.
Tyndall, J. (1874) *Address Delivered Before the British Association Assembled at Belfast, with Additions*. London: Longmans, Green & Co.

Useful website

www.plato.stanford.edu/entries/epiphenomenalism

ERGONOMICS

A sub-discipline which emerged from British Applied and Industrial Psychology in the 1950s, pioneered by K.F.H. Murrell (who coined the word in 1949) and A.T. Welford. The Ergonomics Research Society was also founded in 1949. The earliest book-length publication on the topic appears to be Floyd and Welford (1953). Ergonomics is concerned primarily with the design of artefacts in a way that renders their use as efficient, comfortable and practical as possible. This can include anything from chairs to machines. It can be especially important in contexts such as aircraft cockpit design. Ergonomics has largely shifted from a sub-discipline within Psychology to being a core component of engineering and design-related disciplines. Karkowski (2006) should tell you all you need to know. There is a specialist journal *Ergonomics. An International Journal of Research and Practice in Human Factors and Ergonomics*, founded in 1957.

References and further reading

Floyd, W.F. and Welford, W.F. (1953) *The Ergonomics Research Society: Symposium on Fatigue*, London: H.K. Lewis.

Karkowski, W. (2006) *International Encyclopedia of Ergonomics and Human Factors*, 2nd edn, London: Taylor & Francis (incl. CD-ROM).

Moray, N. (2005) *Ergonomics: Major Writing*, London: Routledge.

Murrell, K.F.H. (1965) *Ergonomics: Man in his Working Environment*, London: Chapman & Hall.

ESP (EXTRASENSORY PERCEPTION)

The **paranormal** acquisition of information without the use of the normal senses. The most commonly researched form of ESP has been *telepathy* or 'thought transference', using tasks in which a 'transmitter' hidden from the experimental participant looks at a succession of stimuli (such as cards from the Zenner Card set specially designed for this purpose) or a picture. The 'receiving' participant then reports or draws the stimulus the transmitter is looking at. A topic of perennial fascination, experimental Psychological research was pioneered in the 1930s by Rhine (1935, 1938) and his wife Louisa (Rhine, 1962). The upshot has been forever indecisive in confirming whether the phenomenon actually exists in these conditions, with statistically significant results, and results verging on significance, being tantalisingly mingled with non-significant ones. For a recent sceptical view, see Charpak and Broch (2004). Other forms of ESP include 'clairvoyance' in which the individual reportedly has a visual image of events occurring elsewhere, 'clairaudience' in which speech beyond earshot is heard, and 'precognition' or knowledge of future events (although strictly speaking, this would not be ESP in the usual sense). Undergraduate students often want to do projects involving ESP research but this is unwise. Methodological standards of research in this field have become extremely stringent in order to overcome cheating, exclude covert or subliminal communication channels, and ensure randomness of stimulus presentation. Undergraduate research on ESP will thus almost certainly be worthless, although much can be learned from an acquaintance with the methodological issues. Sorting out the wheat from the chaff in the multitude of publications on ESP is not easy.

References and further reading

Charpak, G. and Broch, H. (2004) *Debunked! ESP, Telekinesis and other Pseudoscience*, Baltimore, MD: Johns Hopkins University Press.
Hansel, C.E.M. (1966) *ESP: A Scientific Evaluation*, London: MacGibbon.
—— (1989) *The Search for Psychic Power: ESP and Parapsychology Revisited*, New York: Prometheus Books.
Rhine, J.B. (1935) *Extra-Sensory Perception*, London: Faber & Faber.
—— (1938) *New Frontiers of the Mind*, London: Faber & Faber.
Rhine, L.E. (1962) *Hidden Channels of the Mind*, London: Gollancz.
Smythies, J.R. (1971) *Science and ESP*, London: Routledge & Kegan Paul.
Tart, C.E. (2002) *The Applications of Learning Theory to ESP Performance*, New York: Parapsychology Foundation.

ETHNOCENTRISM

Viewing things from the point of view of the values and attitudes of one's own ethnic group or culture. While to some degree inevitable for everybody, it becomes problematic in cases where one uncritically takes such values and attitudes as somehow 'natural' or inherently superior to everybody else's. It can often of course arise unwittingly simply out of ignorance of the existence of alternative perspectives.

See also: **prejudice**.

ETHOLOGY

A discipline on the boundary between Psychology and Zoology concerned with the study of animal behaviour in natural (as opposed to experimental) settings. Although an age-old interest, this topic began to assume more scientific form in the late nineteenth century, a major early figure being the German von Uexkull (1909, 1926). Julian Huxley (1914) and Solly Zuckerman (1932) were important British pioneers. The term itself, however, only became widely adopted in the 1950s and is primarily associated with the work of Konrad Lorenz and Nico Tinbergen. The rise in popularity of ethology after the 1950s signified an important cleavage in the nature and role of Animal Psychology. Its commitment to field-study observational methods was, as noted above, in marked contrast to the experimental methods used, especially in North America, but this was rooted in a profound difference in scientific goals. Experimental use of animals in Psychology was generally intended to test hypotheses about general psychological processes or phenomena, such as, most prominently, **learning** and the comparison of animal and human performance in these areas (hence the common term *Comparative Psychology* as a near synonym for Animal Psychology). Ethologists, however, addressed the whole repertoire of animal behaviour for its own sake as a central topic in Zoology and Natural History. The range of species ethologists have studied has thus been enormously varied, from sticklebacks to wolves and chimpanzees. A deeper theoretical issue, however, was that most experimentalists were working within an *environmentalist* and **behaviourist** tradition which had little time for concepts of **instinct** and innate determinants of behaviour. The ethologists, by contrast, were absolutely intrigued by the extent to which behaviour was, or could be, innate and the nature of species-specific behavioural patterns. The upshot was a return to prominence within Psychology of a revised version of the instinct concept. And while initially eschewing direct comparisons between human and animal behaviour, the parallels, similarities and analogues in human behaviour with their discoveries in the animal kingdom proved irresistibly fascinating. In the 1970s, ethology was to some extent assimilated into **sociobiology,** although in the long run it escaped being fully captured in this theoretical net and with the current popularity of everything to do with 'wild life' and huge advances in photographic and tracking technologies, the ethology research tradition continues to boom. Meanwhile, the application of ethological methods to human behaviour has also become a significant strand (see Eibl-Eibsfeldt, 2007). The books published on individual species from gorillas to fish are too numerous to reference here.

Ethologists introduced several concepts which psychologists found useful in understanding human social behaviour and child development, the following being among the more important (see also **displacement activity**):

- *Imprinting*. The phenomenon of bonding between a neonate and the closest moving organism it encounters after being born or hatched. Under normal circumstances, this will be its mother and it ensures that the new-born animal recognises and maintains close proximity to her during its most vulnerable phase of life, since the mother (or parents) are its sole source of nourishment, this is absolutely essential if it is to survive. This is to be understood as a two-way process, however, as the mother (usually) reciprocally imprints on the neonate. This became famous from the popular best-selling work by Konrad Lorenz *King Solomon's Ring* (Lorenz, 1952) in which he reported his success in getting newly hatched ducks to imprint on him, as a result of which they followed him about in file as they would normally have followed their mother. See **attachment**.

- *Innate releasing mechanism (IRM)*. A stimulus which elicits a highly specific response from an organism without prior learning. The assumption is that this is genetically 'hard-wired' at a neurological level. IRMs typically take the form of particular colours, smells or movements in the environment to which the animal responds with aggression, avoidance behaviour, submission or sexual arousal, for example. They may be aspects of the appearance, sound or odour of other members of the same species, but also of environmental phenomena. Two examples would be: (1) inhibition of aggressive behaviour in dogs when one submissively exposes its neck to the other during combat; and (2) primate avoidance of snakes which appears to occur spontaneously in young primates on their first encounter with a snake.

- *Pecking order*. Identified initially in chickens in 1922 by Norwegian psychologist T. Schjelderup-Ebbe (using the German word *Hackordnung*), this term originally referred to the existence in domestic poultry of a clear power hierarchy in terms of the order in which flock members gained access to food. It was soon generalised to other contexts for the apparent power hierarchy existing in many social species (including primates) which determines priority of access to food, mates and other resources, especially among males. This hierarchy may, as in gorillas and deer, be headed by an *Alpha male* whose power may enhance that of his mate (or mates) and offspring. His dominance will eventually be challenged by a younger male, often during the mating season when ritualised fighting between males serves to reaffirm or change the dominance hierarchy. The term *dominance hierarchy* is more commonly used than 'pecking order' for higher mammals, and the latter should preferably be restricted to bird behaviour, the context in which it arose. 'Alpha male' and 'pecking order' have of course entered everyday psychological language.

- *Territoriality*. Many species exhibit territoriality, which takes a variety of forms such as male robins (European, not American) vigorously defending their own territory from other intruding males, or wolves marking a pack territory by urinating on trees. One important common feature of territoriality is that the further an intruder penetrates, the fiercer the defender's behaviour becomes, and the less 'confident', so to speak, the invader's efforts. This effect can very largely offset any apparent advantage the invader has in terms of physical strength. Social psychologists were quick to see analogies between this and human responses to invasion, particularly in the context of the Vietnam War.

References and further reading

Burkhardt, R. W. (2005) *Patterns of Behavior: Konrad Lorenz, Nico Tinbergen and the Founding of Ethology*, Chicago, IL: The University of Chicago Press.

Eibl-Eibsfeldt, I. (2007) *Human Ethology*, Edison, NJ: Aldine Transaction.

Huxley, J. ([1914] 1968) *The Courtship Habits of the Great Crested Grebe*, London: Jonathan Cape (first published as a journal paper).

Lorenz, K.Z. (1952) *King Solomon's Ring*, London: Methuen.

——— (1981) *The Foundations of Ethology*, Vienna: Springer.

Tinbergen, N. (1951) *The Study of Instinct*, Oxford: Clarendon Press.

———(1975) *The Animal in its World: Explorations of an Ethologist, 1932–1972*, 2 vols, Cambridge, MA: Harvard University Press.

von Uexkull, J. (1909) *Umwelt und Innenwelt der Tiere*, Berlin: Julius Springer.

——— (1926) *Theoretical Biology*, New York: Harcourt Brace. (None of his other works have apparently been translated into English.)

Zuckerman, S. (1932) *The Social Life of Monkeys and Apes*, London: Kegan Paul, Trench & Trubner.

EUGENICS

This term was coined by the British scientist, and cousin of Charles Darwin, Francis Galton, as a name for a programme in which the quality of the human, and especially British, 'stock' would be improved by scientifically controlled selective breeding in which the best people were encouraged to breed and the worst discouraged from so doing. Eugenics represented a rather crude application of evolutionary ideas to contemporary social problems and its ultimately disastrous applications remain a cautionary lesson. From the 1880s until the 1920s, eugenics became a European and North American obsession, although it lost momentum after the First World War. It is closely related to the concept of **degenerationism**. Eugenics was seen as taking two forms: the first, 'positive eugenics' was promoting breeding by the evidently 'fit'; the second was prevention of the 'unfit' and 'degenerate' from breeding by measures such as compulsory sterilisation of those with learning difficulties, mental illness or other 'degenerate' tendencies such as criminality. Initially the idea was as keenly promoted by as many on the political left as on the right, but its hijacking by the Nazis to justify extermination of such groups as the mentally handicapped and homosexuals and then the entire Jewish 'race' resulted in the collapse of left-wing support by the late 1930s. From then on, it became seen as essentially an extreme right-wing doctrine. On the scientific front, any credibility it possessed also declined with greater understanding of genetics. Psychology was closely involved in the eugenics episode from the start, Galton being a prominent pioneer in British Psychology. Throughout the late nineteenth and early twentieth centuries, Psychology's concerns with issues such as mental illness, criminality and intelligence meant that work in these areas was often framed by eugenic concerns and expressed as a contribution to the eugenics project. Complacency is, however, dangerous and the spectre of what might be termed 'neo-Eugenics' has begun hovering over the last decade or so due to the ever-increasing possibilities of 'genetic engineering'. A few countries, such as Singapore, have also introduced financial 'positive eugenics' measures to encourage the most intelligent to have more children.

References and further reading

Kevles, D.J. (1985) *In the Name of Eugenics. Genetics and the Uses of Human Heredity*, Cambridge, MA: Harvard University Press.

Pick, D. (1989) *Faces of Degeneration: A European Disorder, c.1848 – c.1919*, Cambridge: Cambridge University Press.

EVOLUTIONARY PSYCHOLOGY

While the phrase 'Evolutionary Psychology' occurs intermittently from the late nineteenth century onwards, and while evolutionary perspectives on human psychology have appeared fairly frequently, modern Evolutionary Psychology emerged in the late 1980s as a direct result of the earlier rise of **sociobiology.** Psychologists such as J. Barkow, L. Cosmides and J. Tooby began exploring in detail how sociobiological concepts such as *inclusive fitness* and **kin selection** could be used to explain human behaviour, particularly sexual behaviour, **altruism**, and gender differences, although they threw their net somewhat more widely than these (Barkow *et al.*, 1995). This development followed a period of about ten years or so during which the study of behavioural aspects of human evolution had, while enjoying a great revival after decades of near neglect, been quite multi-faceted and eclectic in its theoretical character (see Richards, 1987). As a sub-discipline, Evolutionary Psychology has expanded considerably since 1990, some exponents even claiming it could provide the discipline's long-sought 'unifying paradigm', but this remains highly controversial. While often suggestive and provocative, it faces problems and challenges of several kinds. One is that while, indisputably, there are genetic parameters for the variability of human behaviour, these do not necessarily cause any specific behavioural event. A second is that it is unclear what practical use can be made of knowledge of such parameters, and they may in fact be treated as an excuse for not doing anything. Third, there is a subtler argument that knowing the hitherto unknown determinants of one's behaviour liberates one from their tyranny, hence if hostility to step-children is, as evolutionary psychologists claim, a deeply rooted primate reaction explicable in kin-selection terms, then realising this might come as a great relief to a step-parent who feels an apparently irrational level of irritation and dislike of their step-children. Now they may feel that they understand and can do something about it. Fourth, stemming in part from the second point, there are inevitable ideological and philosophical tensions between evolutionary psychologists and, for instance, many feminist psychologists and social constructionists. Having said that, it has undoubtedly been valuable for Psychology that the evolutionary perspective has a presence within the discipline and, like all scientific controversies, the current debates are necessary if a balanced grasp of the roles of our evolutionary past in our current lives is to be achieved. A further final critical point is, however, necessary, whereas many of its immediate precursors were primarily concerned with contributing to the multidisciplinary project of understanding human evolution itself, Evolutionary Psychology is essentially concerned with explaining the present, especially topics of current cultural concern, in what are essentially speculative terms suggested by Sociobiological theory.

See Rose and Rose (2000), for a selection of critical perspectives.

References and further reading

Barkow, J., Cosmides, L. and Tooby, J. (1995) *The Adapted Mind. Evolutionary Psychology and the Generation of Culture*, Oxford: Oxford University Press.

Barrett, L., Dunbar, R., Dunbar, R.I.M. and Lycett, J. (2002) *Human Evolutionary Psychology*, Princeton, NJ: Princeton University Press.

Buss, D. (2005) *Handbook of Evolutionary Psychology*, Chichester: John Wiley & Sons, Ltd.

Clamp, A. (2001) *Evolutionary Psychology*, London: Hodder Arnold.

Holcomb, H.R. (2001) *Conceptual Challenges in Evolutionary Psychology*, Amsterdam: Kluwer.

Richards, G. (1987) *Human Evolution: An Introduction for the Behavioural Sciences*, London: Routledge & Kegan Paul.

Rose, H. and Rose, S. (eds) (2000) *Alas, Poor Darwin: Arguments Against Evolutionary Psychology*, New York: Harmony Press.

EXISTENTIALISM

This mid-twentieth-century school of philosophy was primarily French but drew considerably on the earlier work of the German philosophers Edmund Husserl and Martin Heidegger, generally referred to as **phenomenology**. These thinkers were concerned with the nature of existence or 'Being' itself as directly experienced and related issues of personal identity and freedom. The existentialists, of whom the best known was Jean-Paul Sartre (1905–80), author of *Being and Nothingness* ([1943] 1957) were, however, not concerned with these as purely intellectual questions. They were, rather, driven by a preoccupation with the meaning (or lack of it) of life itself. Sartre was a novelist and playwright as well as philosopher and one of the most influential works generally classified as embodying the existentialist mood was Albert Camus's novel *The Plague* (1948, in French, 1947 as *La Peste*). In many respects, the topics they dealt with were psychological ones, such as emotion and imagination (both of which were topics of books by Sartre). Most profoundly, however, they held that for humans, unlike other creatures, 'existence precedes essence'. That is to say that, whereas a cat never has an issue about what it is to be a cat, for humans the question of our identity is deeply problematic. This implies that we are in a situation of radical freedom, each of us chooses who and what we are through our actions and choices. And we are always 'becoming', never arriving at a final answer to the question 'who am I?' This burden is too heavy for many people and they employ numerous tactics to evade and deny such responsibility (they act 'in bad faith'). In doing so they become 'inauthentic', (a concept with affinities to the Marxist notion of **false consciousness)**. To cease striving to 'become', moving on from our present, is to opt out of genuine living. A short account such as this cannot do justice to the full range of existentialist thought or its complex relationships with other contemporary systems of thought such as *Marxism* and **psychoanalysis**. It is helpful though to see existentialism's pessimistic and inward-looking mood, if not its specific doctrines, as encapsulating and addressing that of the immediate post-Second World War European intelligentsia. Confused and traumatised by recent events, for this generation, many multiply bereaved and uprooted from their lands of origin, the 'meaning of life' was no abstract philosophical issue but one of urgent personal psychological concern. While Paris was its epicentre, existentialism's influence soon spread to the English-speaking world, influencing psychiatrists such as R.D. Laing in Britain and the American **Humanistic Psychology** School. As it did so, its doctrines gradually came to be construed more positively, and by the 1960s many had been assimilated into the optimistic outlook behind much of the **growth movement** in psychotherapy.

References and further reading

Allers, R. (1961) *Existentialism and Psychiatry: Four Lectures*, Springfield, IL: C. C. Thomas.

Blackham, H.J. (1951) *Six Existentialist Thinkers*, London: Routledge & Kegan Paul.

Camus, A. (1948) *The Plague*, London: Hamish Hamilton.

Dreyfus, H. (2005) *A Companion to Phenomenology and Existentialism*, Oxford: Blackwell.

Raymond, D. (1990) *Existentialism and the Philosophical Tradition*, New York: Pearson.

Reynolds, J. (2006) *Understanding Existentialism*, Ottowa: McGill Queen's University Press.

Sartre, J.-P. (1950) *Psychology of the Imagination*, London: Rider.

—— (1957) *Being and Nothingness*, London: Methuen.

EXPERIMENTER EFFECT(S)

Given the inescapably social character of any research involving interaction between human experimenters and human subjects or 'participants', the quest for 'scientifically objective' research methods has always presented Psychology with a problem. Initially, the solution seemed to lay in ensuring that research was rigorously designed to include such factors as administrator ignorance as to which experimental group subjects had been assigned, subject ignorance regarding the purpose of the research (especially the nature of the hypothesis being tested), and so on. This, as Danziger (1990) described in an important historical study, resulted in a sort of myth being created that the subjects of Psychological experiments (particularly, as was very often the case, university students) could be considered as non-social behavioural units, and their broader social existence and individual motivations ignored. In 1966, R. Rosenthal published *Experimenter Effects in Behavioural Research*, which challenged such complacency (Rosenthal, 1966). More specifically he identified what he called 'experimenter expectancy effects', showing how experimenters could unwittingly give clues as to the kinds of result they were seeking. Such features of the experimental situation have come to be known as 'demand characteristics'. This takes seriously the fact that some participants at least will be actively interested in what the experiment is about and seek clues regarding this. Experimenter effects are not restricted to 'expectancy' effects, however. Such factors as experimenter (or administrator) ethnicity and gender and/or participants' attitudes towards them, can come into play. In addition, though not 'experimenter effects' as such, extraneous social and cultural factors can affect performance. The notion that one can ever find an experimental subject or participant – or even group – whose performance is neutrally representative of all humanity, is clearly an illusion. The implication is not that experimental research is useless, but that, as well as being technically designed in such a way that experimenter effects are eliminated or controlled for, only very cautious generalisations can be made as to how widely findings apply in the outside world (see **validity**: *external validity*). Statistically, a partial solution lies in 'meta-analysis' of large numbers of studies with different kinds of participants. However, pure replication is rare in Psychology beyond **psychophysics** and such studies are unlikely to all be strictly comparable. The problem is, at heart, not a technical one, but theoretical and conceptual. In a recent unpublished conference paper, Morawski (Morawski, 2007) suggests that we need to consider Rosenthal's original work in a Cold War context, and further argues that while he in effect let the genie of **reflexivity** out of the bottle, the experimental research tradition he initiated was primarily aimed at luring it back in and replacing the stopper.

References

Morawski, J.G. (2007) 'Robert Rosenthal's Studies of Experimenter Bias: from Cold War Anxieties to Civil Rights Democracy', paper given at the Joint European Society for the History of the Human Society/Cheiron Conference, University College, Dublin, June.

Rosenthal, R. (1966) *Experimenter Effects in Behavioral Research*, New York: Appleton-Century-Crofts.

EXTRAVERSION/INTROVERSION

Extraversion refers to the psychological orientation and direction of interests, attention and concerns towards the outside world, while introversion refers to the reverse, an orientation and direction of these towards one's own feelings and ideas. The terms were introduced into modern Psychology primarily by C.G. Jung (see **Analytical Psychology**) for whom they characterised two distinct **personality** types, everyone being one or the other (and the opposite unconsciously). H.J. Eysenck adopted the terms but viewed them as dimensions rather than types, with everyone falling somewhere on the continuum between extreme introversion and extreme extraversion. His Eysenck (later, Maudsley) Personality Inventory (EPI, later MPI) claimed to measure degree of extraversion (along with **neuroticism**, considered to be a separate, uncorrelated dimension). It should be stressed that the everyday stereotype of extraverts (or 'extroverts') as jolly, talkative and outgoing in their behaviour somewhat distorts its Psychological meaning, which primarily refers only to psychological orientation rather than overt behaviour, although the EPI/MPI scales do include behavioural items. Similarly, there is a popular assumption that introversion in some way signifies neurotic self-absorption, but this is quite erroneous. Eysenck believed there was a physiological basis for the difference between the two tendencies, introverts being very easily aroused or stimulated, extraverts requiring greater stimulation and excitement. The concepts are now almost universally used by psychologists concerned with personality and *individual differences*. Eysenck's first major statement on the topic was Eysenck (1947).

See also: **personality** references.

Reference

Eysenck, H.J. (1947) *Dimensions of Personality*, London: Routledge & Kegan Paul.

EXTRINSIC VS INTRINSIC

Usually used to describe **motivation**, but may be used in other contexts where appropriate. Activity engaged in as a means to an end is 'extrinsically' motivated, but if engaged in for its own sake, because it is pleasurable or rewarding in its own right, is 'intrinsically' motivated. The first is typical of much paid work, the latter of playing a musical instrument or sport without any other reward.

FACTOR ANALYSIS

Statistical technique for identifying the number of factors involved in determining the variance of a set of data. Generally considered to have been initially devised by Charles Spearman (1904a, 1904b) to analyse his data on intelligence, it was subsequently adopted by Cyril Burt (who later contested Spearman's priority) and refined by other statisticians. Widely used by psychologists in the fields of intelligence and personality theory, it always remained controversial as a statistical technique due to there being two basic approaches to the analysis, one aimed at minimising the number of factors and the other aimed at extracting as many as possible. Technically it is a 'parametric' procedure, which is to say that it assumes the data to be 'normally distributed' in a 'bell curve' fashion.

References and further reading

Child, D. (2006) *Essentials of Factor Analysis*, London: Continuum International.

Cudeck, R. and MacCallum, R.C. (2007) *Factor Analysis at 100: Historical Developments and Future Directions*, London: Taylor & Francis.

Lovie, A.D. and Lovie P. (1993) 'Charles Spearman, Cyril Burt, and the Origins of Factor Analysis', *Journal of the History of the Behavioral Sciences*, 29: 308–21.

Spearman, C.E. (1904a) '"General Intelligence" Objectively Determined and Measured', *American Journal of Psychology*, 5: 201–93.

—— (1904b) 'Proof and Measurement of Association between Two Things', *American Journal of Psychology*, 15: 72–101.

FACULTY PSYCHOLOGY

A view of the mind as divided into a set of specific 'faculties', rejected by the British **associationist** school but common to **rationalist** and other philosophical schools, dating back to antiquity and medieval

Scholasticism. With slight degrees of variation, these were Thinking, Sensation, Imagination, Feeling (or Emotion), Memory and Will (although Will was often cast in mediating role between others). The far more elaborate list developed by **phrenology** was also essentially a faculty theory. In modern Psychology, Jung's *psychological functions* (see **Analytical Psychology**) derived from this, but he did not consider them as 'faculties' in the traditional sense. By the end of the nineteenth century, Faculty Psychology had fallen into disuse in the discipline. Its major shortcomings were that it was descriptive rather than explanatory, over-simplistic in the light of greater understanding of the complexities of psychological functioning, and reified (see **reification)** qualities or properties of behaviour into thing-like entities. Insofar as the notion of faculties was retained, they were translated into 'abilities' or 'functions'. Discussed in most histories of Psychology (and, indeed, philosophy) but Klein (1970) is particularly good.

Reference

Klein, D.B. (1970) *A History of Scientific Psychology: Its Origins and Philosophical Background*, London: Routledge & Kegan Paul.

FALSE CONSCIOUSNESS

Having an erroneous understanding or consciousness of the social world and one's place within it. This concept was introduced by Marxist sociologists and refers primarily to the way social class position falsifies or distorts the individual's image of the overall nature of the society they live in and thus their own identity. So, for the working class, false consciousness might take the form of acceptance of their position as the natural order of things, for the middle class, a failure to understand the exploitative nature of their work and feelings of superiority over the working class. This Marxist class-based analysis of false consciousness can now be seen as highly over-simplified, but the concept itself, though rarely used in academic Psychology, is not without value. For Marxists, the cure was to grasp the inherent nature of the class struggle within capitalist societies and to identify oneself with this. One might now view the task of grasping the effects on one's consciousness of one's social class, ethnic, gender, generational, etc. positions more broadly as a universal component of achieving a fuller self-knowledge. There are links here with **existentialism** and the goals of **psychotherapy** and **counselling**.

FALSE MEMORY SYNDROME (FMS)

One of the most controversial topics in Psychology in the past two decades. What appears to have happened is that the huge expansion of **psychotherapy** from 1970 onwards, combined with a dramatic increase in **multiple personality disorder** cases, resulted in a growing number of people engaging in 'recovering' long forgotten memories in therapeutic contexts, or using therapeutic techniques such as **hypnosis**. Most dramatically, these frequently produced 'recovered memories' of child sexual abuse, often by parents or relatives. When both client and therapist became convinced of the validity of these memories, serious consequences obviously began to ensue. Families broke up, people (usually, but not always, men) found themselves accused of child abuse and court cases sometimes ensued. In some cases, it became all too evident that, however intensely believed, the 'memory' was false. Therapists were in turn accused of colluding with clients or engaging in a *folie à deux* to create such memories. The status of both *recovered memories* and FMS continues to be a matter for heated debate. False Memory Syndrome Foundations were set up on both sides of the Atlantic during the 1990s as a lobby and resource for those claiming to be falsely accused on the basis of purported 'recovered memories', while others believe over-scepticism will discredit all accusations of child abuse in which 'recovered memory' is part of the evidence. What is at issue here is not whether 'false memories' can occur, or whether forgotten memories can be recovered – they obviously can in both cases. It is rather the status, character and credibility of a sub-category of memories recovered in psychotherapeutic contexts which pertain specifically to child (sometimes adolescent) sexual abuse. It must be patent folly to proceed on anything other than a careful case-by-case basis, but in a world of bandwagons and media panics, this has become exceptionally difficult. The literature on FMS is extensive and closely intertwined with that on child sexual abuse and multiple personality disorder. Brainerd and Reyna (2005) is the most recent academic overview of the topic.

References and further reading

Bjorklund, D.J. (2000) *False Memory Creation in Children and Adults: Theory, Research and Implications*, Hove: Psychology Press.

Brainerd, C. and Reyna, V.F. (2005) *The Science of False Memory: An Integrative Approach*, New York: Oxford University Press.

Brown, D.P., Hammond, D.C. and Scheflin, A.W. (1998) *Memory, Trauma Treatment and the Law*, Scranton, PA: W. W. Norton.

Schachter, D.L. (2000) *Cognitive Neurospsychology of False Memory*, Hove: Psychology Press.

FAMILY THERAPY

Collective term for psychotherapeutic techniques in which families are treated as a whole. This is usually undertaken when it is felt that the psychological problems of a family member are in some way related to the family dynamics as a whole. The problems of the 'identified' individual may thus prove to be symptomatic of wider issues concerning how the family operates. Analysing these generally involves using a 'systems' approach in which families are viewed as dynamic wholes. A wide range of theoretical perspectives have been developed, however, and therapists now tend to be eclectic in how they use them. Many psychotherapists and counsellors would argue that, ideally, nearly all cases, especially those involving younger people and children, should be dealt with in this way, since their problems cannot be understood in isolation. In reality, this is unfeasible for resource reasons, as well as the practical difficulties in obtaining family collaboration. The term 'family therapy' is usually also considered to cover *marital therapy* and *couples counselling*. While the role of the family in creating psychological problems had long been acknowledged, it was only in the 1950s that family therapy began to emerge as a distinct field of practice. Early figures included Gregory Bateson (who is credited with coining the term itself in 1960) and Murray Bowen, while **attachment theory** was another major influence. Family therapy appeared at the same time as **anti-psychiatry** and reflected similar concerns, without, however, sharing anti-psychiatry's confrontational approach and critical political agendas. There is now a large literature on the topic, including many popular books, but those listed below are a sample of more recent serious publications.

References and further reading

Carr, A. (2006) *Family Therapy: Concepts, Process and Practice*, New York: Wiley.

Dallos, R. (2005) *Introduction to Family Therapy: Systemic Theory and Practice*, Milton Keynes: Open University Press.

Lowe, R. (2004) *Family Therapy: A Constructive Framework*, London: Sage.

Nichols, M.P. and Schwartz, R.C. (2000) *Family Therapy: Concepts and Methods*, 5th edn, Tappan, NJ: Allyn & Bacon.

Rivett, M.C. (2003) *Family Therapy in Question*, London: Sage.

FATIGUE

From the late nineteenth century till the 1930s, fatigue was a major topic of research especially in the field of Industrial and Applied Psychology, most of the literature appearing in journal paper form. This was partly because fatigue was an important factor in determining the workers' efficiency and productivity. An additional factor, however, was the availability of new technologies such as the 'kymograph' and the 'ergograph' which enabled shifts in physical performance to be recorded as curves, using a smoked-paper covered cylinder. Obtaining a scientific picture of how and at what rate fatigue developed, and its relationship to other psychological factors, was in any case felt to be a basic task of **psychophysics**. This topic has never entirely vanished from Psychology, and clearly remains important in fields such as Sport Psychology, but its prominence as a research field declined after c.1930. Mosso (1906) was a very successful work from the heyday of fatigue studies. In more recent decades a somewhat different aspect of the topic came to general prominence, *chronic fatigue syndrome*. This is often reported by, or identified in, patients seeking medical treatment for some unde-fined malaise. It is generally considered **psychosomatic**, and sig-nifying **depression** or some other psychopathological condition (see Shorter, 1993, Jason *et al.*, 2003). See Rabinbach (1992) for a study of its broader historical significance.

References and further reading

Hockey, R. (ed.) (1983) *Stress and Fatigue in Human Performance*, Chichester: Wiley.
Jason, L.A., Fennell, P.A. and Taylor, R. (eds) (2003) *Handbook of Chronic Fatigue Syndrome*, New York: Wiley.
Mosso, A. (1906) *Fatigue*, London: Swan Sonnenschein.
Rabinbach, A. (1992) *The Human Motor: Energy, Fatigue and the Origins of Modernity*, Berkeley, CA: University of California Press.
Shorter, E. (1993) *From Paralysis to Fatigue: A History of Psychosomatic Illness in the Modern Era*, New York: Free Press.
Simonson, E. and Weisner, P.C. (eds) (1976) *Psychological Aspects and Physiological Correlates of Work and Fatigue*, Springfield, IL: CC. Thomas.
Thorndike, E.L. (1914) *Mental Work and Fatigue and Individual Differences and Their Causes*, New York: Columbia University Press.

FEAR OF FAILURE (FOF)

During the 1960s and 1970s, researchers on **achievement motivation** and related phenomena such as *level of aspiration* observed that some people were inhibited from maximising their test performance due to what came to be called fear of failure. In other words, while valuing success, this was offset to some degree by anxiety that, by setting their aspirations too high, they would experience failure. The roots of FoF vary across individual cases. It can sometimes be the flip-side of extreme perfectionism, but it may also relate to shyness, fear of embarrassment or some other **personality** trait. Additionally, it was found to be somewhat more common among women than men, and became of concern to feminist psychologists (see Rothblum and Cole, 1988). FoF has obvious bearings on performance in educational settings and willingness to engage in risk-taking and, unsurprisingly, is currently a prominent topic in Sport Psychology. There is a less-studied opposite, *fear of success*.

References

Birney, R.C., Burdick, H. and Teevan, R.C. (1969) *Fear of Failure*, New York: Van Nostrand-Reinhold.
Galbraith, J.M. (1993) *Fear of Failure*, San Marino, CA: Benchmark.
Rothblum, E.D. and Cole, E. (eds) (1988) *Treating Women's Fear of Failure*, New York: Haworth Press.

FEAR OF STRANGERS (FOS)

Infants and young children typically go through a phase, more or less prolonged, during which they exhibit fear or extreme shyness in the presence of strangers. This is related to **attachment**. FoS became the subject of psychological research during the 1960s and 1970s and is usually covered in more general works on Child Psychology (see **attachment** references). The phrase is also used to refer to fear of foreigners (*xenophobia*).

FEELING

This has fallen from prominence as a technical term in Psychology, but was one of C.G. Jung's *psychological functions* (see **Analytical Psychology**). While overlapping with **emotion** in many of its uses (for Jung, being almost synonymous with it), it is perhaps too vague a word to serve any rigorous explanatory function. (The *New Oxford English Dictionary* takes about nine columns to cover 'feel' and 'feeling'.)

In everyday use it can refer to the experience of almost any psychological or physical state or sensation – we can feel sick, dizzy, bored, relaxed, alarmed, apprehensive, uneasy, and so on *ad infinitum*, as well as that a texture is smooth or rough. In pre-twentieth-century philosophical and psychological writing, however, feeling typically figured as one of the major faculties (see **Faculty Psychology**).

FIELD DEPENDENCY

The extent to which perception is affected by the structure of a stimulus situation or 'spatial field'. This actually has some affinities with the older concepts of **suggestibility** and **conformity** but is primarily used in perceptual contexts. Field dependent individuals are highly affected by this structure while the field independent are not, or far less so. Level of field dependency is assumed to be indicative of a more general **cognitive style**, and is related to the distinction between 'analytical' and 'globalising' or **convergent** and **divergent thinking**, the latter being less field dependent. These are not, however, precisely synonymous, having different theoretical connotations and ranges of application. The term was introduced by H.A. Witkin, following work with S. Asch in the late 1940s, and has become one of the most researched topics in the study of cognitive style. The main methods for measuring field dependency are Witkin's own 'rod and frame test' (RFT) and the 'embedded figures test'. The former requires that a rod be aligned vertically within a variably tilting rectangular frame. Field dependency is indicated by the extent to which the rod deviates from the vertical in the direction of tilt. As its name indicates, in the embedded figures test, a line figure embedded in a larger set of lines has to be identified. The concept is not non-controversial because it has proved difficult to tease out the respective roles of cognition and simple spatial ability. The simplicity and versatility of the tests have nonetheless ensured their widespread and continuing use in research on topics as varied as gender differences, cross-cultural differences and memory.

References and further reading

Witkin, H.A. (1978) *Cognitive Styles in Personal and Cultural Adaptation*, Worcester, MA: Clark University Press.

Witkin, H.A. (1981) *Cognitive Styles, Essence and Origins: Field Dependence and Field Independence*, Madison, CT: International Universities Press.

FLICKER FUSION

Term used in **psychophysics** to refer to the rate of flicker in a visual stimulus at which the flickering appears to 'fuse' into continuity. The point at which this happens is called the 'flicker fusion rate'.

FOLK PSYCHOLOGY

Phrase used to refer to the psychological beliefs of the general public. An interesting example of the ambiguity of the word 'psychology' mentioned in the Introduction, since insofar as it refers to ideas and theories about the psychological, it should be Psychology (discipline sense), but since it is an overt expression of the psychological character of the 'folk' it could be 'psychology' (subject-matter sense). Folk psychology thus produces Folk Psychology (see **reflexivity**). Many terms originating in Psychology or medicine also become assimilated into everyday language (e.g. 'nervous breakdown', **motivation**, **attitude**), often enduring long after they have been abandoned as scientific concepts. The expression became widely used in the late twentieth century by those such as Stephen Stich (Stich, 1983) who wanted to argue that scientific Psychology could in principle replace 'unscientific' Folk Psychology (see also Churchland, 1988, and for a critique of their position, Richards, 1996). The Stanford website entry (dated 1997) is especially useful, summarising the historical and philosophical issues extremely well.

References and further reading

Churchland, P.M. (1988) *Matter and Consciousness*, Cambridge, MA: MIT Press.

Hutto, D. and Ratcliffe, M. (eds) (2007) *Folk Psychology Re-Assessed*, Berlin: Springer.

Ohreen, D.E. (2004) *The Scope and Limits of Folk Psychology: A Socio-linguistic Approach*, Bern: Peter Lang.

Richards, G. (1996) 'On the Necessary Persistence of Folk Psychology', in W. O'Donohue and R. Kitchener (eds) *Philosophy and Psychology,* London: Sage.

Stich, S. (1983) *From Folk Psychology to Cognitive Science: The Case against Belief,* Cambridge, MA: MIT Press.

Thomas, R.M. (2001) *Folk Psychologies across Cultures*, London: Sage.

Useful website

www.plato.stanford.edu/entries/folkpsych-theory/

FRUSTRATION

State induced by inability to achieve one's goals, master a task or solve a problem. Typified by high **arousal**, irritability, and general bad temper. Often accompanied by displaced aggression (see also **aggression, displacement activity**). May occur in almost any life-context from personal relations to assembling a wardrobe from IKEA. Sometimes induced by external facts beyond one's control such as traffic jams, sometimes internally by what one feels is one's own inadequacy. Does not have any clear technical Psychological meaning beyond its every-day one, but is widely used.

FUNCTIONALISM

Like **structuralism**, with which it is variously contrasted and asso-ciated, this is a slippery 'weasel word' of the first order, deployed in Anthropology and Sociology as well as Psychology. An initial source of difficulty is that the word 'function' has a mathematical meaning, referring to the level of correlation between two variables. If, given measurement x, we can predict measurement y, then y 'is a function of' x'. This appears to be quite distinct from the everyday meaning in which 'function' refers to purpose or use, 'the function of the heart is to keep the blood circulating'. But in evolutionary (or any other) theorising, in which adaptation plays a central explanatory role, the distinction can become blurred, especially in relation to behaviour. In these contexts we may want to say that behaviour y is a function of (i.e. correlated with) stimulus x, with the implication that it must have a function in the usual sense. In short, it can refer both to a relationship between two phenomena or to the purpose of a single phenomenon. It is the latter which has given the concept explanatory appeal in the human sciences, but the linkage with the former remains, especially in Psychology (in which correlational statistics abound). The following three senses need to be distinguished.

- From around 1900 into the 1930s it was used in US Psychology to differentiate theories which focused on learning and the adapta-tional functions of behaviour from those (such as E.B. Titchener's and **Gestalt Psychology**) concerned with such things as the structure of consciousness and experience. (See also under **Schools of Psychology**: *Chicago, Columbia.*) By the 1930s, the 'Structuralism' versus 'Functionalism' polarity had become almost obsolete due to the dominance of the latter.

- In Anthropology and Sociology, it refers to the explanation of social institutions, customs, beliefs, etc. in terms of the function (purpose or role) they play in maintaining the society in question. A distinction is usually made here between 'manifest' and 'latent' functions. Thus, the manifest function of a dietary prohibition on eating e.g. pork may be to remind society members of their collective religious identity, but latently may have originated to prevent people eating a meat which, in their region, posed health risks. Rituals such as religious services may serve numerous latent functions such as facilitating regular information exchange and reinforcing the social status hierarchy. In Anthropology, there is a less clear-cut opposition with structuralism and the early twentieth-century British School of A. Radcliffe-Brown, E.E. Evans-Pritchard and B. Malinowski is often called the 'Structuralist-Functionalist' school, differentiating it from previous social evolutionary approaches.
- As a common phrase, 'functionalist explanation' now typically means an explanation in terms of the role a phenomenon serves either consciously or unconsciously, overtly or covertly, for the individual, group or society ('social function') in question.

Most general histories of psychology contain a chapter on the first of these.

GAME THEORY

Branch of mathematics which came to the fore during the 1950s, in which J. von Neumann was the leading figure, along with John 'Beautiful Mind' Nash. This analysed the strategies people used, or could use, in competitive contests involving decision-making. It was taken up politically during the Cold War in the context of 'war-gaming' exercises by military strategists. In Psychology, it became incorporated into the repertoire of **Cognitive Psychology** – and the pioneers of both were often in close intellectual contact. See also **prisoner's dilemma**. Von Neumann and Morgernstern (1944) is effectively the founding text. For a recent overview, see Varoufakis (2001).

References and further reading

Dimand, M.A. and Dimand, R.W. (eds) (1997) *The Foundations of Game Theory*, Cheltenham: Edward Elgar.

Varoufakis, Y. (2001) *Game Theory*, London: Taylor & Francis.
Von Neumann, J. and Moergenstern, O. (1944) *Theory of Games and Economic Behavior*, Princeton, NJ: Princeton University Press.

GESTALT PSYCHOLOGY

A major early twentieth-century school of Psychology centred on Max Wertheimer (1880–1943) and his two younger close associates and colleagues, Kurt Koffka (1886–1941) and Wolfgang Köhler (1887–1967). Generally dated to 1911, the Gestalt School flourished, first in Germany until the early 1930s, and then in the United States until around 1940, where all three were then based. Also closely associated with the school was Kurt Lewin (see **Topological Psychology**). The key feature of Gestalt theorising was its 'top-down', holistic character (the word itself being the German for 'form' or 'shape'). It is often crudely summarised in the phrase 'the whole is greater than the sum of its parts', but this description is inadequate. A little more accurate would be 'the structure of the whole determines what the parts are', in other words, one should begin with the 'whole'. A key starting point for their work was the fact that forms (such as tunes, faces or printed letters) remain recognisable even although the actual content may vary widely (a cartoon of a face and a photograph, or a tune played on the piano and on the violin at twice the speed). Gestalt theory had three main areas of impact: *perception*, **cognition** and **learning**. In each of these, they deployed a number of concepts which referred to aspects of a more general principle of *Prägnanz*, roughly meaning 'goodness of form'. These included such things as *contrast, closure, figure–ground distinction*. These are most easily demonstrated in perceptual phenomena. In relation to cognition, they showed how the structure of the way a problem was presented affected how easily it was solved, and that re-structuring of the problem was sometimes required (see also *lateral thinking*, under **divergent thinking**). Köhler's early studies of chimpanzee learning famously challenged behaviourist learning theory (**behaviourism, learning theory**) by drawing attention to 'insight learning' – how a behaviour could suddenly be learned rather than acquired over a number of trials during which it was progressively perfected. The best-known cases of this were Sultan's sudden realizations that a stick could be used to pull a banana into the cage and that boxes could be piled up to reach one hanging from the ceiling (later parodied in the film *Planet of the Apes*). Despite yielding much fascinating and influential work, which had enduring covert effects on social psychology as well as cognition and perception, the school as such largely disappeared after Köhler's death, although Mary Henle continued to ensure it was never forgotten. Typically seen as the main rival to behaviourism during the 1920s, the two schools are expressions of fundamentally different sets of cultural values and concepts of the nature of science. Gestalt Psychology was, explicitly, an attempt to apply to psychological phenomena the new 'field theory' approach in Einsteinian physics (Wertheimer being a friend of Albert Einstein and Köhler having been a student of Max Planck). The Gestalt psychologists were urbane and self-confident with few anxieties about the scientific status of their work but passionately opposed to what they saw as behaviourism's philistine reductionism. Three especially enduring works are Koffka (1935), Köhler (1925) and Wertheimer ([1945] 1959). The role of the school in the rise of **Cognitive Psychology** is well covered in Murray (1995).

References and further reading

Ash, M.G. (1996) *Gestalt Psychology in German Culture 1890–1967: Holism and the Quest for Objectivity*, Cambridge: Cambridge University Press.

Koffka, K. (1935) *Principles of Gestalt Psychology*, London: Kegan Paul, Trench & Trubner.

Kohler, W. ([1917] 1925) *The Mentality of Apes*, London: Kegan Paul, Trench & Trubner.

Murray, D.J. (1995) *Gestalt Psychology and the Cognitive Revolution*, New York: Harvester Wheatsheaf.

Wertheimer, M. ([1945] 1959) *Productive Thinking*, New York: Harper.

GROUP THERAPY/PSYCHOTHERAPY

Pioneered by British psychotherapist W.R. Bion in the 1940s, when working with hospitalised soldiers. Although psychoanalytically influenced, Bion's work moved beyond this framework to explore the way in which, under a therapist's direction, groups of patients or clients could collectively address their problems. In some respects, this anticipated later **encounter group** approaches but was explicitly intended to deal with genuine psychological problems rather than self-development or 'growth', as well as being theoretically grounded in a far more detailed fashion. Bion's pioneering efforts remain highly respected and the Group Therapy techniques he developed continue to be widely used.

References and further reading

Bion, W.R. (1961) *Experiences in Groups and Other Papers*, New York: Basic Books.

Ettin, M.F. (1999) *Foundations and Applications of Group Psychotherapy*, London: Jessica Kingsley.

Foulkes, S.A. and Anthony, E.J. (1965) *Group Psychotherapy: The Psychoanalytic Approach*, 2nd edn, London: Penguin Books.

Yalom, I.D. and Leszcz, M. (2006) *Theory and Practice of Group Psychotherapy*, 5th edn, New York: Basic Books.

GROWTH MOVEMENT

A somewhat catch-all expression referring to the many new schools of psychotherapy which emerged in the United States and, to a lesser extent, Britain during the 1960s and early 1970s, including some which had originated a little earlier, particularly the **Humanistic Psychology** of Abraham Maslow and Carl Rogers. If there is a unifying feature to these, it is to be found in their common belief in ongoing psychological growth and development, the ability to overcome psychological problems resulting from past experience, and, in many cases, the possibility of finding one's 'true self'. If none of this was entirely new, having been anticipated by e.g. C.G. Jung's concept of *individuation* (see under **Analytical Psychology**) and in some respects by French **existentialism**, what was new was the scale and variety of the techniques being introduced. The main approaches included Fritz Perls's **Gestalt Psychology**, Arthur Janov's **primal therapy**, Eric Berne's *transactional analysis*, 'T-Groups', and Viktor Frankl's *logotherapy*. Somewhat detached from these, and more hard-headed, was the late Albert Ellis's *rational-emotive therapy,* which later mutated into today's **cognitive behavioural therapy** (CBT). By the end of the 1970s, the situation had somewhat settled down and **counselling**, as it is currently known, was becoming established, often drawing eclectically on the insights of these various schools. Historically, what was most crucial was that it became acceptable for 'normal' people to seek psychological help, and broke the stigmatising popular association of psychotherapy with mental illness and madness. For references, see other entries cited here plus those under **anti-psychiatry**.

HALO EFFECT

First named as such in a 1920 journal paper by American psychologist E. Thorndike, although the phenomenon was reported as early as 1907 in a paper by F.L. Wells. The tendency of people to ascribe general positive or negative motives or personality characteristics to others on the basis of one such trait or characteristic alone. Most familiar is generalisation from physical attractiveness to believing the person to be honest, caring, warm, etc. Conversely, dishonesty may be ascribed on the basis of an unattractive facial feature. Handwriting, dress and accent are among other factors which can generate positive or negative halo effects. Similarly, a single altruistic act, or a single well-cooked meal, may result in someone being seen ever after as generous or an excellent cook. Closely related to **stereotyping**. The phenomenon has been of particular interest to criminological psychologists for two reasons: (1) physically unattractive people are more likely to be suspected of criminal behaviour and thus arrested or searched by police; (2) physically attractive people, especially women, are likely to be treated more leniently, and their testimony more likely to be believed. Another area in which halo effects may be pernicious is in the way teachers perceive pupils in primary and secondary education. Although commonly referred to in Psychology textbooks, the topic has received hardly any modern book-length treatments. Rommetveit (1960) is the only one I have identified apart from Rosenzweig (2007) − a popular work aimed at business managers.

References

Rommetveit, R. (1960) *Selectivity, Intuition and Halo Effects in Social Perception*, Oslo: Oslo University Press.

Rosenzweig, P.M. (2007) *The Halo Effect and Eight Other Business Delusions that Deceive Managers*, London: Simon & Schuster.

HANDEDNESS

One of the consequences of **lateralisation of function** in humans has been to differentiate between the ways in which we use our two hands. This primarily takes the form of one hand being dominant or preferred and the other being used in an auxiliary fashion. Most commonly it is the right hand which is dominant, but about 9 per cent of the population are left-handed and a small minority genuinely ambidextrous or able to use either hand with equal facility. Around 76 per cent of identical twin pairs have one who is left-handed. Right-handedness is considered to result from left-hemisphere dominance in the brain, and left-handedness from right-hemisphere dominance. This is perhaps somewhat circular, however, as it is handedness which is the primary signifier of 'dominance' in the first place – maybe early-life 'handedness' preferences produce the direction of hemispheric dominance? There is a fairly high degree of potential flexibility in this, however, as right-handed people who lose their right hand can relearn to rely on their left in a relatively short period of time. Many people are also left-handed in some tasks but right-handed in others. Left-handedness is slightly commoner among males (10 per cent) than females (8 per cent). Chris McManus of University College London is currently considered to be the leading British researcher on the topic.

References and further reading

Annett, M. (2001) *Handedness and Brain Assymetry: The Right Shift Theory*, Hove: Psychology Press.

Cohen, S. (ed.) (1990) *Left-Handedness: Behavioural Implications and Anomalies*, Oxford: Elsevier.

Herron, J. (ed.) (1980) *Neuropsychology of Left-Handedness*, New York: Academic Press.

McManus, C. (2002) *Right Hand, Left Hand The Origins of Assymetry in Brains, Bodies, Atoms and Cultures*, Cambridge, MA: Harvard University Press.

HEDONIC TONE

Simply a jargonistic expression meaning how pleasurable or otherwise something is.

HORMIC PSYCHOLOGY

Title chosen by one of the leading early twentieth-century British psychologists, William McDougall (1871–1938), for his theoretical approach. Hardly amounting to a school, since McDougall signally failed to attract any follower or devotees of note. The key features of his hormic psychology are its holistic approach (shared with **Gestalt Psychology**), the prominent role ascribed to instincts, and, more heretically, acceptance of purposive explanations. In fact, by the end of his life, McDougall was claiming that he had anticipated or independently arrived at virtually all the major conclusions of other contemporary Psychological schools and theories. The best account of his mature theory is McDougall (1923), while McDougall (1908) laid the basis for all his subsequent work and was one of the most successful

Psychology textbooks of all time. Heidbreder (1939) includes a useful introduction to the topic. Despite his contemporary eminence and productivity, McDougall is now less well remembered than many of his equally eminent contemporaries.

References

Heidbreder, E. (1939) *Seven Psychologies*, New York: Appleton–Century.
McDougall, W. (1908) *An Introduction to Social Psychology*, London: Methuen.
—— (1923) *An Outline of Psychology*, London: Methuen.

HUMANISTIC PSYCHOLOGY

Identified primarily with the psychotherapeutic approaches of Abraham Maslow and Carl Rogers in the 1950s, and the tradition they initiated. Influenced by **existentialism** and sharing more widespread misgivings about reductionist and 'dehumanising' tendencies within Psychology, Humanistic Psychology adopted a holistic and compassionate, non-medicalising, approach to psychological distress and endorsed an explicit set of values rather than pose as neutral and value-free. The *Journal of Humanistic Psychology* is the school's main academic forum. Many of the **growth movement** therapies should be considered as representing Humanistic Psychology. There is a large literature, especially from the 1970s and 1980s, but the references are restricted to some more recent works.

References and further reading

DeCarvalho, R. (1991) *The Founders of Humanistic Psychology*, Westport, CT: Greenwood Press.
Moss, D. (1999) *Humanistic and Transpersonal Psychology: A Historical and Biographical Handbook*, Westport, CT: Greenwood Press.
Rowan, J. (2001) *Ordinary Ecstasy: The Dialectics of Humanistic Psychology*, 3rd edn, London: Taylor & Francis.
Schneider, K. J., Bugental, J.F.T. and Fraser Pierson, J. (eds) (2002) *The Handbook of Humanistic Psychology: Leading Edges in Theory, Research and Practice*, London: Sage.

HYPNAGOGIA

Hypnagogia or a 'hypnogogic state' is a semi-awake **REM** (see **rapid eye movement**) state during which the brain's alpha-rhythms become especially strong and induce powerful flashing visual imagery. It has attracted the attention of a wide range of people interested in meditation techniques, etc. and is sometimes given mystical significance or seen as a route for exploration of the deep unconscious. Book-length texts on it are, however, very few, but Grey Walter (1953) still remains a useful introduction, while fuller coverage may be found in Mavromatis (1987).

References

Grey Walter, W. (1953) *The Living Brain*, London: Duckworth.
Mavromatis, A. (1987) *Hypnogagia: The Unique State of Consciousness between Wakefulness and Sleep*, London: Routledge & Kegan Paul.

HYPNOSIS

From F.-J. Mesmer's (1734–1815) highly publicised and controversial 'discovery' of '*animal magnetism*' onwards, hypnotism has never ceased to attract both popular and scientific attention. While *mesmerism* itself was largely discredited by the 1840s, since his 'animal magnetism' theory proved unsustainable, the phenomenon of induced trance states was evidently real enough. British doctor James Braid, in his *Neurypnology* (Braid [1843] 1994) argued that it was a psychological phenomenon, a 'nervous sleep', based on **suggestion** rather than caused by some enigmatic physical 'force' emanating from the hypnotist and introduced the word 'hypnotism'. By the late nineteenth century, the topic was again attracting wide attention, especially in France, as a psychotherapeutic technique (see *Nancy School* under **Schools of Psychology**). It remains in use for a variety of purposes such as helping people stop smoking, and among a few psychotherapists as a technique for accessing deep memories and inducing *regression* (see under **psychoanalysis**). Among psychologists who have studied the topic are E.R. Hilgard (1904–2001), arguably the most solidly 'mainstream' (as well as long-lived) eminent academic American psychologist of the twentieth century, who devoted much of his later career to it, establishing a Laboratory for Hypnosis Research at Stanford University. Precisely how and why hypnotism 'works' continues to be controversial, but hypnotic techniques are now highly refined. Dangers of abuse have always been a concern, and 'stage hypnotists' can still make mistakes – accidently leaving 'hypnotic suggestions' in place, for example. Hypnotism and kindred phenomena should always be treated with caution and not treated as a party game. The literature on hypnotism is particularly vast and variable in both content and quality. For a recent academic review of the topic, see Heap and Kirsch (2006) and for the current state of play, Jamieson (2007).

References and further reading

Braid, J. ([1843] 1994) *Neurypnology; Or, the Rationale of Nervous Sleep, Considered in Relation to Animal Magnetism*, New York: Gryphon Editions.

Gauld, A. (1992) *History of Hypnotism*, Cambridge: Cambridge University Press.

Heap, M. and Kirsch, I. (2006) *Hypnosis: Theory Research and Application*, Aldershot: Ashgate.

Hilgard, E.R. and Hilgard, J.R. (1983) *Hypnosis in the Relief of Pain*, Los Altos, CA: Kaufmann.

Jamieson, G. (ed.) (2007) *Hypnosis and Conscious States: The Cognitive Neuroscience Perspective*, New York: Oxford University Press.

HYPOTHETICAL CONSTRUCT

Any concept referring to a process or phenomenon, the existence of which cannot be empirically demonstrated but which nevertheless seems to be required on theoretical grounds or for pragmatic descriptive purposes. It is very similar to, and can be almost synonymous with the term *intervening variable*. Their relationship, use and meanings were the topic of a classic paper by MacCorquodale and Meehl (1948), and during the late 1940s and 1950s, in the light of this paper, the two concepts became the focal point of a complex and philosophically technical conceptual controversy in US Psychology. Their respective roles, status, definitions, and methods of validation were all contested. Put somewhat crudely, the difference between them is that hypothetical constructs refer to quasi-concrete 'entities' while intervening variables are defined in terms of the role which the hypothesised 'variable' plays. Thus, Freud's *super ego* (see under **psychoanalysis**) is a hypothetical construct whereas the **cognitive map** concept refers to an intervening variable. This distinction is nevertheless a little elusive and ambiguities persist. Hypothetical constructs and intervening variables are unavoidable in Psychology due to our inability to directly observe internal psychological phenomena. Many scientific concepts begin as hypothetical constructs, in the physical sciences however these typically end by being empirically confirmed or validated, or, alternatively, abandoned. In Psychology, their hypothetical status is often more recalcitrant. A common strategy is then to define them operationally (see **operationalism**). In Psychology, the term itself first became widely used during the 1930s in **learning theory** contexts (especially in the context of C.L. Hull's work) to refer to events, etc. assumed to be taking place within the organism. The debate about the nature and role of hypothetical constructs has long since fizzled out, but some of the issues at stake remain open – particularly those related to how we state and test hypotheses about internal psychological processes.

Reference

MacCorquodale, K. and Meehl, P.E. (1948) 'On a Distinction between Hypothetical Constructs and Intervening Variables', *Psychological Review*, 55: 95–107.

HYSTERIA

One of the oldest psychopathological categories, dating back to the ancient Greeks. The word is derived from the Greek term for 'uterus'. This was because it was long considered an exclusively female condition caused by 'wandering' of the uterus. The symptoms of hysteria are typically wild, emotional and irrational, sometimes violent, ravings. In the seventeenth century the English physician Thomas Sydenham proposed that men too could display hysteria but the image of it as typically affecting women persisted. The concept has attracted considerable attention from historians of Psychiatry since it played a major role in the work of the French psychiatrist J.-M. Charcot and the emergence of **psychoanalysis**. Feminist historians have also been interested in the way changing notions of the nature of hysteria have reflected the social place of women in western cultures (see Mitchell, 2000). 'Hysteria' is now rarely used in medical contexts, and the classic symptoms are somewhat rarely encountered. It remains in popular use, often in the phrase 'mass hysteria' to denote collective outbreaks of alarm, panic or, as with the death of Princess Diana, extreme emotion. Even this can retain a gender link since media use of this expression is almost automatically triggered in relation to events in all-female institutions such as girls boarding schools. For many years, Veith (1965) was the only book-length history of the concept, but while this remains a handy introduction, its approach is now considered obsolete. M. Micale's work has substantially changed the picture (Micale, 1989), along with J. Mitchell's subsequent account (Mitchell, 2000).

References

Micale, M.S. (1989) 'Hysteria and its Historiography: A Review of Past and Present Writings', in 2 parts, *History of Science* 17: 223–62, 319–51.

Micale, M.S. (1995) *Approaching Hysteria: Disease and its Interpretations*, Princeton, NJ: Princeton University Press.

Mitchell, J. (2000) *Mad Men and Medusas: Reclaiming Hysteria*, New York: Basic Books.

Veith, I. (1965) *Hysteria: The History of a Disease*, Chicago, IL: The University of Chicago Press.

IDEALISM

In everyday language, we usually use 'idealism' simply to mean pursuing high ethical principles, but it also has important philosophical uses of a more technical kind. In relation to the **mind–body problem** of how mind and body are related it refers to positions which argue for the primacy of mind. This is typically understood to imply that everything somehow exists 'in the mind', and was classically expounded with great power by the British philosopher George Berkeley (Berkeley, [1710] 2004). In this sense, it is opposed to **materialism** and **dualism**. It can also sometimes refer to the doctrine, dating back to Plato (c.428–348 BCE), that ideas exist separately from their objects. The opposite of this kind of idealism is *nominalism*, the argument that words do not refer to abstract 'ideas' but are simply names for real-world objects and phenomena. This is actually related to everyday use, for Plato argued that all horses, for example, are imperfect manifestations or embodiments of a perfect 'ideal' horse existing in an 'ideal' realm. Hence the use of 'idealist' to refer to someone pursuing, or believing in the possibility of, perfection. In academic philosophical or psychological contexts, however, it usually refers to someone espousing an idealist position on the mind–body relationship. Idealism is covered in general histories of philosophy, and there is a large literature on specific varieties of the doctrine such as German idealism in the nineteenth century. For a general introduction, Vesey (1982) remains probably the best option.

References

Berkeley, G. ([1710] 2004) *The Principles of Human Knowledge*, New York: Kessinger.

Vesey, G. (1982) *Idealism Past and Present*, Cambridge: Cambridge University Press.

IDENTIFICATION

To identify with someone is to believe their personality and character to have such affinities with one's own that one can understand their situation, behaviour, motives, interests, etc. It also involves a close emotional *empathy* with their lives and fate, although identification exceeds empathy as such. Identification can be transient or enduring, and may occur simply when you become aware of somebody being in a situation very similar to one you have experienced. More broadly, however, and in a somewhat looser sense, one can be said to identify with a particular cause, one side in a controversy, or a football team, etc. In William James's (1890) terms, to identify with someone or something is to treat it as an extension of one's **Self**. (For another more technical sense, see also *identification*, under **psychoanalysis**.)

IDENTITY

In Psychology, debates about this concept usually arise in the context of the question as to whether people possess a constant, enduring, personal identity or 'I'. Sceptics argue that although we nearly all assume this to be the case, it is actually illusory, that our identity is in flux and constantly being recreated or reconstituted. This case is most powerfully raised by some in the **social constructionism** camp. It is very closely related to the **Self** concept, which has been the centre of a similar controversy, and the two terms are not always clearly differentiable. Basically, 'Identity' denotes the general principle of sameness over time, while 'Self' more specifically refers to the individual's core character or personality. Identity is thus an 'all or nothing' thing – either we possess a single identity from the start or we do not – but 'Self', for many psychologists, is more of a comprehensive psychological integration we strive to achieve, or modify over time. In the phrase **dissociative identity disorder** (see **multiple personality disorder**), however, the term is in effect synonymous with 'Self'. Here, 'identity' is being used more in its everyday sense of 'who one is' (as in 'identity cards', 'identity theft' or 'false identity'). Another, philosophical, meaning is met with in the **mind–body problem**, in the phrase 'mind–brain identity theory', U.T. Place's argument that mind-events or processes and brain-events or processes are identical.

References and further reading

Burke, P.J. (ed.) (2003) *Advances in Identity Theory and Research*, Amsterdam: Kluwer.

Leary, M.R. and Tangney, J.P. (eds) (2003) *Handbook of Self and Identity*, London: Guilford.

Paranjpe, A.C. (2000) *Self and Identity in Modern Psychology and Indian Thought*, New York: Plenum Press.

Yancy, G. and Hadley, S. (2005) *Narrative Identities: Psychologists Engaged in Self-Construction*, London: Jessica Kingsley.

IDIOGRAPHIC AND NOMOTHETIC

Terms introduced by Allport (1937) for opposing research methods in the field of **personality** research. Ideographic is approximately synonymous with the 'case study' method, involving in-depth exploration of the individual. Allport felt this was necessary in order to capture the full complexity of individual personalities and the inter-relatedness of people's various traits and abilities. Nomothetic methods, by contrast, use large numbers of subjects/participants and are usually aimed at establishing norms and commonalities, seeing them as complementary. Ideographic and nomothetic methods are generally qualitative and quantitative respectively.

Reference

Allport, G.W. (1937) *Personality: A Psychological Interpretation*, New York: Holt.

IMAGERY

Visual images 'in the mind'. A long-standing topic of Psychological interest, dating back to British pioneer psychologist Francis Galton's famous studies of people's visual imagery for numbers and days of the week (Galton, 1883). There is huge variation in ability to form visual images, from those who seem to be completely incapable of it to those apparently capable of forming highly detailed images almost at will. The term *eidetic imagery* is used to refer to what is often commonly called 'photographic memory', the ability to retain near-perfect images of what they have seen and even scan them for details not consciously noticed at the time. While there have been controversies in the past as to how significant imagery was and whether it actually played any real role (the **behaviourists**, for example, were extremely sceptical), it is now appreciated that it can play an important part in **memory**. In *paired associate* learning, for example, the creation of a visual image incorporating both terms (e.g. for 'parrot' and 'trumpet' an image of a parrot blowing a trumpet) can result in quite long lists of word-pairs being learned in only one or two trials. Luria (1969) was an extended case report of a man whose exceptional memory was entirely based on visual imagery, over which he had little real control, to the extent that in order to forget something he had to imagine it being disposed of by e.g. erasing the word from a blackboard. While, strictly speaking, dreaming is a form of imagery, the term is not usually used to refer to dreams except in the explicit phrase 'dream imagery'. In recent years the value of actively using mental imagery has been explored in relation to psychotherapy, sport, Health Psychology and other applied areas.

References and further reading

Betts, G.H. (2007) *The Distribution and Function of Mental Imagery*, Whitefish, MT: Kessinger.

Galton, F. ([1883] 2005) *Inquiries into Human Faculty*, Whitefish, MT: Kessinger Publisher.

Kosslyn, S.M., Thompson, W.L. and Ganis, G. (2006) *The Case for Mental Imagery*, Oxford: Oxford University Press.

Luria, A.R. (1969) *The Mind of the Mnemonist*, London: Jonathan Cape.

Morris, T. (2005) *Imagery in Sport: The Mental Approach to Sport*, Champaigne, IL: Human Kinetics Europe.

Roeckelein, J.E. (2004) *Imagery in Psychology: A Reference Guide*, Westport, CT: Praeger.

Singer, J.L. (2005) *Imagery in Psychotherapy*, Washington, DC: American Psychological Association.

IMITATION

Copying the behaviour of someone else, an animal or a natural phenomenon. Imitation differs from **identification** in involving only overt simulation of the other's behaviour, without necessarily entailing any insight or **empathy** with them, indeed, it can take derisive or mocking forms. There is nevertheless a sense in which imitation may be considered a route towards deeper understanding of the other, behaving like somebody (or something) potentially providing insight into what it feels like to *be* them (see **physiomorphism**). For

learning theory based on the accumulation of discrete *S-R* connections, the holistic nature of imitative behaviour posed considerable theoretical difficulties.

References

Dautenhahn, K. (ed.) (2002) *Imitation in Animals and Artefacts*, Cambridge, MA: MIT Press.

Hurley, S. and Chater, N. (eds) (2005) *Perspectives on Imitation*, Cambridge, MA: MIT Press.

Nehaniv, C. and Dautenhahn, K. (eds) (2007) *Imitation and Social Learning in Robots, Humans and Animals: Behavioural, Social and Communicative Dimensions*, Cambridge: Cambridge University Press.

IMPLICIT PERSONALITY THEORY (IPT)

This topic appears to have first emerged in the 1970s and has, since the 1980s, become an established issue in Social Psychology (see **social cognition**). It refers to the implicit assumptions which everyone makes about **personality** and their 'theories' about how different traits are related and/or their presence indicated by e.g. physical appearance or demeanour. This varies from simple stereotypes such as a high forehead indicating high intelligence to assuming that if someone is shy, they are also naturally anxious. There appears to be a fairly high social consensus about many of these, and debate has tended to focus on such issues as how valid IPT actually is, and how similar it is across cultures. Since we rely heavily on IPT in everyday social situations, an understanding of how it operates – and especially how and when it can be misleading – is clearly of some importance. IPT applies not just to individuals but groups, and thus merges into the broader topics of **stereotyping** and **prejudice**. There are no book-length texts on the topic but it is now generally covered in the context of **attribution theory**.

INDIVIDUAL PSYCHOLOGY (ADLERIAN)

The third of the major schools of dynamic **psychotherapy** along with S. Freud's **psychoanalysis** and C.G. Jung's **Analytical Psychology** which emerged in the early twentieth century. Alfred Adler (1870–1937) split from Freud in 1911. Although ultimately less successful than these, Individual Psychology had a distinct impact and left its own legacy of insights. For Adler, the central motivation in human life was neither sex nor *individuation* but an aspiration to mastery or power (in a general rather than Machiavellian sense). We live in a future-oriented, goal-directed, fashion. We seek success in a social context and thus our behaviour can only be understood in terms of *social interest*. This led Adler to produce quite distinctive accounts of the significance of dreams, the nature of sex, and the importance of social factors (which Freud left largely unexplored). Some cast Adler as a forerunner of **Humanistic Psychology** and both his stress on the social embeddedness of human life and belief in human autonomy, as against unconscious determinism,' have continued to appeal to many psychotherapists and lay people alike. Uniquely Adlerian concepts include *inferiority complex, organ inferiority, compensative striving,* and *sibling rivalry,* although unlike Freud and Jung he was reluctant to coin an elaborate technical vocabulary, aiming his writings as much towards the general readership as to his professional peers. The 'inferiority complex' is created when we realise that we are physically or psychologically unable to achieve the kind of mastery or goals we are seeking, especially when those around us appear able to do so. 'Organ inferiority' refers explicitly to physical shortcomings. 'Compensative striving' refers to the efforts we make to overcome organ inferiority and the 'inferiority complex' – the classic example being the stammerer or stutterer who, like the Greek Demosthenes, becomes a great orator. The small individual who cultivates their aggressive abilities would be another case. In some way or other, however, we all engage in compensative striving. 'Sibling rivalry' is important because it is often in the context of the sibling group that the individual's shortcomings are brought home to them, and towards which their first compensative efforts are played out. A British 'Adlerian Society and Institute for Individual Psychology' (ASIIP) and an International Adlerian Society continue to remain highly active and offer training courses. In some respects the schools' fortunes are perhaps better now than they were between the 1940s and 1980s.

References and further reading

Adler, A. (1921) *The Neurotic Constitution,* London: Kegan Paul, Trench & Trubner.
—— ([1925] 1999) *The Practice and Theory of Individual Psychology,* London: Routledge.

Ansbacher, H. L. and Ansbacher, R.R. (eds) (1956) *The Individual Psychology of Alfred Adler: A Systematic Presentation in Selections from his Writings*, New York: Harper.

Grey, L. (1998) *Alfred Adler, the Forgotten Prophet: A Vision for the 21st Century*, Westport, CT: Greenwood.

Hoffman, E. (1994) *The Drive for Self: Alfred Adler and the Founding of Individual Psychology*, Reading, MA: Perseus.

Way, L. (1956) *Alfred Adler: An Introduction to his Psychology*, Harmondsworth: Penguin.

INFORMATION PROCESSING

This expression entered Psychology in the late 1950s in the wake of the interlinked rise of information theory and computing technology. It marked the application to psychological processes, initially at the perceptual and sensory level, of the image that these involved processing incoming information in the technical information theory sense of the term. This was soon being extended to **memory** and **cognition** and hence became a fundamental concept in **Cognitive Psychology**. Explanations of psychological processes in terms of information channels and levels of processing thus provided the standard theoretical framework for cognitivist approaches. For references, see cross-referenced topics.

INHIBITION

As a general term for any suppression, conscious or not, of any psychological or psycho-neurological process, inhibition has a long and tortuous history within Psychology (see Smith, 1992). In the nineteenth century its primarily neurological sense was integrated into a hierarchical image of the mind in which a rational controlling **Self** (or some such agency) operated in a top-down fashion by inhibiting undesirable **instincts** and impulses. From this emerged the everyday use of the terms 'inhibited' and 'uninhibited' to describe personality or behaviour. It also corresponded with a much wider view of society itself as requiring top-down management and control by rulers over potentially unruly masses, and almost invisibly the term could slide from neurological into social discourse. In **psychoanalysis**, the concept became widely used in the early twentieth century in relation to *repression*, *suppression*, and *ego-functioning* (see under psychoanalysis). **Perceptual defence** was also seen as involving the inhibition of conscious awareness of unwelcome stimuli. Unsurprisingly, **Cognitive Psychology** has also found a role for the concept, particularly in relation to **memory** where it figures as a factor in preventing recall, and more positively as being required by efficient cognitive functioning in order to remain focused on tasks in hand. Providing a clear-cut technical definition of 'inhibition' is, fairly obviously, thus rather difficult, but Psychology is unlikely to shed the term in the near future.

References and further reading

Gorfein, D.S. and MacLeod, C.M. (eds) (2007) *Inhibition in Cognition*, Washington, DC: American Psychological Association.

Reznick, J.S. (ed.) (1989) *Perspectives on Behavioral Inhibition*, Chicago, IL: The University of Chicago Press.

Smith, R. (1992) *Inhibition. History and Meaning in the Sciences of Mind and Brain*, London: Free Association Books.

INSPECTION TIME

The time taken for a stimulus to be processed sufficiently for it to be identified or discriminated from the total sensory input. Inspection time tasks are widely used in *perception*, **cognition** and **memory** research. Closely related to **reaction time**.

INSTINCT

The concept of 'instinct' has had a somewhat tortuous career in Psychology. From the late nineteenth century to around 1920 there was a general assumption that the behaviour of all animals, including humans, was controlled and determined by a relatively small number of basic instincts which ensured their survival and reproduction. Typically these would include sex, hunger, shelter, aggression and nurturing (although not all species would possess all of these). They might differ somewhat between the sexes, thus women would have 'maternal instincts' (including nurturing) and men have 'paternal instincts' such as protection. It was often assumed that somehow there were specific energies devoted to these at the physiological level. They were also, in the work of William James and later William McDougall (1908), considered as underlying **emotion**. The first challenge to this may perhaps be said to be Sigmund Freud's theory that there was a single, sexual, instinct at the heart of all others (see *Eros, Pleasure Principle* under **psychoanalysis**). But even more seriously, within experimental Psychology, with the advent of **behaviourism** and the turn, from around 1912, towards radical environmentalism (especially in the USA), the concept itself came to be rejected as unnecessary and misleading. All that was required was the reward versus pain principle around which **learning theory** was built. By the 1930s, the adequacy of this solution was beginning to come under pressure from ethologists (see **ethology**) such as Julian Huxley who were becoming increasingly aware that complex species-specific behaviour could often only be explained as genetic in origin, since it was displayed spontaneously without prior learning or, in many cases, exposure to adult models.

This required a concept of 'instinct', but rather different from the earlier one. Instead of a few general categories, there were numerous 'instinctive' behaviours frequently restricted to one or a few species. The older categories came to be understood simply as labels for the necessary conditions of survival which any species had to meet, but did not imply that they all shared a common 'sex' or 'feeding' instinct. During the 1950s this new meaning became widespread in the popular works of German ethologist Konrad Lorenz and the Norwegian Nico Tinbergen (Timbergen, 1951). While topics such as 'aggression' remained thus labelled, their analysis required a species-by-species approach. A new technical vocabulary replaced the old instinct list, referring to categories of behaviour and responses rather than some supposedly inner sources shared by all creatures who displayed them (see ethology).

The term 'instinct' has now largely lost any clear-cut technical meaning, although its everyday use in expression such as 'I instinctively knew what to do', 'I survived by pure instinct' and the like remains useful in referring to behaviour which seems to emerge spontaneously without any reflective forethought. As genetics proceeds apace in unravelling the genetic origins of behaviour, the 'instinct' concept becomes ever more redundant as a scientific term. Book-length texts on the topic in its technical sense virtually disappear after the 1960s, although it still figures in popular book titles.

References and further reading

Birney, R.C. and Teevan, R.C. (eds) (1961) *Instinct: An Enduring Problem in Psychology*, New York: Van Nostrand.

Drever, J. (1917) *Instinct in Man*, Cambridge: Cambridge University Press.
Fletcher, R. (1968) *Instinct in Man: In the Light of Recent Work in Comparative Psychology*, London: Allen and Unwin.
McDougall, W. (1908) *Introdcution to Social Psychology*, London: Methuen.
Tinbergen, N. (1951) *Study of Instinct*, Oxford: Clarendon Press.
Wozniak, R.H. (1998) *Habit and Instinct: Classics in Psychology, 1855–1914*, Bristol: Thoemmes.

INTELLIGENCE

Intelligence has proved surprisingly difficult to define in a rigorous fashion. Clearly it refers in a general fashion to the level of ability to reason, solve problems, successfully respond to situations and so forth, but these range from mathematics to handling social situations, from understanding machines to solving crosswords and Sudoku puzzles. Psychologists such as Francis Galton (using the expression 'natural ability') and the American Raymond B. Cattell began attempting to study intelligence in the late nineteenth century, this culminating in the pioneering statistical studies of C. Spearman (see **factor analysis**) and, most famously, Alfred Binet and H. Simon in France who produced the first intelligence test in 1904, to which all subsequent *IQ* (intelligence quotient) tests trace their origins. These all focused primarily on reasoning ability and academic performance, ignoring social intelligence and *emotional intelligence*. One should stress here that it was the advent of universal education which created the climate in which an assessment scale applicable to all children was required, IQ tests being Psychology's response to this. Throughout the twentieth century, IQ testing and theories of intelligence enjoyed a chequered and controversial history. IQ testing itself evolved quite rapidly after Binet and Simon's work. Initially IQ was defined as the ratio between mental age (MA) and chronological age (MCA) but it was obvious from the outset that this was inapplicable to people much over 15 years old and so was replaced by a statistical definition in terms of standard deviations from population norms. The term 'IQ' itself was introduced by the German psychologist Wilhelm Stern who converted the MA:CA ratio into a simple quantitative scale, defining MA = CA as 100. The definition of mean intelligence as 100 has continued ever since.

A second, practical, problem was that the original Binet–Simon tests and their derivatives were time-consuming, having to be administered on a one-to-one basis. In 1917, when the United States entered the First World War, it was felt necessary rapidly to assess the intelligence levels of conscripts. A clutch of leading psychologists were co-opted who famously produced the first 'group intelligence test', which could be administered to large numbers over a short period of time.

However, theoretical questions came to the fore during the 1920s and 1930s as controversy broke out between those who argued that intelligence was general (*general intelligence*, termed '*g*' by C. Spearman) and those who held that there were a multiplicity of different types of intelligence, such as verbal, mathematical and spatial, which did not necessarily correlate with each other at all strongly and needed separate assessment. This centred on complex debates about statistical procedures involved in factor analysis. Less profound, but important in relation to the study of alleged 'racial' and cultural differences, was a challenge by Otto Klineberg (Klineberg, 1928) to the prioritisation of speed over accuracy as an index of intelligence, since he found that some Native American groups were slower, but took fewer trials, to solve problems.

By the end of the 1940s, it had become customary, in education particularly, to use tests of specific abilities, to provide a 'profile' of the child's performance, while retaining general IQ tests, in which a variety of types of ability were included, to produce an overall IQ score. Even so, the range of abilities remained restricted to those involving formal reasoning of some kind. It had also, by then, become customary for psychologists in the field to define intelligence 'operationally' as 'what intelligence tests measure' (see **operationalism**). The Australian-born S.D. Porteus, working with 'subnormal' children had, in the early 1920s, already diverged from this and developed a social rating scale of 'social sufficiency' which he felt was far more useful for assessing how well such children could manage than a formal IQ score. It was, however, only from the 1980s onwards that attention really began to turn towards emotional and social intelligence, while the distinction between **convergent** and **divergent thinking** was additionally complicating the picture.

Those outside the **psychometric** tradition, such as developmental psychologists working in the **Piagetian theoretical** framework were meanwhile adopting quite different approaches which did not lend themselves easily to quantification. Robert J. Sternberg's influential *Metaphors of Mind: Conceptions of the Nature of Intelligence* (Sternberg, 1990) signalled the declining dominance of the older IQ testing paradigm. Creativity, emotional intelligence, social intelligence, even spiritual intelligence, are now firmly on the agenda.

Finally, it should be noted that the intelligence issue has, from early in the twentieth century, frequently become bound up with other topics such as 'race differences', gender differences, the **nature–nurture controversy** and ideological challenges to the social function played by Psychology itself.

References and further reading

Ciarrochi, J. (2006) *Emotional Intelligence in Everyday Life*, Hove: Psychology Press.

Klineberg, O. (1928) 'An Experimental Study of Speed and Other Factors in "Racial" Differences', *Archives of Psychology Monograph No. 93*, New York: Columbia University Press.

Mackintosh, N.J. (2004) *IQ and Human Intelligence*, New York: Oxford University Press.

Minton, H.L. (1988) *Lewis M. Terman: Pioneer in Psychological Testing*, New York: New York University Press.

Oliver, W. and Endle, R.W. (eds) (2004) *Handbook of Understanding and Measuring Intelligence*, London: Sage.

Porteus, S.D. (1921) 'The Social Rating Scale', *Training School Bulletin*, 19.

Spearman, C. (1921) *The Nature of 'Intelligence' and the Principles of Cognition*, London: Macmillan.

Sternberg, R.J. (1990) *Metaphors of Mind: Conceptions of the Nature of Intelligence*, Cambridge: Cambridge University Press.

Zenderland, L. (1998) *Measuring Minds: Henry Herbert Goddard and the Origins of American Intelligence Testing*, Cambridge: Cambridge University Press.

INTENTIONALITY AND INTENSIONALITY

'Intentionality' is fairly unproblematic, meaning simply 'having intentions'. It thus enables the basic distinction between acting in intended and unintended ways. In **AI**, one of the central issues has been whether or not intentionality in the full sense can ever be programmed into a computer system. Can a computer ever, in other words, be said to *mean* to do something? (J. Searle, in a classic, and controversial, 1980 paper, argued not (Searle, 1980).) At this point 'intention' and 'intension' can become blurred. 'Intension' is a much more technical philosophical and theoretical term which refers to the features, etc. of whatever a word (or other symbol) refers to. The question then arises as to whether, although it may appear to be using words correctly, an AI system can actually be said to 'understand them', i.e. has 'intensional' understanding. The confusion between the two terms thus centres on the notion of 'meaning': what we mean to do are our 'intentions' and what words, etc. mean are, to put it crudely, their 'intensions'.

References and further reading

Bratman, M. (2004) *Faces of Intention: Selected Essays on Intention and Agency*, Cambridge: Cambridge University Press.

Gustafson, D.F. (1986) *Intention and Agency*, Dordrecht: D. Reidel.

Martin, R.M. (1963) *Intension and Decision: A Philosophical Study*, Englewood Cliffs, NJ: Prentice Hall.

Searle, J. R. (1980) 'Mind, Brains and Programs', *Behavioral and Brain Sciences*, 3(3): 417–57.

INTERPERSONAL ATTRACTION

This topic became prominent in US Social Psychology during the 1960s (e.g. Pepitone, 1964). The central goal is to identify the factors involved in determining whether two people will be attracted to each other (often, but not exclusively, in establishing potentially sexual relationships). One aspect of this has been to look at 'first impressions'. Numerous factors are now considered to be involved. These include similarity (both psychological and physical), physical attractiveness as such, and biological attraction working at the pheromonal level (body odour). **Learning theory** principles can also be applied in this area, attraction being considered to involve mutual reinforcement of some kind. There is now a very large literature on this subject, covering both 'romantic' attraction and friendship. Most current book-length coverage is in more general works on interpersonal relationships.

References and further reading

Dwyer, D. (2000) *Interpersonal Relationships*, London: Routledge.

Hendrick, C. and Hendrick, S. (1993) *Loving, Liking and Relating*, Pacific Grove, CA: Brooks/Cole.

Knapp, M.L. and Miller, G.R. (eds) (1994) *The Handbook of Interpersonal Relating*, Thousand Oaks, CA: Sage.

Pepitone, A. (1964) *Attraction and Hostility: An Experimental Analysis of Interpersonal and Self-evaluation*, New York: Atherton.

Vohs, K.D and Finkel, E.J. (2006) *Self and Relationships: Connecting Intrapersonal and Interpersonal Processes*, New York: Guilford.

INTERVENING VARIABLE *see* hypothetical construct.

INTROSPECTION, INTROSPECTIONISM

In everyday language, 'introspection' refers to a 'looking inwards', observing and reflecting upon one's own mind, and 'being introspective' is a tendency to engage in such self-scrutiny and self-examination. In Psychology, this acquired a more technical character in the late nineteenth century when the German pioneer Wilhelm Wundt (1832–1920) included a form of systematic disciplined introspection in his experimental studies of the nature of consciousness. This would, it was argued, overcome the problem that the 'mind' was private and not open to objective scientific study, and is now known as 'introspectionism'. It has, however, been a much mythologised topic in Psychology's understanding of its history and origins, routinely being characterised as its initial experimental approach or phase before being overthrown by **behaviourism**. As Alan Costall (Costall, 2006) has shown, this is far from being the case, even within Wundt's own work introspection played a fairly minor role in comparison with other methods, such as use of **reaction times**, nor did the pragmatic use of introspection ever disappear. The numerous difficulties which introspection poses as an objective scientific method were well known to late nineteenth-century psychologists such as the American William James (1840–1910) as well as Wundt himself. In practical terms, it was impossible to resolve conflicting findings, more profoundly, however, it was increasingly realised that, on logical and philosophical grounds, it was impossible to observe what was going on in one's mind, let alone report it, in a totally neutral 'objective' way. Experience is always interpreted in terms of the concepts we have available, our expectations and prior knowledge. We can never even experience 'raw' uninterpreted sensations, or at least we cannot describe them without interpreting them. This does not mean that introspection is valueless, the very act of trying to understand psychological discourse involves us in applying to ourselves what we reading or hearing, for example. It does, however, mean that we cannot use introspection alone as a viable scientific method. Another factor limiting introspectionism's applicability was that the kinds of phenomena it could be used to study were quite restricted (such as the nature of sensations or what it was like to try and remember something). Long before 1900, numerous psychologists were turning their attention to a far wider range of topics such as child development, learning and animal behaviour, to which introspective methods were largely irrelevant. The endurance of the 'introspectionism' myth is a complex historical issue of some psychological interest in its own right, and readers are advised to consult Costall's on-line paper for a fuller exposition. The most ardent introspectionist was Edward Bradford Titchener (1867–1927), an English student of Wundt who spent his subsequent academic career at Cornell University in the United States. Although he cast himself as Wundt's disciple and follower, his approach soon diverged significantly from Wundt's, who criticised him strongly in later years. The topic is naturally covered in all general histories of Psychology but has received scant recent book-length coverage, however, Costall's paper should be consulted to counter the orthodox story.

Reference

Costall, A. (2006) '"Introspectionism" and the Mythical Origins of Scientific Psychology', *Consciousness and Cognition*, 15(4): 634–54.

JUST WORLD BELIEF/HYPOTHESIS

The belief that the world is fundamentally just and that people ultimately get what they deserve is deeply rooted in many human cultures although can take different forms. Perhaps most commonly it is a component of religious beliefs in which the injustices of this world will become balanced either posthumously or in a later incarnation ('the law of karma'). When held to apply to *this* world, it can also have religious connections in that good events may be viewed as 'rewards' and bad ones as 'punishments'. Whether religiously backed or not, the belief that this world is just can also lead to blaming victims and withholding of sympathy. More positively, it may be argued that creating a 'just world' is an aspirational goal and as such plays a positive motivational role in human affairs. In Psychology, the topic appears to have gradually emerged in Social Psychology during the 1950s before being taken up by M. J. Lerner (Lerner and Simmons, 1966; Lerner, 1980), the most prominent authority on the topic. It has subsequently received attention from several different directions. While the broad consensus is that the just world belief is false (at least for *this* world), there is some ambiguity as to whether or not it is entirely bad to hold it. Fighting injustice is likely to be more determined and passionate if it is viewed as in some way an offence against the natural order of things. As has recently been pointed out by L.L.P. Gellert, one version holds that while the world at large is unjust, it does deal fairly with oneself, and this can have positive psychological effects on the ability to cope with misfortune. There is thus some linkage with the topic of **locus of control**. The emphasis of research is now shifting from the belief itself to the 'justice motive' as such, two aspects of the issue which had been rather confusingly conflated in earlier work.

References and further reading

Gellert, L.L.P. see www.jjay.cuny.edu/docket/941.php

Lerner, M.J. (1980) *The Belief in a Just World: A Fundamental Delusion*, New York: Plenum Press.

Lerner, M.J. and Simmons, C. (1966) 'Observer's Reaction to the "Innocent Victim": Compassion or Rejection?', *Journal of Personality and Social Psychology*, 4: 203–10.

KIN SELECTION

Introduced by evolutionary biologist W.D. Hamilton (Hamilton, 1964) and taken up by **sociobiology**, then **Evolutionary Psychology**, kin selection is the theory that organisms behave in a way which enhances the survival chances of those most closely related to the actor. Thus, for example, the more distant the genetic relationship, the less likely the occurrence of **altruism**. While the ethological evidence on non-human species if impressive, the application of this to humans is controversial. See also *inclusive fitness* under sociobiology.

See also: **Evolutionary Psychology, sociobiology**.

References

Hamilton, W.D. (1964) 'The Evolution of Social Behavior I & II' *Journal for Theoretical Biology*, 7: 1–52.

KINESICS

The study of body movement, especially expressive and communicative body and facial movement. Kinesics was named and pioneered by ex-ballet dancer turned anthropologist Birdwhistell (1952, 1970). It has, however, failed to establish itself as a flourishing subdiscipline (and there is very little work on the psychology of dancing, for instance, which is really quite remarkable considering its near universality and cultural prominence). Birdwhistell's work has now been incorporated as one strand in the broader field of studies on **non-verbal communication**.

References and further reading

Birdwhistell, R.L. (1952) *Introduction to Kinesics*, Louisville, KT: University of Louisville Press.

—— (1970) *Kinesics and Context: Essays on Body-Motion Communication*, London: Allen Lane.

Poyatos, F. (2002) *Nonverbal Communication across Disciplines: Paralanguage, Kinesics, Silence, Personal and Environmental Interaction*, Amsterdam: John Benjamins.

LANGUAGE ACQUISITION DEVICE (LAD)

Innate mechanism hypothesised by the linguist Noam Chomsky (1957, 1965) to explain why language is acquired so readily and quickly by small children. This process far exceeds anything explicable using conventional **learning theory** concepts and indeed displays some features contrary to these (such as using grammatical rules in ways they would never have heard, e.g. adding the plural 's' to words like *mouse* where the plural is not formed this way). Nobody has yet actually identified the LAD in any physical form, but if it exists in this way it is presumably at the level of the genetically determined neurological organisation of the human brain. The LAD serves: (1) to underpin grammar; and (2) to provide a generalised sense of 'meaning' or 'reference'. Although of less concern to Chomsky himself, who was primarily interested in proving that there was a universal 'deep structure' to the grammar or syntactic rules of all human languages, this last point is important. As Wittgenstein demonstrated (Wittgenstein, 1953), the notion of words having a meaning or referent cannot itself be acquired in the same way as individual word meanings. There has to be some notion of 'meaning' there in the first place. You cannot teach a cat the meaning of the word moon by pointing at the moon – it will just look at the end of your finger, having no notion of what pointing itself means.

References and further reading

Chomsky, N. (1957) *Syntactic Structures*, The Hague: Mouton.

—— (1965) *Aspects of the Theory of Syntax*, Cambridge, MA: MIT Press.

Cook, V.J. and Newson, M. (2007) *Chomsky's Universal Grammar: An Introduction*, Oxford: Blackwell.

McGilvray, J. (ed.) (2005) *The Cambridge Companion to Chomsky*, Cambridge: Cambridge University Press.

Smith, N. (2004) *Introducing Chomsky: Ideas and Ideals*, Cambridge: Cambridge University Press.

Wittgenstein, L. (1953) *Philosophical Investigations*, Oxford: Blackwell.

LATERALISATION OF FUNCTION

Since the 1860s (see **Broca's area**), it has been increasingly understood that the brain hemispheres differ in many respects regarding the psychological functions they control. Most typically, in right-handed individuals, the left hemisphere (LH) controls language and logical reasoning while the right hemisphere (RH) controls visual-spatial awareness and ability, plus, to some degree, emotional reasoning and face recognition. There are, however, enormous individual differences in this and these are reversed to a greater or lesser extent in left-handed people (see **handedness**). For many years, a simplistic image was widespread that equated the LH with logic, reason, sequential thinking, and manual gripping and the RH with spatial thinking, artistic ability, emotion and manual manipulation. This is no longer entirely sustainable in the light of finer-grained studies using high-tech brain scanning and imaging techniques which reveal great individual variation in precisely which functions are localised where. They also suggest that there is some degree of plasticity in this, so that an individual's pattern of localisation and brain-functioning generally may change, or be changeable, over time.

References and further reading

Bradshaw, J.L. and Nettleton, N. (1983) *Human Cerebral Asymmetry*, New York: Prentice-Hall.

Gordon, E. (2000) *Integrative Neuroscience: Bringing together Biological, Psychological and Clinical Models of the Human Brain*, London: Taylor & Francis.

Molfese, D. and Segalowitz, S.J. (eds) (1988) *Brain Lateralization in Children: Developmental Implications*, New York: Guilford.

Ramachandran, V.S. (2002) *Encyclopedia of the Human Brain*, 4 vols, New York: Elsevier.

LEADERSHIP

A topic that received much attention from Social Psychologists during the mid-twentieth century. Various aspects of leadership were studied such as types of leader, effects of leadership style on group performance, personality characteristics of leaders, etc. In some work, the concept of 'leader' somewhat dissipated into the identification of a set of roles (see **role theory**) necessary for efficient group-functioning, so *socio-emotional leadership* and *task leadership* roles had to be differentiated. The former was responsible for keeping up morale and articulating the group's goals and character, the latter for organising the implementation of the tasks involved in pursuing group goals. Which type of leadership is overtly seen as embodied in the official 'leader' can vary depending on circumstances and the nature of the group. There is also an applied literature on leadership skills (e.g. Clark, 2003) The topic is more fully elaborated in the **social power** entry.

References and further reading

Clark, C.C. (2003) *Group Leadership Skills*, 4th edn, New York: Springer.
Messick, D.M. and Kramer, R.M. (eds) (2004) *The Psychology of Leadership: New Perspectives and Research*, Hove: Psychology Press.

LEARNING AND LEARNING THEORY

Pioneered by E.L. Thorndike's studies of cats escaping from 'puzzle boxes' (Thorndike, 1898), learning research came to dominate American laboratory-based experimental Psychology down to the early 1960s. A major boost came with the rise of **behaviourism**, reinforced a few years later by the incorporation of concepts developed by the Russian physiologist Ivan Pavlov in his studies of the conditioning of canine salivatory responses. The topic's popularity was due to three inter-related factors. First, it was ideally suited to laboratory research with animals (notably the white rat). Second, it was believed learning could be analysed as a purely behavioural phenomenon without invoking mentalistic concepts. Third, it could be viewed as the most fundamental psychological issue of all, underlying all adaptive behaviour and having a bearing on all other psychological topics from perception to personality and language. Following the first phase of highly **reductionist** 'radical behaviourism', up to about 1930 a wave of '*Neo-behaviourist*' theorists took learning theory in a variety of different directions. These included W. Guthrie, E.C. Tolman, B.F. Skinner, E. Hilgard and, most ambitious of all, Clark L. Hull. During the 1950s and early 1960s, the project was continued by K. Spence and W.K. Estes. However, the rise of **Cognitive Psychology** fairly rapidly displaced learning from its central place in experimental Psychology thereafter, although it has remained very prominent. Essentially the phrase 'learning theory' denotes theories in the behaviourist tradition, although other approaches to learning itself have been explored, especially since the 1970s. Despite their variety, all behaviourist learning theories deployed a common core set of technical concepts, although some of those listed below are more theoretically specific. In the case of Clark Hull and other later theorists, many of these were rendered into algebraic form.

- *avoidance learning*. Learning to avoid an unpleasant or negatively reinforcing stimulus. Theoretically interesting because it is anticipatory in nature, obviously occurring, once established, in the absence of the stimulus itself.
- *conditioning*. The central Pavlovian concept. There are two kinds of conditioning. The first is known as *classical conditioning* and refers to the original Pavlovian paradigm. In this, an *unconditioned stimulus* (UCS) such as a food elicits an *unconditioned response* (UCR) such as salivation. If, however, presentation of food is accompanied by or 'paired with', a bell ringing (the *conditioned stimulus*, CS), then salivation will subsequently occur when the bell is rung without food being presented – in these circumstances the salivation has become a *conditioned response* (CR). The second form is *operant conditioning* in which the organism learns that a certain behaviour is rewarding, for example, pressing a bar with its nose releases a food pellet. In this context, the behaviour in question is the conditioned response. Learning theorists came to see conditioning as the very core of the learning process and believed that chains of conditioned responses (CRs) could be built up to form the most complex of behaviours in an associative fashion (see **associationism, associative learning**). By the mid-1950s, it had, however, become clear that this mechanism was insufficient to account for complex behaviours such as language or e.g. playing arpeggios on a piano, while some behaviours could never be conditioned as responses to certain kinds of stimuli (the organism being said to be *counter-prepared*). On an etymological note, the original Russian term meant 'condition*al* response' – i.e. a response 'conditional' on certain 'conditions' being met. The English term 'conditioned' is thus a little misleading regarding what Pavlov meant.
- *contiguity*. Direct proximity in space or time. Used technically by associationist philosophers (see associationism), the principle of contiguity became central in E.R. Guthrie's (1886–1959) version of behaviorist **learning theory** who used it to explain how all *S-R* connections were established. He began developing his ideas during

the 1920s and first fully stated the theory in Guthrie (1935), the final version being a 1952 revision of this. This in fact echoed the conclusions of the early nineteenth-century associationist philosopher James Mill.

- *experimental neurosis* (see also *learned helplessness* below). In a series of experiments on dogs in the 1940s (Gantt, 1944), it was shown that when no response enabled it to avoid a negative stimulus (such as an electric shock) the animal became, as it were, 'neurotic' (see **neurosis**), and ceased making any attempt to avoid it. This persisted even when it was subsequently placed in a situation where an avoidance response could have been acquired.

- *extinction*. The disappearance of a learned *response*. This typically arises either when *positive reinforcement* ceases, is replaced by *negative reinforcement* or with repeated presentation of the CS in the absence of the UCS. Extinction of the first kind occurs more slowly in *intermittent (positive) reinforcement* situations.

- *habit formation*. Nearly synonymous with Thorndike's *law of exercise*. The establishment of a response so firmly and deeply that the organism displays it virtually automatically, even perhaps in situations where it is inappropriate. In some respects the establishment of desirable behaviour to the level where it becomes habitual, and, conversely, the *extinction* of undesirable habits, have been one of the goals of applied learning theory in fields as varied as **psychotherapy** (see also **aversion therapy**) and *Sport Psychology*.

- *habituation*. Similar to, but not identical with, *extinction*. Cessation of response to a stimulus when the latter is constant or highly frequent and the response itself has been inconsequential. This extends to perception as such as well as behaviour. Thus people living near a loud waterfall cease responding to, or even hearing, it. In jobs where the environment initially elicits a negative *unconditioned response* (e.g. of disgust or fear), workers typically become *habituated*, e.g. happily jumping from girder to girder 200 metres up.

- *insight learning*. Sudden solution of a problem without, a prior (or very minimal) *trial and error* phase. The most famous example in the history of Psychology was the research undertaken by German *Gestalt* psychologist Wolfgang Köhler with chimpanzees, which were required to gain access to bananas either beyond their reach outside their cage or hanging from its ceiling. They appeared to realise quite suddenly that use of a stick or building a stack of boxes could provide the solution. This phenomenon raised serious difficulties for learning theory as it did not appear to involve the establishment of complex associative chains of *conditioned responses*.

- *latent learning*. Where learning occurs incidentally in the course of other activities, only becoming manifest when the situation requires it to be used. Thus rats allowed to wander around a complex maze will later learn the route through the maze to a food reward faster than those unfamiliar with it. This phenomenon was explored in detail by E.C. Tolman and led him to propose the notion of the **cognitive map**.

- *law of effect and law of exercise*. These two 'Laws' were first suggested by Thorndike in 1898, though only formally stated a little later. Constantly cited thereafter their use declined as learning theory got into its stride in the late 1920s. Put simply, the law of effect is simply that the likelihood of a behaviour recurring is a function of its outcome for the organism, while the law of exercise states that the more often a behaviour occurs, the greater its likelihood of being repeated in the future. In the 1930s Thorndike back-tracked on the second of these. A third 'law of readiness' was also proposed but received little subsequent attention.

- *learned helplessness*. Concept developed by M.E.P. Seligman during the late 1960s, most fully expounded in Seligman (1991). This refers to circumstances in which there is a perceived, or real, lack of relationship between responses and patterns of reinforcement, whatever is done having no effect on outcomes. The upshot may be to meet any positive suggestions with a 'Yes, but … ' response, explaining why the suggestion would not work in their case or how they have tried it in the past and it failed. Seligman believed the phenomenon of learned helplessness (originally demonstrated in dogs) could shed particular light on the nature of **depression**. (See also *experimental neurosis* above.)

- *learning curve*. The graph showing the rate at which a learned response was acquired. Thus, the now-popular expression 'a steep learning curve' to refer to situations in which someone is having to learn rapidly.

- *maze-learning*. Researchers on learning rapidly learned that one of the easiest and most versatile techniques was the use of mazes. Initially they used fairly complex mazes but eventually discovered that a simple T-maze could serve the majority of uses they required. This method dominated animal learning research from around 1910 into the 1960s, but has declined since with the near exhaustion of this research tradition.

- *one-trial learning*. Where behaviour is acquired in a single trial. Typical where *negative reinforcement* is involved – a single 'punishment' being sufficient to ensure *avoidance learning*. May, however, occur in *positive reinforcement* situations also, particularly if the 'reward' is especially powerful and the behaviour quite simple.

- *operant conditioning.* Distinct from *classical* (Pavlovian) conditioning in that the reinforcement is delivered following a behavioural response ('operation') by the organism – pressing a bar resulting in delivery of food, for example. Classical conditioning, by contrast, essentially involves only the passive association of a UCS (e.g. food) with a CS (e.g. bell ringing).

- *reflex.* An automatic behavioural response, usually biologically determined and beyond conscious control. In the Pavlovian experiment, salivation on the sight of food is a canine reflex. Many human facial expressions, vocalisations, and gestures are of a reflex nature (e.g. raising one's eyebrows when surprised or shocked). When the subject of conditioning procedures, the term *conditioned reflex* is often used rather than *conditioned response*. Well-established habitual responses can also acquire a characteristically 'reflex' immediacy.

- *reinforcement.* The nature of the effect of a *response*. This may be of two kinds: *positive reinforcement,* for situations in which the likelihood of the response recurring is increased (i.e. it was in some way 'rewarding') and *negative reinforcement* for those with the opposite effect (i.e. it was in some way 'punishing').

- *reinforcement schedule.* Used in experimental contexts to refer to the patterning of the delivery of reinforcement. There are four basic types of schedule: (1) constant, where the reinforcement is delivered on every occasion the desired response occurs; (2) *fixed interval,* where it is delivered on, say, every third or every fourth occasion; (3) *fixed ratio,* where it is delivered on a certain percentage of occasions but randomised within that; and (4) *random,* where delivery is more truly randomised, although clearly this has to have some constraints. All except the first are known technically as *intermittent reinforcement* schedules.

- *response.* A general term for any behaviour elicited by a *stimulus.* The limits of the term's application are actually somewhat blurred – technically one could refer to someone's becoming a physicist as a result of a childhood excitement by an introductory book on the topic as a 'response' to that 'stimulus'. In most contexts, however, it is restricted to a more or less immediate behavioural response to the presentation of a stimulus. The terms 'independent variable' (IV) and 'dependent variable' (DV) largely entered Psychology in the context of the stimulus-response distinction (IV and DV respectively).

- *stimulus.* A very general term which in effect refers to any perceptual input or sensation to which the organism responds. Typically this will originate externally to the organism but also includes internal sensations like pain and dizziness. The stimulus–response relation is invariably abbreviated as *S-R* or *S-O-R* when, as in most later learning theories, an intervening 'organic' process is believed to occur.

- *stimulus generalisation.* Where the *conditioned response* occurs in the presence not only of the exact *conditioned stimulus* but to others which resemble it to a greater or lesser extent. Thus conditioned avoidance of a particular dog after having been bitten by it may easily extend to avoidance of all dogs.

- *trial and error learning.* The importance of trial and error was recognised by the British pioneer psychologist Alexander Bain in the mid-nineteenth century. It was also the focus of Thorndike's cat experiments. *Operant conditioning* may be considered as a major example of trial and error learning since essentially it requires the subject to try out, more or less randomly, a variety of behavioural responses until it hits on one which works.

See also: **behaviorism**.

References and further reading

Gantt, W.H. (1944) *Experimental Basis for Neurotic Behavior: Origin and Development of Artificially Produced Disturbances of Behavior in Dogs*, New York: Paul B. Hoeber.

Guthrie, E.R. ([1935] 1952) *The Psychology of Learning*, New York: Harper.

Jarvis, P. (2005) *Towards a Comprehensive Theory of Human Learning* London: Routledge.

Olson, M. and Hergenhahn, B.R. (2004) *Introduction to the Theories of Learning*, New York: Prentice-Hall.

Schwartz, B., Robbins, S.J. and Wasserman, E.A. (2001) *Psychology of Learning and Behavior*, New York: Norton.

Seligman, M.E.P. (1991) *Helplessness: On Depression, Development and Death*, 2nd edn, New York: Freeman.

Thorndike, E.L. (1898) 'Animal Intelligence: An Experimental Study of Associative Processes in Animals', *Psychological Review Monograph Supplement* II(4).

LEARNING DIFFICULTIES

How to refer to people of very low intelligence or ability in a non-derogatory, respectful, fashion has been a perennial problem for those concerned with their care and interests. It is perhaps surprising to discover that the word 'moron', for example, was introduced by

H.H. Goddard in 1910 as a neutral technical term with just this in mind (although it was derived from the Greek word for 'foolish'). 'Idiocy', 'imbecility', 'retardation' and 'subnormality', 'mental deficiency' and 'mental handicap' have all been used in the past and each of course either possessed or acquired a pejorative connotation. The expression 'learning difficulties' was widely adopted to solve this in the early 1990s, although its precise origin is difficult to identify. The expression 'moderate learning difficulties' was used as early as the 1978 Warnock Report to replace 'educationally subnormal to a moderate degree'. There is a serious confusion, however, since British and US usages have different meanings; in Britain, it is used more or less as a direct replacement for the earlier terms whereas in the USA (where its adoption has been more recent) it is used, on the contrary, more literally for learning difficulties such as **dyslexia** and **ADHD,** which do *not* involve impaired intelligence. 'Severe', 'moderate', 'mild' and 'specific' are frequently used to qualify the term as appropriate. So far, the expression has survived quite well in the UK, presumably because it is both neutrally descriptive and not easily converted into an insult term in the way 'mental retardation' yielded 'retard' in the USA. Yet it is not entirely unproblematic since 'learning difficulties' in the strict sense may often describe only some of an individual's dysfunctional behaviour. But while it can thus seem like a rather contrived euphemism, it is the best term we currently have along with the widely used alternative '*learning disability*'. The majority of the current literature is concerned with applied, especially educational, issues rather than theoretical ones.

References and further reading

Deponio, P. and Macintyre, C. (2003) *Identifying and Supporting Children with Specific Learning Difficulties: Looking beyond the Label to Support the Whole,* London: Routledge.

Kelly, N. and Norwich, B. (2004) *Moderate Learning Difficulties and the Future of Inclusion,* London: Routledge.

Swain, J. and French, S. (1999) *Therapy and Learning Difficulties: Advocacy, Participation and Partnership,* London: Elsevier Health Sciences.

LEVEL OF ASPIRATION (LOA)

Although this can reasonably be read simply as a technical-sounding synonym for 'ambition', it refers more specifically to score on a test designed to quantify this. Tests of LoA typically involve the person taking them setting themselves a performance target and then comparing this with their actual performance. The higher their stated target, the higher their LoA, of course, but such tests can also identify both unrealistically high LoA, where the target proves to have been a substantial over-estimate, and 'under-achievement' where the target set is reached very easily or greatly exceeded. Use of the term usually indicates that writer is working within the **achievement motivation**, or **N–Ach,** research tradition, although it is now often treated as a discrete phenomenon with few theoretical connotations. The term appears to have gradually entered Psychology's vocabulary from the 1930s onwards but does not appear to have received any general book-length treatment.

See also: **achievement motivation, fear of failure**.

LEVELS OF PROCESSING

A theory of memory first developed by Craik and Lockhart (1972). Levels of processing emphasises that what is remembered, and how well, are largely a by-product of the kind of cognitive activity – processing – engaged in when the remembered material was encountered. Thus, typically, identifying the number of letters in words leads to poorer recall of those words than if you had to think of a word similar in meaning. Tasks such as counting letters in words are regarded as requiring a shallow level of processing; tasks requiring engagement with the word's meaning were regarded as requiring deep processing. The theory hit two main problems: it was difficult to establish an agreed, independent measure of the depth of processing and findings emerged suggesting that sometimes we remember things processed shallowly better than we remember things processed deeply. Nevertheless, the theory remains an attractive alternative to store models of memory.

See also: **information processing, memory**.

Reference

Craik, F. and Lockhart, R. (1972) 'Levels of Processing: A Framework for Memory Research', *Journal of Verbal Learning and Verbal Behavior*, 11: 671–84.

Useful website

See also www.tip.psychology.org/craik.html for a good summary.

LIMEN

Another term for threshold, a term used in **psychophysics** for the level of stimulus intensity below which the organism ceases to respond (or, conversely, above which they do). In humans, this is equated to conscious awareness. The possibility that below this level the individual may be unconsciously aware of it or somehow responding to it has long been debated and researched (see **subliminal perception)**. Usage of the concept in psychophysics itself has somewhat declined since the advent of **signal detection theory** which rejected the notion of clear-cut thresholds.

LOBOTOMY

Also known as leucotomy. A now notorious psychiatric procedure in which the prefrontal cortex of the brain was severed from the remainder, used to treat conditions of extreme emotional distress, anxiety, schizophrenia. Although initiated in 1936 by a Portuguese neurologist A.E. Moniz, it only became widely adopted in Britain and the USA in the late 1940s and early 1950s. In the USA, Dr Walter Freeman had begun using this form of psychosurgery, inspired by Moniz, in 1936 with an associate James Watts and became its most passionate advocate. The momentum of his work increased after 1945 with his adoption of a new quicker procedure known as 'ice-pick lobotomy'. (Watts was so aghast at the grisly nature of this he broke with Freeman.) Moniz's 1949 Nobel Prize consolidated the respectability of the procedure, however, and use of lobotomy became so widespread as to amount almost to a craze (a figure of 18,000 is given for US cases alone from 1939–51, the majority in the final years of this period). By 1950, however, the omens for its future fortunes were becoming bad. Success rates were barely above spontaneous remission rates, and the frequently negative psychological effects on patients' personalities and emotional lives were becoming increasingly evident. As the ethical objections mounted, the appearance of new kinds of drugs like Thorazine offered alternatives to irreversible psychosurgery. (Interestingly, lobotomy was illegal in the Soviet Union.) Among the victims of the procedure were President Kennedy's sister Rosemary, operated on by Freeman himself. As a curious side-note, in the 1950s, the Kenya-based Dr J.C. Carothers proposed a theory of race differences in which he claimed African 'negroes' resembled lobotomised Europeans (see Richards, 1997). While lobotomy has never entirely disappeared from medical psychiatry's therapeutic repertoire, its use is now restricted to a handful of extremely recalcitrant and problematic cases *per annum*. In popular culture it has figured widely in drama (Harold Pinter's *The Caretaker*), film (*One Flew Over the Cuckoo's Nest*) and pop music (in lyrics by the Ramones and Pink Floyd, for instance). Valenstein (1986) provides a sufficient introduction to the topic, and the Wikipedia entry on it is quite good. (An 'Official Lobotomy Site' turns out, however, to be about a defunct Swedish rock group.)

References

Richards, G. (1997) *'Race', Racism and Psychology: Towards a Reflexive History*, London: Routledge.

Valenstein, E.S. (1986) *Great and Desperate Cures: The Rise and Decline of Psychosurgery and Other Radical Treatments for Mental Illness*, New York: Basic Books.

LOCALISATION OF FUNCTION

Used by physiological psychologists to refer to the ways in which different regions of the brain govern different psychological and behavioural processes. The extent to which brain functioning is localised was long controversial (see **phrenology**). Although phrenology was largely discredited by the 1860s, physiologists and neurologists studying the brain began identifying a number of specific brain regions which appeared to govern such things as speech and motor-movements. While the earliest findings (such as **Broca's area** in the left hemisphere) were based on post-mortem examination of the brains of people affected by a relevant behavioural pathology, by the end of the nineteenth century, electrical stimulation techniques were beginning to appear (an 1870 German journal paper by G.T. Fritsch and E. Hitzig introduced this method). During the 1930s, the American physiological psychologist Karl Lashley, however, challenged the extent of localisation on the basis of experimental studies of rats, proposing that the brain was in fact highly generalised and that the functions of damaged areas could be transferred to others. In the 1950s, R. Penfield, a brain surgeon, was engaged in an extensive study using electrical stimulation of the exposed brains of patients, revealing what seemed to be an extraordinarily high degree of localisation. Since then, the field has progressed dramatically, with today's high-tech MRI and CAT scan methods revealing an ever increasing amount of information regarding the localisation – or not – of many different psychological functions.

It should, however, be remembered that everybody's brain is unique, reflecting their psychological and general physical uniqueness, and that generalisations from such findings require caution.

See further references under **lateralisation of function.**

References and further reading

Gordon, E. (2000) *Integrative Neuroscience: Bringing Together Biological, Psychological and Clinical Models of the Human Brain*, London: Taylor & Francis.

Ramachandran, V.S. (2002) *Encyclopedia of the Human Brain*, 4 vols, New York: Elsevier.

von Bonin, G. (ed.) (1960) *Some Papers on the Cerebral Cortex Translated from the French and German*, Springfield, IL: Charles C. Thomas.

LOCUS OF CONTROL

Since its introduction by Julian Rotter in 1966, the 'locus of control' or LoC concept has further developed and continued to attract attention. Basically, it refers to the extent to which people believe events are under their own control (internal locus of control) or under that of others (or chance) (external locus of control). Rotter devised a Locus of Control Scale questionnaire for assessing this as a personality dimension. The implicit evaluation of course is that it is better to be high on 'internal LoC', although where, objectively, control really does lie needs to be taken into account in specific circumstances. Levenson (1973) later proposed that 'control by powerful others' and 'control by chance' needed to be differentiated and that high 'internal control' could be compatible with high 'control by powerful others'. Rotter's original work was undertaken in the theoretical context of social **learning theory**.

References

Levenson, H. (1973) 'Multidimensional Locus of Control in Psychiatric Patients', *Journal of Consulting and Clinical Psychology,* 41: 397–404.

Rotter, J.B. (1966) 'Generalized Expectancies for Internal Versus External Control of Rinforcement', *Psychological Monographs*, 80(1), Whole No. 609.

MALE GAZE

Term introduced by Laura Mulvey (Mulvey [1975] 1999) and taken up by feminist psychologists such as J.G. Morawski and R.S. Steele

(Morawski and Steele, 1991) to refer to the implicit assumption that e.g. readers of a text will be male. This is signalled by the way women are described and characterised from an obviously male perspective. Literally, it refers to males looking at females as sexual 'objects', especially when this becomes a routine way of looking at women in general. It was powerfully argued that unconscious adoption of a 'male gaze' orientation in Psychology texts could seriously undermine their supposedly 'objective' scientific character.

References

Morawski, J.G. and Steele, R.S. (1991) 'The One or the Others? Textual Analysis of Masculine Power and Female Empowerment', *Theory and Psychology*, 1: 107–31.

Mulvey, V. ([1975] 1999) 'Visual Pleasure and Narrative Cinema', in L. Braudy and M. Cohen (eds) *Film Theory and Criticism: Introductory Readings*, New York: Oxford. University Press, pp. 833–44 (originally published in the film journal *Screen*, 16(3): 6–18).

MANIC/MANIA

To be 'manic' is to be extremely and irrationally, perhaps violently, active or obsessed, hence the term 'maniac' for someone displaying such behaviour. In the phrase 'manic-depressive' (now replaced by the blander **bi-polar disorder),** it refers to oscillation between periods of restless hyperactivity and depression. 'Mania' refers to the target or content of manic behaviour and is often used with a prefix (as in 'nymphomania', 'dipsomania' – an obsolete synonym for alcoholism, or 'pyromania' – fascinated by fire and with a tendency to commit arson). Some uses of 'mania' as a separate word are less obviously negative, denoting only passionate interest, such as 'football mania'. 'Mania', 'manic' and 'maniac' have a long history and were common in medical discourse and classifications of madness from the eighteenth century onwards, declining in popularity during the twentieth century although being retained for a few psychiatric conditions.

MATERIALISM

'Materialism' is used in a wide range of contexts. Most relevant for Psychology are: (1) in relation to the **mind–body problem** in which it refers to rejection of anything other than material processes being involved, and, closely related to this; (2) belief that all psychological phenomena are reducible to physiological ones (see **reductionism**). In general usage it also means believing in the value of material goods and wealth over such things as relationships, 'spiritual values', etc. Historically, the term came to philosophical prominence in the context of the rise of the physical sciences, in which it denoted a rejection of immaterial 'forces' and belief that all events are ultimately subject to the laws of physics. In 1872, the German philosopher F.A. Lange published a mighty three-volume work on the history of materialism as a philosophical doctrine (Lange 1877–92). In modern Psychology, **behaviourism** and **neuropsychology** are examples of strongly materialist approaches. Another common usage is in the phrase *dialectical materialism* which is almost synonymous with *Marxism*, and holds, to oversimplify grossly, that ultimately the material conditions of life determine human affairs both historically and individually, rather than some underlying 'human spirit' or autonomous psychological principle.

See also: **mind–body problem** and **reductionism** references.

References and further reading

Lange, F.A. ([1877–92] 2003) *The History of Materialism*, London: Routledge.
Melnyk, A. (2007) *A Physicalist Manifesto: Thoroughly Modern Materialism*, Cambridge: Cambridge University Press.

MATRIARCHY/MATRIARCHAL

Originally an anthropological term for societies in which social and political power was exercised primarily by women and in which descent was traced through the female lineage (and still used in this sense). During the nineteenth century the theory was widely circulated that human societies were originally matriarchal in character, particularly prior to understanding of the male's role in procreation, and that this was then overthrown and 'Patriarchy' established. The classic exposition of this was the German J.J. Bachofen's 1861 *Das Mutterecht* (see Bachofen, 1967). Now used generally for social settings (especially domestic) in which power rests with women, thus references to 'matriarchal families' and 'matriarchs' (for the 'rulers' of such families).

See also: **patriarchy/patriarchal**.

Reference

Bachofen, J.J. (1967) *Myth, Religion and Mother Right: Selected Writings of J.J. Bachofen*, London: Routledge & Kegan Paul.

MEMORY

Memory is one of the relatively few psychological topics to have continually been addressed since antiquity by philosophers, physicians and, eventually, scientists. It is a phenomenon which becomes ever more awesome the more one ponders it, as was beautifully evoked by St Augustine in Book X of his *Confessions*. A variety of metaphors, usually of either a 'container' or 'inscription' kind, were deployed to try and understand it (see Draaisma, 2000; Danziger, 2008). Modern Psychology has come to identify numerous types of memory and memory-related phenomena which we will treat individually. For a picture of the state of the topic in the earlier part of the past century, Edgell (1924) is quite handy and puts later developments in perspective. It is worth noting that while memory and **learning** are obviously very closely related, even partly synonymous, in Psychology, they have been tackled by distinct research traditions. This differentiation owes more to historical accident than to any intrinsic distinction between them as phenomena. It should not be assumed that the categories, processes and distinctions listed below are in any way definitive and settled, indeed, many (such as the short-term memory and long-term memory distinction) continue to be matters of theoretical debate and controversy. In the 1960s, the field became increasingly influenced by information theory concepts and emerged as a central topic in **Cognitive Psychology**, while more recently technological developments such as CAT and fMRI scanning have entered the picture as methods of 'watching' the brain at work during memory tasks. One major difficulty is that memory's centrality to human psychological life makes it difficult to isolate it in any 'pure' form – we are always using our memories for a reason. Similarly, it is difficult to easily define the scope of memory: does it include anything where the past affects present behaviour or should it be more narrowly understood? Moreover, there are major individual differences in how memory operates corresponding to the range of human personality as a whole, even if some basic common neurological structures and processes can be identified as underpinning it. For a useful mainstream overview of the topic as a whole, A. Baddeley's *Human Memory: Theory and Practice*

(Baddeley, 1997) remains extremely useful along with his *Essentials of Human Memory* (Baddeley, 1999). His popularly pitched *Your Memory: A User's Guide* (Baddeley, 1996) is also helpful for beginning students. More recently he has co-edited *The Handbook of Memory Disorders for Clinicians* (Baddeley, 2004) and *Working Memory, Thought and Action* (Baddeley, 2007). Baddeley is acknowledged as the leading British authority on the topic and these can provide a reliable entry into the work of other researchers and relevant literature, although may be usefully supplemented by the more socially constructionist works such as Middleton and Edwards (1990) and Wyer (1995) referenced under *collective memory* below. See also **levels of processing**, **aphasia** and **agnosia**.

- *amnesia.* Loss of memory. The study of amnesia and related memory disorders has played a large research role in recent decades as brain functioning has become accessible to high-tech scrutiny. Amnesia is generally a result of brain damage induced by disease or physical accident, but is an umbrella term covering a fairly wide range of conditions. Baddeley (1990), for example, lists post-traumatic amnesia, retrograde amnesia and anterograde amnesia, each of which may affect any or all of the various memory systems we consider below. 'Anterograde' amnesia refers to the inability to acquire new memories as opposed to inability to recall material from before the event which caused the amnesia ('retrograde').
- *auditory memory.* Now subdivided into *echoic memory* (see below), auditory short-term memory and auditory long-term memory. Auditory short-term memory, lasting up to 20 seconds, is the period during which an accurate memory of auditory material can be sustained. Auditory long-term memory refers to our enduring memory of particular sounds, music and voices which remain recognisable long after they are first heard. The most impressive cases of this are probably the abilities of some professional musicians and conductors.
- *autobiographical memory.* Fairly self-explanatory, memory of the events in one's own life. This does not, however, refer to events (such as one's birth) which are remembered simply as facts, only to memories in a visual, auditory or other sensory mode. In other words, it involves a 'replaying' of the events as they were apparently experienced. The reliability of autobiographical memory is often quite low and probably becomes less so the more a memory is subsequently rehearsed. Closely related to *episodic, flashbulb,* and, to some extent, *eidetic* memory.

- *collective memory*. Not a strictly technical term, this phrase is never-theless sometimes encountered in Psychological texts as well as in everyday use. It is important because it focuses attention on the extent to which memory is a collective social process as well as an individual one. Many memories, especially *autobiographical* ones, are sustained and shaped by reminiscing with others, by using external stimuli such as photographs or music, and, on a larger scale, by ritualised public ceremonies and restatements of past events. The latter include Remembrance Day ceremonies for example, as well as less formal story-telling. Dramatic collective experiences such as wars, disasters or great national sporting achievements are especially subject to collective remembering processes which in the long term yield a shared memory of the atmosphere and most salient features of the event. These may actually come to depart significantly from the reality of individual experiences at the time, especially given the prominent role the mass media can now play. Naturally **social constructionist** psychologists have been inter-ested in exploring the topic, seeing it as offsetting the individualist character of traditional experimental memory research. Two par-ticularly useful works from this angle are Middleton and Edwards (1990) and Wyer (1995). The French writer M. Halbwachs (1877–1945) is another important figure, and is credited with coining the phrase 'collective memory' in 1925. His *On Collective Memory* is most accessible in the 1992 edition cited below (Halbwachs, 1992).
- *echoic memory*. The most transient phase of *auditory memory*, lasting probably not more than 300 milliseconds, during which the sound persists at the sensory level.
- *eidetic* (or *'photographic'*) *memory*. The ability to retain a detailed visual image of a visual stimulus, which may be experienced as fixed and scannable. Although sometimes mythologised, the capacity for eidetic memory and eidetic image formation is com-monly exploited by menomonists (see *memory improvement* and *menomonic* below), A.R. Luria's *The Mind of the Mnemonist* (Luria, 1969) reports a particularly notable case. There are great individual differences in eidetic ability or functioning, and in many it is altogether absent.
- *episodic memory*. Aspect of *autobiographical memory* required for cer-tain kinds of learning. While the original learning episode (e.g. being taught to tie shoe-laces) may be forgotten once its lesson is well established, the initial acquisition of the learned material requires some conscious autobiographical recall. While this persists,

it is an 'episodic memory'. It is distinct from *semantic* memory for facts in involving recall of actual events. See also *procedural memory*.

- *eyewitness testimony*. Although some early twentieth-century research was done on the reliability of eyewitness memory, 'eyewitness testimony' became a major topic in the 1980s and has remained so ever since. This interest arose primarily in the context of legal and forensic concerns, initially particularly regarding the court testimony of children. It has since been found, for example, that while children may be poorer on memory for detail, their general reliability is as good as that of adults. Both children and adults, however, are prone to inaccuracies arising for a number of reasons such as **stereotyping** and general fallibility of judgements of e.g. car speed and time duration as well as, rather worryingly, recognition of unfamiliar faces. The usual distorting processes affecting *autobiographical* memory are also in play. A further interesting finding has been that under many circumstances a witness's level of certainty regarding the accuracy of their recall is unrelated to the likelihood of it being correct.

- *facial recognition*. Over the past two decades the topic of facial recognition has received substantial experimental attention. It has become clear that we possess an especially highly tuned ability to distinguish and memorise faces. This is almost certainly genetically determined due to the extremely high importance in all social life of ability to recognise other individuals, and to 'read' their facial expressions. Facial recognition thus appears to have become more specialised than simple object recognition. Recognition of faces of those belonging to physically distinct ethnic groups other than our own is famously harder than recognising those of our own. For example, Europeans all tend to look the same (gender aside) to Chinese and people of African ancestry were long viewed as having a common facial appearance by others. This tendency is almost certainly weakening as we become routinely familiar with individuals of other ethnicities. See Bruce and Young (1998).

- *false memory*. *Autobiographical* type memory of events which actually did not occur. See **false memory syndrome**.

- *flashbulb memory*. Especially vivid memories of dramatic events in which they seem to be relivable in minute detail, notably the circumstances in which one first heard or saw them. Typically these might be of one's first learning of the 9/11 destruction of the Twin Towers in New York or the death of Princess Diana (the canonical example for many years was President Kennedy's assassination). The apparent accuracy of these is somewhat illusory however. My wife and I forever disagree over who first registered and commented on the 9/11 news coming over a shop radio. (One moral of doing Psychology is never to insist on the accuracy of one's memory too doggedly!)

- *forgetting*. Forgetting has often been studied as a phenomenon in its own right rather than simply as the converse of memory. Several issues have figured in the literature. One is the extent to which genuine, permanent, forgetting normally occurs. It may be argued that forgotten material still remains in storage but that it is the access mechanisms which have failed. A second is the extent to which forgetting can be an active process, which links with the concept of *repression* in **psychoanalysis**, and has led to a research topic called 'motivated forgetting'. Third, for current cognitivist theorists, the challenge is to identify where in the broader information processing system forgetting of various kinds can take place. It should not be forgotten that forgetting is not necessarily a bad thing – total recall of everything would be intolerably oppressive, while memories might interfere with performance in new situations only partially similar to ones recalled.

- *implicit memory*. Memory or knowledge acquired unconsciously or subconsciously simply in the course of everyday life. The operation of implicit memory may also be unconscious in that a person's behaviour may well indicate that they 'know' something, but they would be quite unaware of this. Knowing how to open doors would be an example of implicit knowledge, but so too would be a culturally specific mode of greeting someone which the actor simply took for granted as natural.

- *long-term memory (LTM)/long-term system (LTS)*. Usually conceived of as the storage system in which memories are retained in some more or less permanent and accessible fashion. This may be divided into sub-systems such as auditory long-term memory, visual long-term memory, autobiographical memory, semantic memory, etc. and, given the sheer diversity of memory's contents and the complexities of their interconnections, the overall structure and organisation of LTM remain far from clear.

- *memory improvement*. Somewhat surprisingly, until recently Psychology paid relatively little attention to the issue of how to improve or train memory, although this has always been a popular commercial field for self-proclaimed experts. One early twentieth-century technique which enjoyed great success was Pelmanism, a fairly sophisticated course in memory-training. The various methods which professional entertainers use are now receiving more attention. By associating words or numbers with images, for example, it is quite easy to learn word pairs as used in some Psychological tests – for 'badger' and 'hat' one imagines a badger wearing a hat, for 'star' and 'ladder' a ladder ascending to the stars, etc. Another common method is *mnemonics* (see below). While applicable to *short-term memory*, especially of verbal material, these are harder to apply to *long-term memory*. Much current work concerns memory training in the elderly, to offset declining memory abilities, and **ADHD** sufferers. In the ancient world and during the Renaissance, however, a very sophisticated memorising technique was developed based on linking the material to be remembered to places, particularly the architectural features of the monastery or church in which the scholar lived. The classic study of this was Francis Yates (1966).

- *mnemonics*. A technique for enhancing especially *verbal* and *factual* memory. This usually takes the form of constructing a memorable sentence of words beginning with the first letter of the items in question. Thus '**m**en **v**ery **e**asily **m**ade **j**ugs **s**erve **u**seful **n**eeds **p**rettily' is a mnemonic for the order of planets from the Sun – Mercury, Venus, Earth, Mars, Jupiter, Saturn, Uranus, Neptune, Pluto (if you wanted to add the asteroid belt you could insert '**a**ll' before 'jugs' of course). The term is also sometimes used for the imagery based techniques described in the previous entry.

- *organic memory*. Now rarely used, the notion of organic memory was popular among some early twentieth-century theorists. It referred to the supposed storage of memories at a general physiological level, often with the assumption that these could then become hereditary. Such memory was unconscious. The last major advocate of this was Semon ([1904] 1921).

- *procedural memory*. Memory for how to do things such as riding a bike. Acquisition of procedural memory is a topic of debate among psychologists, particularly the respective roles of *episodic memory* and *implicit memory*.

- *recall* and *recognition*. Recall is the conscious retrieval of a memory, while recognition only manifests itself in the presence of the original stimulus. It is, as it were, a weaker form of memory in that we cannot recall the stimulus at will but do know, when it is present, that we have seen it before and may then be able to access other associated memories. *Face recognition* is an especially interesting phenomenon in this latter respect since we frequently recognise faces as having been met before but are unable to 'place' them. (It is perhaps time for someone to research the irritating and distracting phenomenon of trying to remember film and TV actors' names and previous roles at the expense of enjoying their current performance!) Much experimental research on memory involves recognition tasks.

- *rote memory*. Memory instilled by repeated, normally verbal, rehearsal of the material to be learned. The material may itself be purely verbal (e.g. a list or a piece of verse) but rote learning may also be used to ensure a grasp of rules or certain facts, the alphabet and the multiplication tables being obvious instances. Rote learning is typically enhanced by using rhythm and rhyme, as in both of these cases as traditionally taught.

- *semantic* (or *lexical* or *vocabulary*) *memory*. Semantic memory, while including lexical or vocabulary memory of words and their meanings is also considered to include factual memories such as 'The Nile runs through Egypt' and 'Abraham Lincoln was a US President' as opposed to *autobiographical* and *episodic* memory. It also extends to memory of the meanings of non-verbal signs and symbols. Research has primarily addressed how this kind of memory, particularly its linguistic component, is structured. Language acquisition is a complex topic which has received much attention from developmental psychologists. It clearly involves both memory for sounds and for meanings but the relationship between the two is not straightforward – we can, when learning another language, map meanings onto different sounds, while in our own language we can give the same sound a multiplicity of meanings (e.g. 'match', 'fast', 'peal/peel') and the same meaning a multiplicity of near synonymous words (e.g. 'sad', 'down', 'depressed', 'miserable', 'blue'). It might be noted here that estimates of the typical size of the human vocabulary store are misleading because they omit the proper names of people, etc. we can recall and might be nearly doubled if we consider speakers fluent in two languages as having two vocabularies. This latter would suggest that there is a core 'semantic' memory capable of being lexically encoded in a variety of ways, however, the structure and content of the semantic memory are also presumably determined in part at least by the categories, etc. deployed in the first language one acquires. Language also involves syntax or grammar, but it is unclear if this should be considered as part of the memory system. Since N. Chomsky's classic *Syntactic Structures* (Chomsky, 1957) (see **language acquisition device**), it has been broadly accepted that there is some innate level of syntactic structuring, with a universal set of 'rules' underlying all actual languages.

- *short-term memory (STM)/short-term system (STS)*. The memory system which briefly stores current on-going events and stimuli. It is experimentally or empirically assessed by performance on tasks such as recalling a series of numbers ('digit span'). All sensory input initially enters the STS which is now generally understood to function, at least in part, as an initial 'information processor' determining whether or not the information will be retained for 'deeper' level processing in *long-term memory* (LTM). This aspect of its functioning is thus now known as *working memory*. It also serves to facilitate continuity of monitoring of, and engagement with, what is actually going on, e.g. when holding a conversation. There is some ambiguity in the expression 'short-term memory', however, since it is commonly used also to refer, in a less technical fashion, to memory for recent events occurring in the past few days or weeks. When this ability reduces, as typically occurs in one's later years, it may be ascribed either to a failure of STS-level processing to transfer information or of LTM to retain it, but is nevertheless typically described as a failure of STM. In fact, the latter explanation seems in some respects more plausible. STS functioning is currently understood to involve looping processes (e.g. 'phonological loops' for acoustic material). Whether or not STM/STS and LTM/LTS are genuinely distinct or levels of a single system operating at various 'levels of processing' has been a matter of much theoretical debate in recent decades.
- *situation-specific memory*. It has long been noticed that memories can be activated by specific situations (see *memory improvement* and *collective memory* above). We particularly talk of long-dormant autobiographical memories being suddenly 'triggered' or 'jogged' when we revisit a place for the first time in many years or rehear a piece of music after a long interval. It is also a familiar experience to return to the same train of thought or topic when walking a regular route. Halbwachs (see Halbwachs, 1992, under *collective memory*) at one point notes how he regularly rattled a stick along a fence as a child, but repeating this as an adult to try and evoke the original experience failed until he crouched down to the same height as he had been when a child and repeated the exercise. Then, as we say, 'It all came back to him.'
- *unconscious memory*. Memory which is currently inaccessible but which may be activated in the course of psychoanalysis, under **hypnosis** or some similar condition. It is also claimed that such unconscious memories can affect our current behaviour and feelings in certain circumstances. Not a term used in cognitivist approaches.

- *verbal memory*. Memory for verbal material. Experimental research on memory was for a long period primarily focused on verbal memory due to the ease of using verbal stimuli in experimental situations, a tradition famously initiated by Ebbinghaus (1885). It is a fair criticism that this focus biased Psychological research on memory until the latter half of the last century. In particular, the use of 'nonsense' syllables in an effort to isolate 'memory' in some pure form meant that the kind of memory tasks which participants were engaged in bore little relationship to memory in everyday life. Verbal memory is nevertheless one of the most important types of memory for obvious reasons, being the primary mode in which we encode and store factual *memory* and communicate about it. It is not, however, an entirely unitary phenomenon as distinct *lexical, syntactic* and *semantic* aspects of verbal memory can be distinguished.

- *visual memory*. A multi-faceted topic. As with *auditory memory*, there appear to be three levels: (1) a very transient 'iconic' memory phase during which the visual sensation persists after presentation; (2) a rather elusive short-term visual memory phase during which differences between successively presented stimuli remain identifiable; (3) and long-term visual memory in which stimuli remain recognisable or reproducible for periods extending up to and beyond a year. There are, however, a number of complexities relating to *eidetic memory, facial recognition* and *flashbulb memory*.

- *visuo-spatial scratchpad/sketchpad*. Hypothesised component of the *working memory* model proposed by A.D. Baddeley and G. Hitch in the 1974 and further developed in subsequent work by Baddeley and various associates. As the name suggests, its function is to retain and manipulate visual information. It has been suggested that it has two sub-components, a 'visual cache' in which visual memories are stored and a 'spatial mechanism' of some sort responsible for planning physical engagement with the visual environment and perhaps sustaining the visual cache in a looping process. These two components are now increasingly considered to be separate systems.

- *working memory*. This term has now effectively replaced *STM* in most research contexts, denoted a much more elaborate and complex system than *STM* as traditionally conceived. See also **central executive, level of processing**.

References and further reading

Baddeley, A.D. (1990) *Human Memory. Theory and Practice*, Hove: Lawrence Erlbaum.

—— (1996) *Your Memory: A User's Guide*, London: Prion Books.
—— (1999) *Essentials of Human Memory*, London: Taylor & Francis.
—— (2007) *Working Memory, Thought and Action*, Oxford: Oxford University Press.
Baddeley, A.D. and Hitch, G. (1974) 'Working Memory', in G.H. Bower (ed.), *The Psychology of Learning and Motivation: Advances in Research and Theory*, vol. 8, New York: Academic Press, pp. 47–89.
Baddeley, A.D., Kopelman, M. and Wilson, B.A. (eds) (2004) *The Handbook of Memory Disorders for Clinicians*, Chichester: John Wiley & Sons, Ltd.
Bruce, V. and Young, A. (1998) *In the Eye of the Beholder: The Science of Face Perception*, Oxford: Oxford University Press.
Danziger, K. (2008) *Marking the Mind: A History of Memory*, Cambridge: Cambridge University Press.
Draaisma, D. (2000) *Metaphors of Memory: A History of Ideas about the Mind*, Cambridge: Cambridge University Press.
Ebbinghaus, H. ([1885] 1987) *Memory: A Contribution to Experimental Psychology*, New York: Dover.
Edgell, B. (1924) *Theories of Memory*, Oxford: Clarendon Press.
Halbwachs, M. (1992) *On Collective Memory*, Chicago, IL: The University of Chicago Press.
Logie, R.H. (1995) *Visuo-spatial Working Memory*, Hove: Lawrence Erlbaum Associates.
Luria, A.R. (1969) *The Mind of the Mnemonist*, London: Jonathan Cape.
Middleton, D. and Edwards, D. (1990) *Collective Remembering*, London: Sage.
Semon, R. (1921) *The Mneme*, London: Allen & Unwin.
Wyer, R.S. Jr (ed.) (1995) *Knowledge and Memory: The Real Story*, Hillsdale, NJ: Lawrence Erlbaum.
Yates, F.A. (1966) *The Art of Memory*, London: Routledge & Kegan Paul.

METACOGNITION

Literally, this refers to 'thinking about thinking', in which sense **Cognitive Psychology** in its entirety is presumably an exercise in metacognition. In practice, however, as a topic of Psychological research, it concerns our ability (or not) to think reflexively about both how, and/or what, we and others are thinking. The classic sequence of 'I know', 'You know I know', 'I know you know I know' is a typical example. That particular mode of metacognition attracted the attention of 'anti-psychiatrist' R.D. Laing (see **anti-psychiatry**) in his book *Knots*, and also Antaki and Lewis (1986). The general conclusion is that the infinite regress involved here becomes senseless after four or five steps. More practically, metacognitive ability is involved in effectively managing interpersonal tasks (which require taking into account how others might be thinking), and in successful **problem solving** (which often requires one to step back and 'metacognitively' analyse the strategies one is adopting and ponder what others might be used). Metacognition may be either conscious or unconscious, and, as a research topic, partly overlaps with **cognitive style** issues and **learning** generally. More profoundly, the capacity for metacognition is widely considered to be an aspect of, if not synonymous with, distinctively human reflexive self-consciousness itself.

Reference

Antaki, C. and Lewis, A. (eds) (1986) *Mental Mirrors: Metacognition in Social Knowledge and Communication*, London: Sage.

MIND–BODY PROBLEM

The difficulty of formulating any fully satisfactory account of how the mind and body are related. See **dualism, epiphenomenalism, idealism, materialism, neutral monism, parallelism**. Historically this began receiving intense philosophical attention with the French philosopher Descartes' 'dualist' theory (Descartes, [1641] 2006), remaining a topic of active debate ever since among philosophers and, since the mid-nineteenth century, psychologists. The number of answers which have been proposed runs well into double figures, although until 1949 most were variants of those just listed. In 1949, Gilbert Ryle's *The Concept of Mind* proposed the first new solution for 400 years, arguing that the entire issue was rooted in a basic linguistic misunderstanding which led us to think about the question in terms of, to use his famous phrase, a 'ghost in the machine'. In a way his answer was a *materialist* theory, but couched in a quite different fashion. The nub of the matter was that we had all been making a *'category mistake'*. Mind and matter were concepts of different logical orders, they did not 'exist' in the same way. His example, which became canonical, was of the visitor to Oxford being shown the various colleges and institutions such as the Bodleian Library, the Ashmolean Museum, only to then ask bemusedly, 'But where is the university?'. That is, he (it was a male in the example) had failed to understand that these colleges and institutions *were* the university and that 'Oxford University' did not exist separately from them. It did of course exist, but in a different sense. Exploring this concept of the category mistake Ryle strove to demonstrate that mental concepts, including mind itself, did not refer to some immaterial realm but were ways of characterising the various qualities of behaviour. It is a brilliant, fascinating and, to many, infuriatingly frustrating, book. It was, however, widely rumoured that Ryle himself never experienced genuine visual imagery, the paradigm evidence for most of us of the existence of a genuinely subjective realm, in whatever sense it might be said exist. (Evaluating this further here would sidetrack us into the so-called 'Other Minds' debate in philosophy about how one can ever know another's experience or even that they have a mind at all.) Some major shortcomings of his account were addressed by Place (1956) in a short paper, in which he proposed his '*mind-brain identity theory*'). This, essentially, was that brain events and mental events were identical, but accounts of them were descriptions of different kinds. They were identical in the sense that a cloud and the water particles comprising it are identical. Most contemporary technical philosophical accounts of the mind–body problem, such as John Searle's, are essentially developments of, and elaborations on, the Ryle–Place position. Debate nevertheless continues, and they have failed to explain their solutions in ways which the majority of outsiders find intuitively satisfactory, including many psychologists. **OBE**s are also a problem! The Wikipedia entry on the topic is quite useful, but not fully adequate.

References and further reading

Crane, T. and Patterson, S. (2000) *History of the Mind–Body Problem*, London: Routledge.

Descartes, R. ([1641] 2006) *Discourse on Method and Meditations on First Philosophy*, Oxford: Oxford University Press. (Many editions, titles slightly vary.)

Kirk, R. (2003) *Mind and Body*, Montreal: McGill-Queen's University Press.

Place, U.T. (1956) 'Is Consciousness a Brain Process?', *British Journal of Psychology*, 47 : 44–50.

Ryle, G. (1949) *The Concept of Mind*, London: Hutchinson.

Searle, J. (1984) *Minds, Brains and Science: The 1984 Reith Lectures*, London: BBC.

Valentine, E. (1992) *Conceptual Issues in Psychology*, London: Routledge.

MONISM

Any answer to the **mind–body problem** which explains one as an aspect of the other, thus covering both **idealism** and **materialism**.

MOOD

Emotional atmosphere or state, generally not directed at anything specific. Psychology has usually subsumed mood under the broader category of **emotion** and paid it relatively little sustained research attention. There are, however, some interesting aspects of mood differentiating it from emotion in the usual sense, for instance, as well as often lacking a specific object, moods can more easily be collective in quality. An individual's moods may also be more obvious to observers than to the individual concerned.

MORAL DEVELOPMENT

The process by which a child acquires an understanding of morality. The best-known theoretical approach is that of Piaget (Piaget, 1932) as developed into a more extended six-stage model by his follower Lawrence Kohlberg in building on his 1958 PhD thesis (Kohlberg, 1981, is the most comprehensive source). In **psychoanalysis**, the topic had previously been dealt with in terms of the development of the *super ego* (see under psychoanalysis). Kohlberg's stages fall into three groups: (1) a 'preconventional' phase where punishment, obedience and then simple self-interest guide moral judgements; (2) a 'conventional' phase in which 'goodness' is defined by rigidly adhering to conventional rules, leading to a more general notion of maintaining social 'law and order'; and (3) a 'post-conventional' phase in which morality is seen as centring on a kind of social contract and understood as more flexible, this culminates – or can culminate – in a grasp of universal moral principles which underlie specific moral rules. In 1982, Carol Gilligan criticised this as male-centred, in that it focused exclusively on principles of fairness and equality but ignored the ethical principle of 'caring' and responsibility for others (Gilligan, 1982). (She noted that the research had been done overwhelmingly using male subjects.) During the 1990s, M.L. Hoffman also stressed the central importance of empathy as crucial for moral development. One significant difficulty is that when defining what counts as maturity of moral understanding, an engagement with the perennially tangled and controversial philosophical debate on the nature of ethics becomes unavoidable. Trying to define moral maturity in a purely formal, 'objectively' value-free way is clearly paradoxical, and whether – or how far – the last of Kohlberg's six stages is ever achieved has long been controversial. It is also perhaps questionable whether it is a unitary topic at all, since different areas of human life (such as sexual behaviour, matters relating to property and standards of interpersonal conduct), while clearly involving 'morality', are psychologically rather different. The topic remains an active and contentious research area, Killen and Smetana (2005) providing the fullest recent overview.

References

Gilligan, C. (1982) *In a Different Voice: Psychological Theory and Women's Development*, Cambridge, MA: Harvard University Press.

Killen, M. and Smetana, J. (eds) (2005) *Handbook of Moral Development*, Hillsdale, NJ: Lawrence Erlbaum Associates.

Kohlberg, L. (1981) *Essays in Moral Development*, New York: Harper & Row.

Piaget, J. (1932) *The Moral Judgment of the Child*, London: Kegan, Paul, Trench & Trubner.

MORALE

Similarity to 'moral' may be confusing. 'Morale' refers to the overall mood of an individual or, more often, a group. If everyone is cheerful, confident and optimistic, then morale is high, if they are depressed, pessimistic, argue among themselves a lot, and are unable to get organised, then it is low. Psychology has usually addressed the topic in one of two contexts. First, in relation to the military and war, either concerning the morale of fighting forces or the 'national morale' of the country as a whole (e.g. MacCurdy, 1943). Psychologists have been asked, for instance, to help devise propaganda enhancing national morale or to reduce the enemy's morale. Second, 'morale' figured in some mid-twentieth-century applied and industrial Psychology work (e.g. Brown and Raphael, 1956; Viteles, 1954). More recently it appears in Sport Psychology in relation to 'team morale', but hardly anywhere else. It has no direct link with 'morals', both high and low morale being symptomatised by particular varieties of immorality. Although commonly discussed in popular self-improvement and advice literature, the topic seems to have been dropped from Psychology's agenda since 1960, indeed, the only post-2000 title yielded by a web search was *Coaching Baseball for Dummies*, issued by the National Alliance for Youth Sports! Morale is presumably low among morale researchers …

References

Brown, W.B.D. and Raphael, W. (1956) *Managers, Men and Morale*, London: MacDonald & Evans.

MacCurdy, J.T. (1943) *The Structure of Morale*, Cambridge: Cambridge University Press.

Viteles, M.S. (1954) *Motivation and Morale in Industry*, London: Staples Press.

MOTIVATION

A very general term adopted by psychologists from the 1930s onwards to refer to whatever drives people to behave in a certain way. Danziger's account of its introduction as a Psychological term is particularly valuable (Danziger, 1997). He argues that it served as a theoretically neutral term, replacing **instinct** and **will**, for example. This enabled the focus of attention to shift from inner sources of behaviour to environmental factors, especially in industrial Psychology. In these, the concern was often with how factors such as wages and work conditions affected worker performance, and how to *motivate* them. It is curious how natural the term has become, given the relatively recent emergence of its current meaning. See also **drive**. Since motivation is so closely linked to emotion, by the mid-twentieth century it had become customary for them to be paired in undergraduate courses on 'Emotion and Motivation'. Peters (1958) remains a valuable philosophical study even though the material he is referencing is now out of date.

References and further reading

Beck, R.C. (2003) *Motivation: Theories and Principles*, New York: Prentice Hall.

Danziger, K. (1997) *Naming the Mind: How Psychology Found its Language*, London: Sage.

Edwards, D.C. (1998) *Motivation and Emotion: Evolutionary, Physiological, Cognitive and Social Influences*, Thousand Oaks, CA: Sage.

Efklides, A., Kuhl, J. and Sorrentino, R.M. (2007) *Trends and Prospects in Motivation Research*, Berlin: Springer.

Peters, R.S. (1958) *The Concept of Motivation*, London: Routledge & Kegan Paul.

MULTIPLE PERSONALITY DISORDER (MPD)/ DISSOCIATIVE IDENTITY DISORDER (DID)

Condition in which an individual appears to have more than one personality, these 'alters' not necessarily being aware of each other. While 'multiple personality disorder' was introduced as a diagnostic term in 1980, it was replaced by dissociative identity disorder in the 2000 'text revision' of **DSM** IV. The first two cases were reported in

1905 ('Miss Beauchamp' and 'Hannah') both in the USA. For decades
it remained a very rare condition with numbers of 'alters' being no
higher than four. It then achieved wide publicity in 1957 with the
publication of *The Three Faces of Eve* (Thigpen and Cleckley, 1957),
attention reviving in 1973, with the case of 'Sybil' (Schreiber, 1973),
filmed in 1977. (This latter was, incidentally, cast into severe doubt in
1998 by R.W. Rieber (Rieber, 1998), whose detective work uncovered
audiotapes of conversations between 'Sybil' and her psychiatrist Cornelia
Wilbur in which it was clear that the latter was actively engaged in
differentiating Sybil's various identities. His conclusions were later
endorsed by H. Spiegel.) Then something odd happened. During the
1980s, in the USA, there was a virtual explosion of the number of
cases and the number of 'alters' being reported – by 1990, they were
averaging 24 and occasionally over 100, and in 1991 the record was
broken with a case in which alters exceeded 1,000. Most of those
diagnosed were women and the 'epidemic' seems to have been a largely
US affair. By then, scepticism was beginning to grow, and concerns
about responsibility in legal contexts also surfaced. While the publicity surrounding the topic has declined, this remains an extremely
controversial topic, with some robustly defending the concept and
the reality of the condition, while others argue that the majority of
cases, if not all, are 'iatrogenic' (i.e. caused, wittingly or not, by the
therapeutic process itself) or that the condition is a social or cultural
construct (**social constructionism**). Historical and cross-cultural
oscillations and variability in its reported occurrence certainly need
explaining by its supporters. As to its causes, there is broad consensus
that it is a variety of **post-traumatic stress disorder** originating in
severe early childhood sexual abuse or wartime experiences. In some
regards this is not at issue, what is as yet unresolved is the degrees to
which the DID mode of presenting these consequences is variously
shaped by autonomous internal processes, active conformity to cultural expectations and therapist–client collusion (albeit inadvertent).
Hacking (1998) has had a major impact on how the phenomenon is
conceptualised, raising numerous philosophical and historical issues.

References and further reading

Hacking, I. (1998) *Rewriting the Soul: Multiple Personality and the Sciences of
Memory*, Princeton, NJ: Princeton University Press.
Haddock, D.B. (2001) *The Dissociative Identity Sourcebook*, New York:
McGraw-Hill.
Rieber, R.W. (1998) see 'Tapes Raise New Doubts About 'Sybil'
Personalities' *New York Times,* 19 August (available on-line).

Schreiber, F.R. (1973) *Sybil*, New York: Warner Books.

Spira, J.L. (ed.) (1996) *Treating Dissociative Identity Disorder*, New York: Wiley.

Thigpen, C.H. and Cleckley, H.M. (1957) *The Three Faces of Eve*, London: Secker & Warburg.

MUTUALISM

Theoretical orientation proposed by several British psychologists and anthropologists including T. Ingold (e.g. Ingold, 2000), J.M.M. Good and A. Still (e.g. Good and Still, 1998), and A. Costall (Costall and Still, 1986). Rooted in ideas variously proposed by perception theorist J.J. Gibson and pragmatists such J. Dewey, it offers an account, transcending crude organism–environment distinctions, in which all factors are mutually interacting in an ecological fashion. From this perspective, **social constructionism** offers too simple an image of a unilinear process. Ingold has applied this perspective in his palaeo-anthropological writings on human evolution, while Costall and Still (1986) is a powerful critique of **Cognitive Psychology**. There are clear affinities with recent ideas being advanced in M. Billig's work on **rhetoric**. Although Mutualism remains in many respects unjustly marginalised, caught between the big guns of cognitivism and social constructionism, it is making headway in **Ecological Psychology** (if not in **Evolutionary Psychology**). Still largely unknown as such in North America, although percolating into US Ecological Psychology. Ian Hacking (Hacking, 1999) also appears to have shifted towards a mutualist position.

References

Costall, A. and Still, A. (1986) *Cognitive Psychology in Question*, Hove: Harvester Press.

Good, J.M.M. and Still, A. (1998) 'The Ontology of Mutualism', *Ecological Psychology*, 10(1): 39–63.

Hacking, I. (1999) *Social Construction of What?* Cambridge, MA: Harvard University Press.

Ingold, T. (2000) *The Perception of the Environment: Essays on Livelihood, Dwelling and Skill*, London: Routledge.

NARRATIVISM

A *social constructionist* theoretical orientation in which narratives, or story-telling, are considered the central process by which **personality**, self-image, and **attribution** judgements are generated. Strong versions of narrativism would claim that all Psychological explanations are, if only covertly, narrative in character and derive their power from how convincingly they tell their 'story'. This is in many ways related to the concept of **rhetoric** as developed by M. Billig. A narrativist approach to understanding an individual would thus involve unpacking the autobiographical story the person has developed in order to explain and interpret their life experiences and thus define their identity.

References and further reading

Emerson, P. and Frosh, S. (2004) *Critical Narrative Analysis in Psychology: A Guide to Practice*, London: Palgrave Macmillan.

Fivush, R. and Haden, C.A. (eds) (2003) *Autobiographical Memory and the Construction of a Narrative Self: Developmental and Cultural Perspectives*, Hove: Psychology Press.

Mueller, D. (2004) *Narrative and Consciousness*, Oxford: Oxford University Press.

Yancy, G. and Hadley, S. (2005) *Narrative Identities: Psychologists Engaged in Self-Construction*, London: Jessica Kingsley.

NATURAL EXPERIMENT

A naturally occurring or historical event which provides an opportunity to study a psychological phenomenon happening in real life as opposed to the laboratory, thus providing *ecological validity* (see **validity**). This is particularly useful regarding social behaviour. Events such as floods, terrorist attacks, assassinations, major sporting events, political demonstrations and the like might all be considered to be natural experiments providing the opportunity to study the social nature of phenomena such as panic, helping behaviour, grief, communication processes, rumour, exultation and shock. Natural experiments are, on the other hand, obviously non-replicable, unique and usually highly complex, somewhat off-setting the value of their ecological validity. Two classic examples in Social Psychology are the news-style 'War of the Worlds' broadcast by Orson Welles in 1938 which caused a brief but widespread panic (Cantril, 1940) and the millennial cult studied by L. Festinger and colleagues (Festinger *et al.*, 1956) (see also **cognitive dissonance**). More generally, the Holocaust, subject of enormous Psychological scrutiny, might come into this category. Recently the reaction to the death of Lady Diana,

Princess of Wales, in 1997, attracted much Psychological attention, regarding both its conspiracy theory and collective grief aspects (e.g. Douglas and Sutton, in press; Ellis and Cromby, 2004).

References

Cantril, H.H. *The Invasion from Mars: A Study in the Psychology of Panic with the Complete Script of the Orson Welles Broadcast*, Princeton, NJ: Princeton University Press.

Douglas, K.M. and Sutton, R.M. (in press). 'The Hidden Impact of Conspiracy Theories: Perceived and Actual Impact of Theories Surrounding the Death of Princess Diana', *Journal of Social Psychology*. (See also a featured article in *The Psychologist,* February 2007).

Ellis, D. and Cromby, J. (2004) 'It's Not Always Good to Talk', *The Psychologist*, 17(11): 630–1.

Festinger, L., Riecken, H.R. Jr. and Schachter, S. (1956) *When Prophecy Fails*, Minneapolis: University of Minnesota Press.

NATURE–NURTURE CONTROVERSY

Perennial controversy regarding the relative importance of heredity and environment in determining individual psychological traits, abilities and behaviour. Most attention has been paid to **intelligence** and, especially since the 1960s, *sex differences*, but **aggression** and other topics have also figured. Although a seductively simple polarity, it is fundamentally problematic and rejected as misleading by most professional psychologists and geneticists. One conceptual difficulty is in how they can be viewed as 'independent variables' in the first place, one (nurture or environment) being only definable as everything which is not the other. Another is that there is a covert infinite regress in that it always makes sense to ask the extent to which something is determined by nature or nurture is *itself* so determined. These go deeper than anything solvable by a simple 'interaction' compromise solution. Geneticists recognise that the extent to which specific genetic traits are affected by developmental circumstances varies enormously, not least between which 'allele' of the trait is in question. There is no single ideal 'phenotypic' outcome of specific 'genotypes', developmental circumstances at specific times can switch this between varying tracks, as it were. In short, one cannot in practice separate genes and environment: without an environment of a suitable kind no organism could survive, without genes there would be no organism in the first place. There are many other arcane twists and paradoxes of both conceptual and methodological kinds inherent in the nature–nurture schema, but these should alert you to the extent of the problem. The 'twin studies' approach provided the main research paradigm for many years, but even in the credible cases of identical twins reared apart in significantly different environments, the findings could only apply to those specific environments, not 'environment' in general. Identical twins are also, by definition, not genetically representative of the population as a whole. Non-partisan book-length reviews of the topic are surprisingly scarce, but in relation to intelligence, see the chapter on 'race differences' in Richards (1997) and references provided there.

Reference

Richards, G. (1997) *'Race', Racism and Psychology. Towards a Reflexive History*, London: Routledge.

NEED

An unremarkable enough word and common in much Psychological discourse, but it figured particularly prominently in the elaborate **personality** theory (or 'Personology') formulated by Harvard-based psychologist H. Murray (1893–1988) in the 1930s (Murray, 1938). He produced a catalogue of 20 (later expanded) human 'psychogenic needs', subdivided into Primary (basically biological) and Secondary (primarily psychological). His definition of 'need' is surprisingly long-winded and technical (perhaps, indeed, pseudo-technical) but amounts to it being an energising and organising force 'in the brain region' directed at changing the situation in a more satisfactory direction. On his account, although universally present, the respective strengths or weightings of Secondary Needs vary enormously, and underlie many of our personality differences. Of special significance were *achievement* (abbreviated **N-Ach)**, dominance, affiliation and nurture. A need's strength may be referred to as its **motivation**, and of all the needs Murray identified, it was N-Ach which subsequently attracted most attention (see **achievement motivation**). Needs differ in several respects such as whether they are enduring or only temporarily activated and whether they are autonomously generated or triggered by the environment or '*press*' as Murray called it. They can be classified as pertaining variously to power, affection, ambition, information or material possessions. His **thematic apperception test (TAT)** was designed as a technique to assess the relative strengths of an individual's needs. Research on some of Murray's 'needs', such as intimacy and affiliation continued into the 1980s. It must be admitted that Murray was a somewhat rum, if charismatic, character (Robinson, 1992).

References and further reading

Murray, H.A. (ed.) (1938) *Explorations in Personality*, New York: Oxford University Press.
—— (1980) *Endeavors in Psychology. Selections from the Personology of H.A. Murray*, New York: Harper & Row.
Robinson, F. (1992) *Love's Story Told: A Life of Henry A. Murray*. Cambridge, MA: Harvard University Press.

NEO-FREUDIAN *see* Post-Freudian/neo-Freudian.

NEUROPSYCHOLOGY

A sub-discipline which has emerged from more general *Physiological Psychology* in recent decades. Neuropsychology is concerned with the neuropsychological bases of psychological phenomena, particularly in relation to the brain. Its origins are a complex mixture of **Cognitive Psychology**, *neural network theory* (see **parallel distributed processing**), and neurological research on the brain. The rapid expansion in this field has been largely due to advances in brain-scanning technology. It is now one of the most flourishing fields of Psychological research, although its cross-disciplinary nature has led many of its advocates to consider it a separate discipline, under the term *cognitive neuroscience* (with which it should now be considered virtually synonymous). If currently the most 'hard scientific' area of Psychology, it should not be thought of as offering the final answers to all questions because many of the issues concerning Psychology do not arise at the physiological level. Obviously a very fast-developing field, the fullest recent overview is Malatesha and Hartlage (2007), for its applications to **memory**, see Squire (2002), for **perception**, see Fahle (2003) and for a general introduction, see Banich (2003), while Rains (2001) is among the more accessible basic works. For those seeking really specialist coverage, there is also a massive 11-volume *Handbook of Neuropsychology* issued under various editors from 1989–97, but a second edition is now in progress (Boller and Grafman, 2007). These volumes cover its applications across all fields from child development to language, brain-functioning and ageing.

References

Banich, M.T. (2003) *Cognitive Neuroscience and Neuropsychology*, New York: Houghton-Mifflin.

Boller, F. and Grafman, J. (eds) (2007) *Handbook of Neuropsychology*, New York: Elsevier.

Fahle, M. (2003) *Neuropsychology of Vision*, New York: Oxford University Press.

Malatesha, R.N. and Hartlage, L.C. (eds) (2007) *Neuropsychology and Cognition*, 2 vols, Berlin: Springer.

Rains, G.D. (2001) *Principles of Human Neuropsychology*, New York: McGraw-Hill.

Squire, L.R. (2002) *Neuropsychology of Memory*, 3rd edn, New York: Guilford.

NEUROSIS/NEUROTIC

'Neurosis' serves as an umbrella term for a wide range of non-psychotic (see **psychosis**) forms of mental distress. It primarily signifies irrationally high levels of anxiety and/or self-preoccupation. There is, however, no clear borderline differentiating neurotic from normal behaviour and H.J. Eysenck identified neuroticism as one of the basic **personality** dimensions along with **extraversion**. In clinical use, the term may be coupled with a word denoting more specifically the nature of the disorder, such as 'compulsion neurosis'. Conditions such as the various **phobias**, **OCD**, and **depression** are all varieties of neurosis. 'Neurotic' is used either as an adjective or as a noun denoting an individual suffering from neurosis.

NEUTRAL MONISM

Any position on the **mind–body problem** which holds that these are differing facets of a single 'substance', without ascribing priority to either. The most famous classical exposition of this was B.B. Spinoza's 'double aspect monism' (Spinoza, [1663] 2007). There have been numerous variations on this notion and it was popular during the first half of the twentieth century.

Reference

Spinoza, B.B. ([1663] 2007) *Theological-Political Treatise*, Cambridge: Cambridge University Press.

NOMOTHETIC *see* **idiographic and nomothetic**.

NON-VERBAL COMMUNICATION (NVC)

Although largely self-explanatory, it should be stressed how large a part of communication is non-verbal. Even speech is accompanied by a host of what linguists call '*paralinguistic features*' such as intonation, facial expression, body posture, hand gestures, and touching, which variously communicate our attitudes to the listener and the message itself, our emotional state and sincerity, etc. In fact, conversations overtly about one topic can covertly be about something quite different being communicated non-verbally. Hand gestures and body posture ('body language') convey a wide range of messages of course, but NVC extends in principle as far as our mode of dress and general appearance. As a research topic in Psychology, NVC emerged in the late 1950s (Ruesch and Kees, 1956) but did not take off until the 1970s (e.g. Siegman and Feldstein, 1978). The majority of Psychological research focuses on conversation and facial expression (often closely integrated). This may be aimed at developing ways of enhancing the social skills of those who are poor at 'reading' NVC. There are of course numerous popular works aspects of the topic, right down to magazine articles on the signals that someone fancies you.

See also: **kinesics**.

References

Knapp, M.L. and Hall, J.A. (2002) *Nonverbal Communication in Human Interaction*, Belmont, CA: Wadsworth.

Manusov, V. (ed.) (2006) *The Sage Book of Nonverbal Communication*, London: Sage.

Poyatos, F. (2002) *Nonverbal Communication across Disciplines: Paralanguage, Kinesics, Silence, Personal and Environmental Interaction*, Amsterdam: John Benjamins.

Riggio, R. and Feldman, R.S. (eds) (2005) *Applications of Nonverbal Communication*, New York: Lawrence Erlbaum.

Ruesch, J. and Kees, W. (1956) *Nonverbal Communication: Notes on the Visual Perception of Human Relations*, Berkeley, CA: University of California Press.

Siegman, A.W. and Feldstein, S. (eds) (1978) *Nonverbal Behavior and Communication*, Hillsdale, NJ: Erlbaum.

NORM, NORMALITY/ABNORMAL, ABNORMALITY

Statistically the 'norm' refers to data falling within about 1 standard deviation from the mean (= c.68 per cent of the data) when data are normally distributed. The term 'normal', when used in psychological contexts, has, however, caused some problems. First, there is a tendency to impose evaluative connotations on its use, if sometimes only covertly. To be 'normal' is invariably considered good, while to be 'abnormal' may, depending on the phenomenon in question and direction of deviance from the norm, be thought either pathological or very good indeed. Where problems have arisen has, historically, been the use of statistically identified norms of e.g. child development, personality dimensions and beliefs as a route for devaluing non-conformity and elevating the 'normal' to an especially esteemed status. Non-statistically based assumptions about what is normal can also prove oppressive, as was long the case with adult-oriented non-heterosexuality. Obviously there are contexts in which viewing deviance as pathological – or at any rate problematic – is perfectly justified. What is dangerous is the loose usage of current social assumptions about what are normal behaviours and beliefs to stigmatise those who do not display or hold them. The term 'abnormal' has proved perhaps even more problematic since the evaluative implication is quite clear. The common use of the phrase 'Abnormal Psychology', sometimes amounting to a subdisciplinary title, has exacerbated the difficulty in clinical settings, but fortunately its use has gradually declined, largely supplanted by 'Clinical Psychology'.

For various critiques of the concept of normality, see Aitken *et al.* (1996).

Reference

Aitken, G. *et al.* (1996) *Psychology, Discourse and Social Practice: From Regulation to Resistance*, London: Routledge.

OBE

An acronym for 'out of body experience'. Although long anecdotally reported, the incidence of OBEs has grown rapidly in recent decades, especially as a result of advances in surgical techniques and medicine which have enabled people, apparently clinically dead, to return to life. Some of those who undergoing such procedures have later reported OBEs (occurring in these circumstances they are known as *near death experiences*, or *NDEs*). These are often quite similar in kind, typically involving a travelling through a tunnel towards a white light and sometimes meeting dead relatives, others have claimed to have been hovering in the operating theatre witnessing the operation. The British analytic philosopher A.J. Ayer, as adamant an atheist as anyone, admitted being forced by such an experience to become at least a little more open-minded. While many neuropsychologists are sceptical, arguing that a neurological explanation is sufficient, surgeons involved have tended to be less so, especially when patients have given detailed descriptions of unusual surgical instruments which they could not have seen. The reporting of OBEs in non-life threatening situations does not appear to have increased. The jury remains out on the nature of OBEs. Most of the books explicitly on OBEs are popular or mystical, often offering techniques for inducing them. For hostile views, see Blackmore (1982) and Woerlee (2005). For NDEs, see also Bailey (1996). There has been relatively scant solid Psychological research on the topic as yet.

References

Bailey, L.W. and J. Yates (eds) (1996) *The Near-Death Experience: A Reader*, London: Routledge.

Blackmore, S.J. (1982) *Beyond the Body: An investigation of out-of-the body experiences*, London: Heinemann.

Woerlee, G.M. (2005) *Mortal Minds: The Biology of Near-Death Experiences*, New York: Prometheus Books.

OBEDIENCE

The topic of what have become probably the two best known Psychology experiments of the post-1950 period: S. Milgram's 1963 'Behavioral study of obedience' (see Milgram, 1974) and Zimbardo's 'Stanford Prison Experiment' (Zimbardo, 1972; Vallone, 1983). The first required subjects (believing themselves to be collaborators with the experimenter) to administer electric shocks of ascending severity to a 'subject' (actually a collaborator), who reacted accordingly. This famously showed that people were prepared to give shocks of a potentially lethal level. This study has now acquired the status of a folk-parable, although it remains controversial (see e.g. Miller, 1986). The second has generated a virtual industry (largely web-based) of debate, attempted replications, and discussion of its relevance to recent events, notably the Abu Ghraib prisoner abuse in Iraq. Its fame is such that it requires only minimal description. Essentially it involved assigning students arbitrarily to prisoner and prison guard roles in a simulated prison environment. The situation deteriorated very rapidly and the experiment was terminated after only six of the planned 14 days. The precise conclusions to be drawn from these two studies remain debatable beyond a loose consensus that such forms of obedience are primarily caused by situational, rather than internal psychological, factors. The latter are not entirely absent, but more relevant in explaining exceptional resistance to authority than to obeying it (in the Milgram case) or exceptional sadism (in the Zimbardo one). Both studies also need to be understood in their social and historical contexts, particularly the Cold War atmosphere at the time of Milgram's experiment. The Milgram experiment is, additionally, an interesting example of research which has rendered itself unreplicable, since any subject sample comparable to that originally used is now likely to have heard of it and, under the same experimental conditions, would nobly refuse to obey from the outset! A 2001 replication of the Zimbardo experiment by British psychologists A. Haslam and S. Reicher for the BBC (transmitted on 2 May 2002 as 'The Experiment') yielded somewhat different results, with more collective resistance from prisoners for example, but its design diverged in many respects from the original. There appears to have been little genuinely innovatory research on the topic since Milgram and Zimbardo.

References

Milgram, S. (1974) *Obedience to Authority*, New York: Harper.

Miller, A.G. (1986) *The Obedience Experiments: A case study of controversy in social science*, New York: Praeger.

Zimbardo, P.G. (1972) *The Stanford Prison Experiment. A simulation study of the psychology of imprisonment*, Philip G.Zimbardo Inc.

Zimbardo, P.G. and Vallone, R. (1983) *Persuasion, Coercion, Indoctrination and Mind Control*, Lexington, MA: Ginn.

OBJECT RELATIONS THEORY

Distinctively British school of **psychoanalysis** developed by Melanie Klein, W.D.R. Fairbairn, H. Guntrip and D.W. Winnicott from the 1930s onwards. Klein radically rethought the psychological nature of infancy and childhood in the context of her psychoanalytic work with children (especially her own!). This approach places far more emphasis on the real relationship between infant and parent and its role in the origins of adult personality than mainstream Psychoanalysis. Although sharing much of the orthodox Psychoanalytic vocabulary, this school has introduced a number of additional concepts.

To oversimplify, Object Relations Theory sees the infant as *introjecting* the objects (primarily people) in its world, initially (up to about 3 months), in the *'paranoid-schizoid position'*, splitting these into good and bad aspects, famously differentiating the 'good mother' or 'good breast' from the 'bad mother' or 'bad breast' for example. This strategy results in feelings of persecution by 'bad objects', destructive anger towards them and fear of retaliation. It has nevertheless introjected both good and bad into itself as rudimentary core elements from which the *ego* (see psychoanalysis sub-entry) will develop. The major defence mechanism employed at this stage is *projective identification* in which 'bad' parts of the self are ascribed to others. With realization that the split objects are in fact a unity (e.g. that there is really only one mother), it enters the *depressive position*, experiencing guilt about its destructive wishes and having to confront the love versus hate dichotomy. At this point *reparation* enters the picture as the infant strives to alleviate its guilt by repairing or preserving the 'whole' object. This is a major step towards integrating the psyche which has become fragmented by the previous *splitting,* although this will be affected by the success of its efforts at reparation. One consequence of this model is that Object Relations Theory sees the *superego* as emerging far earlier than in orthodox Freudian theory in the form of internalised or introjected parent figures. The central dynamic of psychological development thereafter is an effort towards integration of a Self from introjected elements of the psyche which are divergent and often conflicted. The early introjected good and bad parent identities persist as determinants of adult character, affecting modes of relating to others, especially in close relationships. The British (sometimes 'London') school of Object Relations Theory has been among the most successful variants of Psychoanalysis in the UK since the 1950s. Relationships with orthodox Psychoanalysis (identified in the 1930s with Anna Freud and Ernest Jones) have frequently been stormy. The theory continues to develop and has become far more complex than can be indicated here. Although originating in the psychoanalysis of children it is now equally used with adults. The key differences from the Freudian position are (a). its more detailed account of very early stages of psychological development, (b). its attention to real social relationships as determining the course of events, (c). the prominent roles of introjection and projective identification, and (d.) the consequences of these for the timing of developmental stages, such as emergence of the superego. There are, it should be noted, some links to **attachment theory**, the founder of which, John Bowlby, often strove to play a mediating role between the warring camps.

References

Clarke, G.S. (2006) *Person Relations Theory, Fairbairn, Macmurray and Suttie*, London: Taylor & Francis.

Kernberg, O. (1995) *Object-Relations Theory and Clinical Psychoanalysis*, Lanham, Maryland: Jason Aronson.

—— (2004) *Contemporary Controversies in Psychoanalytic Theory, Technqiue and their Applications*, New Haven, CT: Yale University Press.

Scharff, D.E. (1996) *Object Relations Theory and Therapy. An Introduction*, Lanham, MD: Jason Aronson.

Scharff, J.S. and D.E. (2005, 2nd ed.) *The Primer of Object Relations Theory*, Lanham, MD: Rowman & Littlefield.

Summers, F. (1994) *Object Relations Theories and Psychopathology. A Comprehensive Text*, London: Psychology Press.

OBSESSIONAL

Being highly concerned with a particular topic or issue, or pre-occupied with orderliness and neatness. In *Clinical Psychology* it typically refers to the pathological extremes of this, such as repetitive hand-washing, irrational fear for others' safety, or compulsive checking that household appliances are switched off. This is known as *obsessional compulsive disorder*, or *OCD*. See also **anxiety**. A certain degree of obsessionality is perfectly normal and often advantageous in occupations such as accountancy, librarianship, computer programming and writing dictionaries, and is a quite common academic **trait**. Non-anxious obsessionality can also be associated with **Asperger's Syndrome**.

OPEN/CLOSED MIND

While these terms are common in everyday language the phenomenon first received explicit Psychological attention as a personality dimension in M. Rokeach (1960). Closed-mindedness had already been identified as typical of the **authoritarian personality** and open-mindedness was also related to contemporary work on **persuasibility**.

Reference

Rokeach, M. (1960) *The Open and Closed Mind. Investigations into the nature of belief and personality systems*, New York: Basic Books.

OPERATIONALISM (OCC. OPERATIONISM)

Defining concepts in terms of publically visible 'operations' or criteria. Introduced by the American philosopher of science P.W. Bridgman in 1927 and closely related (though independently formulated) to the logical positivist notion of the *verification criterion of meaning*. Rapidly became popular among behaviorist psychologists as a way of evading the 'private' nature of many psychological phenomena and rendering hypotheses 'verifiable'. Thus 'hunger' in the rat may be defined in terms of hours of food deprivation, **intelligence** as 'performance on an intelligence test', **suggestibility** by performance on the 'rod and frame' test. Although pragmatically useful, operationalism lost its authority with the philosophical decline of logical positivism.

References

Bridgman, P.W. (1927) *The Logic of Modern Physics*, New York: Macmillan.
—— (1936) *The Nature of Physical Theory*, New York: Dover Press.

OPTICAL ILLUSIONS *see* Visual illusions.

ORTHOGONAL

A statistical concept referring to a situation where two variables are completely uncorrelated and thus 'at right angles' to each other. When their relationship is graphically depicted on two axes the data points will thus appear randomly scattered.

PANIC ATTACK

A sudden outbreak of anxiety and panic coupled with such physical symptoms as sweating, dizziness, breathing problems and shaking. This occurs either for no apparent immediate reason or is disproportionate to the apparent trigger for the attack. About a quarter of cases are associated with *agoraphobia* (see under **phobias**). There is no clear consensus as to the cause of panic attacks, and it is likely that it is a symptomatic expression of a variety of psychological and physiological conditions. These might range from physiological abnormality in the amygdala, the area of the brain controlling fear, to stressful life events – it can occur in **post-traumatic stress disorder** cases, for example. Around two-thirds of sufferers are affected by **depression**. Although the classification 'Panic Disorder' appears in the **DSM** – with 13 possible symptoms, four or more justifying the diagnosis – it is obviously a descriptive rather than explanatory term. Although sometimes treated as such, it is unclear whether there is a 'pure' condition of panic disorder, or whether it is actually always a symptom of some deeper-rooted problem. Book-length coverage is generally of the more popular 'self-help' kind (e.g. Shoquist and Stafford, 2002), more academic coverage may be found in general clinical Psychology and psychiatry textbooks.

Reference

Shoquist, J. and Stafford, D. (2002) *No More Panic Attacks*, Franklin Lakes, NJ: Career Press.

PARALLEL DISTRIBUTED PROCESSING (PDP)

Major **connectionist** model of brain and neurological functioning in which information processing regarding a particular issue involves more than one path operating simultaneously with respective outputs being intermittently, or only finally, integrated. This overcomes problems of both time and sequencing which would arise if only linear *serial processing* was involved. The key texts in launching this field were the two volumes by Rumelhart and McClelland (Rumelhart and McClelland 1986; Rumelhart, 1986).

References

McClelland, J.L. and Rumelhart, D.E. (1986) *Parallel Distributed Processing: Explorations in the Microstructure of Cognition: Psychological and Biological Models (Computational Models of Cognition)*, Cambridge, MA: MIT Press.
Rumelhart, D.E. (1986) *Parallel Distributed Processing: Explorations in the Microstructure of Cognition: Foundations (Parallel Distributed Processing)*, Cambridge, MA: MIT Press.

PARALLELISM

The argument that mind and body, while not genuinely interacting, run in parallel to one another in a way which gives the illusion they do. The most sophisticated version of this was formulated by the German philosopher G.W.F. Leibniz (1646–1716). Although *prima facie* implausible, like most philosophical theories it can, in the hands of a genius like Leibniz, be made to seem quite logical and reasonable.

See also: **mind–body problem**.

PARANOIA

Irrational feeling or belief that one is being persecuted or covertly monitored. In *paranoid psychoses* (see **psychosis**), this may take such forms as believing one is being personally addressed by the TV, that one's mail is being opened and phone conversations bugged. Cannabis intoxication, especially if excessive or among regular users, can result in feelings of paranoia of a less tangible kind such as concern about the police or mistakenly experiencing comments as being about oneself. Everyone probably feels twinges of paranoia from time to time, and contemporary public surveillance technology hardly helps. In truth, people *are* sometimes persecuted and/or kept under surveillance. Those engaged in political activism and protest groups, etc., of whatever kind, have often made apparently paranoid claims only for these to turn out to have been justified a few decades down the line when official papers and reports come to light. As the old saying goes, 'Just because you're paranoid, it doesn't mean they aren't out to get you.' Strictly speaking, the use of the term should be restricted to contexts where there is clearly some degree of irrationality or psychopathology involved. For a recent overview, see Freeman and Garety (2004), for a recent psychoanalytic account, see Bell (2003). One might additionally note that many conspiracy theories can be considered as collective paranoid delusions.

References

Bell, D. (2003) *Paranoia*, Cambridge: Icon Books.
Freeman, D. and Garety, P.A. (2004) *Paranoia: The Psychology of Persecutory Delusions*, London: Psychology Press.

PARANORMAL

Collective term for all those psychological phenomena (or alleged phenomena) which appear to be inexplicable in terms of orthodox current scientific knowledge. Most of these such as **extrasensory perception** (**ESP**) and clairvoyance are also known as *psychic* phenomena, though a few, **telekinesis** (allegedly being able to affect the physical world by the power of thought alone) for example, do not fit so easily into this category. Out-of-body and near-death experiences (**OBE**s and *NDE*s, for short) are now well attested and also not usually considered as paranormal, even though they cannot as yet be satisfactorily explained. The sub-discipline concerned with the paranormal is *Parapsychology*. Collins and Pinch (1982) present an interesting and challenging **social constructionist** analysis of the whole field. This suggests that the mystery surrounding paranormal phenomena may be dissipated if tackled from a less scientifically orthodox angle. As far as ghosts and hauntings are concerned, however, recent work by Richard Wiseman and colleagues in which such physical factors as temperature, light intensity, and low frequency vibrations are monitored suggests that environmental factors can trigger biologically rooted fear or anxiety responses (see Wiseman *et al.*, 2003).

References

Collins, H.M. and Pinch, T.J. (1982) *Frames of Meaning: The Social Construction of Extraordinary Science*, London: Routledge & Kegan Paul.
Wiseman, R., Watt, C., Stevens, P., Greening, E. and O'Keeffe, C. (2003) 'An Investigation into Alleged "hauntings"', *The British Journal of Psychology*, 94: 195–211.

PARAPHILIA

Sexual arousal by objects, materials and situations not usually considered as normally related to sex. At one time the term included homosexuality but is now used primarily to denote sado-masochism and fetishism. It does, again, raise the issue of **normality**.

PATRIARCHY/PATRIARCHAL

Originally a standard anthropological term for societies in which males, especially fathers, exercised most social and political power, typically with a male ruler, and also in which descent was traced through the male line. (The opposite to this being **matriarchy**.) From the late 1960s onwards, its use somewhat broadened in feminist discourse, to refer in general terms to all societies in which males have a power advantage over females.

PEAK-EXPERIENCE

Term introduced by the **humanistic** psychotherapist Abraham Maslow (Maslow, [1964] 1978) to refer to rare but profoundly meaningful experiences, often ascribed a religious or spiritual significance, which individuals may consider as landmark life-events. Peak-experiences may occur in many contexts, such as an especially moving concert, a feeling of 'being at one with nature' while resting on a mountainside, or being overwhelmed by the 'spiritual' atmosphere in a church.

Reference

Maslow, A. ([1964] 1978) *Religion, Values, and Peak-Experiences*, Harmondsworth: Penguin Books.

PEER GROUP

Term originally used by sociologists and social psychologists to refer to the social group to which an individual belongs and/or identifies with, the attitudes and values of which they tend to accept. Members of their peer group are usually known personally by the individual. Although now typically used to refer to the groups to which children and teenagers feel they belong, more strictly speaking, 'peer' origin-ally meant 'equals', and one's 'peers' are those with whom one shares, for example, a professional or social status. Hence the use of the term in Britain to refer to the aristocracy. It also carries the connotation that one to some degree accepts the authority of this group.

PERCEPTUAL DEFENCE

Failure consciously to perceive unwelcome stimuli (visual or auditory) due to some kind of unconscious censoring. This really shades into the phenomena of biased and erroneous perception identified by social psychologists in which reported perceptions are distorted in a direction consistent with the individual's **attitudes** or beliefs. Classic perceptual defence research typically involved exposure of taboo words using a **tachistoscope** in which findings showed that length of exposure required for these to be identified was longer than for neutral words. The topic became especially popular during the 1940s and 1950s, Brown (1961) providing a useful overview. It has received far less intense attention since, although is typically subsumed under the broader category of *defence mechanisms* (see under **psychoanalysis**).

Reference

Brown, W.P. (1961) *Conceptions of Perceptual Defence*, British Journal of Psychology Monograph Supplement 35, Cambridge: Cambridge University Press.

PERSEVERATION

Related to the everyday word 'perseverance', perseveration is used in Psychology to refer to repetition of a behaviour. It usually occurs in **learning theory** contexts for the persistence of a *conditioned response* after it has ceased being reinforced. Level of perseveration is related to the nature of the *reinforcement schedule*, being greater following intermittent schedules. It should not be confused with **repetition compulsion**, although some theoretical explanations of this may invoke it.

PERSONAL CONSTRUCT THEORY (PCT)/ PERSONAL CONSTRUCTS

Personal construct theory was the brainchild of US psychologist George A. Kelly (1905–67) launched in 1955 in a large two-volume treatise and a short popular paperback (Kelly, 1955a, 1955b). Although not actually identified with the **Cognitive Psychology** 'revolution' itself, Kelly was catching the same wind. His core notion was of people behaving like intuitive scientists constantly engaging in theory-testing and attempts at prediction. The elements in this process were their concepts and ideas about the nature of the world, for which he introduced the term 'personal constructs' (PCs). Each individual's repertoire of PCs is unique and the overall structure of such PC systems can vary widely. Kelly developed an ingenious method of eliciting and identifying PCs known as the *repertory grid*. In this procedure, the individual is repeatedly presented with three stimuli and has to say how one of them differs from the other two. These are typically names of people they know or relatives, but can in principle be words or stimuli of any kind. The results are then analysed to disclose the 'constructs' underlying their responses – which responses correlate in a way indicating a common underlying construct, how varied the PC repertory is, and how it is structured. In the 1960s, Kelly's theory was taken up by the British clinical psychologist Bannister (1928–86) and psychologist F. Fransella to explore its clinical applications for identifying varieties of 'thought disorder'. This brought to light phenomena such as 'loosened construing' in which PCs were being used inconsistently. It was also felt that psychotherapeutic techniques could be developed based on feedback from 'rep. grid' results. A simple example might be when each partner in a couple claims the other does not 'understand' them while denying the other's similar claim. Despite using the same word, 'understand', by using PCT it may be possible to show them that they actually mean something quite different by this word (stereotypically, a male might use it as equivalent to 'how things work' and a female as equivalent to 'empathy'). During the 1980s, Fransella became increasingly evangelical about PCT but despite having some enduring successes with regard to the 'rep.grid' technique itself as a **personality** assessment tool and in providing insights into individual differences in **cognitive style**, it now appears to have diminished as a significant movement. Fransella's Centre for Personal Construct Psychology nevertheless retains a presence in the British Counselling and Psychotherapy scene (http://centrepcp.co.uk/), as well as *The Journal of Constructivist Psychology*. The US long-term impact of the theory appears to have been less than in the UK.

References

Bannister, D.B. and Fransella, F. ([1971] 1985) *Inquiring Man: The Psychology of Personal Constructs*, 3rd edn, Harmondsworth: Penguin.

Bannister, D.B. and Mair, J.M.M. (1968) *Evaluating Personal Constructs*, London: Academic Press.

Burr, V. and Butt, T. (1992) *An Invitation to Personal Construct Psychology*, London: Whurr.

Fransella, F. and Dalton, P. (2000) *Personal Construct Counselling in Action*, 2nd edn, London: Sage.

Kelly, G.A. (1955a) *The Psychology of Personal Constructs*, 2 vols, London: Routledge.

—— (1955b) *A Theory of Personality: The Psychology of Personal Constructs*, New York: Norton.

PERSONALITY

The term 'personality' has a particularly complex history. Originating in the Greek *persona* which referrred to the mask worn by actors, it subsequently acquired a diverse range of uses in widely different contexts, such as the law and grammar, besides psychological ones. These were famously explored in the first chapter of the American psychologist Gordon W. Allport's book *Personality: A Psychological Iinterpretation* (Allport, 1937). This variety remains evident in the contrast between the everyday sense of 'personality' as something of which one may have more less, or meaning someone who is particularly charismatic, and the Psychological sense in which it is a neutral term denoting the totality of an individual's enduring **traits**, and the sub-discipline which studies these. Kurt Danziger (1997) has an interesting analysis of why the term came to be accepted in Psychology during the 1930s, winning out over potential alternatives such as **temperament** and *character*. During the mid-twentieth century 'Personality Theory' was one of Psychology's most important, controversial and productive areas of activity, Hall and Lindzey (1957) and Maddi (1976) providing especially valuable overviews of the topic at this time. During the late twentieth century, however, the term fell somewhat from favour as a sub-discipline title, being replaced by '*Individual Differences*', reflecting the dominance of **psychometric** methods focusing on identifying the number of dimensions along which individuals vary from each other (a **trait**-oriented approach). Nevertheless, theories accepting individual uniqueness and addressing this in terms of complex personality dynamics continued to flourish, especially in relation to the sources of psychopathology. These were influenced both by **psychoanalysis** and Jungian **Analytical Psychology**, Jung's early book *Psychological Types or the Psychology of Individuation* (Jung, 1923, in English) being the ultimate source of the now widely used *Myers-Briggs Type Indicator* (MBTI) test. Jung's typological theory is one a number of type theories or models going back to antiquity. See also **temperament** and **somatotypes**. Hergenhahn and Olson (2006) and Schultz and Schultz (2004) provide recent reviews of the topic (although several similar works may equally well be consulted, the 'Theories of Personality' genre being a perennial favourite of Psychology textbook writers). One might note that the phrase *personality disorder* is widely used as an umbrella term for psychopathological conditions in which the entire personality structure of the individual is implicated (see also **borderline personality disorder**).

References

Allport, G.W. (1937) *Personality: A Psychological Interpretation*, New York: Henry Holt.

Hall, C.S. and Lindzey, G. (1957) *Theories of Personality*, New York: Wiley.

Hergenhahn, B.R. and Olson, M.H. (2006) *An Introduction to Theories of Personality*, New York: Prentice Hall.

Maddi, S. (1976) *Personality Theories: A Comparative Analysis*, 3rd edn, Homewood, IL: Dorsey.

Schultz, D.P. and Schultz, S.E. (2004) *Theories of Personality*, London: Thomson.

PERSUASIBILITY

Introduced as a technical concept by McGuire (1964) as a term for the personality dimension or trait of being easily persuadable. This was, it should be noted, in the wake of a **brainwashing** scare during the Korean War, when some US prisoners of war apparently changed sides and broadcast propaganda messages for the North Koreans. They had allegedly been subjected to an intense psychological programme aimed at persuading them to discard their previous beliefs and adopt those of their captors. The irony was that, in the earlier **authoritarian personality** studies, being 'open-minded' was seen as good and 'closed-minded' bad. To some extent, persuasibility was similar to the authoritarianism dimension but with reversed evaluative loading. (It is, to digress slightly, a common feature of psychological language in general that it has 'good' and 'bad' ways of referring to the same thing – stubborn *vs* strong-willed, tenacious *vs* obsessional, carefree *vs* irresponsible, etc. This has serious implications for Psychology which cannot be pursued here.) Nevertheless, being 'open-minded' is not exactly the same thing as being, what would commonly be called 'easily led', nor is being reluctant to change your mind without overwhelming evidence the same as being 'closed minded' or dogmatic. As a distinct topic, persuasibility soon became absorbed into the broader field of **attitude** studies, particularly theories of attitude change.

Reference

McGuire, W.J. (1964) 'Inducing Resistance to Persuasion: Some Contemporary Approaches', in L. Berkowitz (ed.), *Advances in Experimental Social Psychology*, vol. 1, New York: Academic Press, pp. 191–229.

PHENOMENOLOGY

Phenomenology is a rather general term denoting the study of the nature of conscious experience itself, and 'how something is experienced'. Thus we might talk of 'the phenomenology of fear' meaning how fear is actually experienced by the fearful individual or oneself. Since Psychology has (with the exception of hard-line **behaviourism**) invariably considered consciousness as part of its remit, there has always been a tension between its phenomenological interests and its behavioural ones. In mainland Europe a number of philosophers resisted the behavioural direction Psychology was taking during the early 1900s and persisted in trying to develop a rigorous science of the nature of pure experience. The founder this phenomenological school was E. Husserl (1859–1938), with his two-volume *Logical Investigations* (Husserl, 1900/1901), but his most original and influential work appeared in the 1920s and 1930s (notably Husserl, 1928, 1931, 1936). (The on-line Stanford Encyclopedia entry on Hussserl is excellent.) By the late 1940s, the approached had evolved, via Heidegger, into **existentialism**, notably in the work of M. Merleau-Ponty (e.g. Merleau-Ponty, 1962). See Chung and Ashworth (2006) for an overview of the current state of play.

References and further reading

Chung, M.C. and Ashworth, P. (2006) *Phenomenology and Psychological Science*, Berlin: Springer.

Husserl, E. (1900/1901) *Logical Investigations*, trans. 1973, London: Routledge.

—— (1928) *On the Phenomenology of the Consciousness of Internal Time*, trans.1990, Dordrecht: Kluwer.

—— (1931) *Cartesian Meditations*, trans.1988, Dordrecht: Kluwer.

—— (1936) *The Crisis of European Sciences and Transcendental Phenomenology*, Evanston, IL: Northwestern University Press (also 1970, London: Hutchinson as *The Paris Lectures*).

Merleau-Ponty, M. ([1945] 1962) *The Phenomenology of Perception*, London: Routledge.

Mooney, T. and Moran, D. (eds) (2002) *The Phenomenology Reader*, London: Routledge.

Thompson, E. (2007) *Mind in Life: Biology, Phenomenology and the Sciences of Mind*, Cambridge, MA: Harvard University Press.

PHI PHENOMENON

The apparent movement of light between two adjacent successively flashing lights (as commonly seen in neon signs, for example).

W. Wertheimer's study of this curious perceptual phenomenon provided a starting point for the development of German **Gestalt Psychology** in 1911.

PHOBIA/PHILIA

The technical medical terms (of Greek origin) for 'fear' and 'love' respectively. The implication of their usage is that there is something extreme, a little irrational or even pathological in a person's fear of, or love for, the objects or phenomena in question. 'Phobias' refers collectively to all those conditions in which 'phobia' appears as a suffix such as agoraphobia, claustrophobia and arachnaphobia (fear of spiders). 'Philia' usually only occurs as a suffix – as in paedophilia, necrophilia (sexual attraction to the dead), bibliophilia (love of books), and the like. While the phobias are almost all considered as to a greater or less extent pathological, many of the 'philias' are simply descriptive terms or even positive, bibliophilia, for example. The full list of phobias is surprisingly extensive. Technically, I suppose 'philophobia' and 'phobophilia' could be used for excessive fear of love and love of fear respectively.

PHRENOLOGY

Formulated by a Viennese doctor, Franz Joseph Gall (1758–1828), during the late eighteenth century, phrenology was an early attempt at scientifically describing the functioning of the brain. Gall's first major publications on the topic were in 1808 and 1809. Gall believed he could identify which brain regions controlled the various mental functions or 'faculties' such as language, benevolence, spirituality, love of children, avarice and the like (initially the list was 28 items long). The level of an individual's capacity for each of these was reflected in the size of the brain-part or 'organ' in question, which in turn determined the shape of the cranium. Examining this, a skilled phrenologist would therefore be able to ascertain someone's character in terms of the strengths and weaknesses of each faculty. Gall's follower J.G. Spurzheim travelled widely expounding his system, finding an especially sympathetic audience in Scotland, where George Combe (1788–1858) became its leading advocate. Initially a serious scientific theory, phrenology gradually degenerated after the 1840s into little more than a popular fortune-telling trade, although retained some serious advocates well into the twentieth century, Dr Bernard Hollander being its last major British exponent (Hollander, 1931). It also flourished in the USA, though had met its demise by about 1900. Phrenology is historically significant for several reasons besides its role in the development of studies of brain functioning. In some respects, as a scientific approach to human nature widely applicable in contexts requiring the assessment of people's abilities and temperaments, it represented a 'dry run' for Psychology. It also involved an early use of descriptive statistics and rating scales. Since the 1960s, it has attracted a considerable degree of historical attention as a case study in the relationship between science and social context. While generally receiving some coverage in standard histories of Psychology, the works referenced below set phrenology more fully in its historical contexts.

References and further reading

Cooter, R. (1984) *The Cultural Meaning of Popular Science: Phrenology and the Organization of Consent in Nineteenth-Century Britain*, Cambridge: Cambridge University Press. Reprinted 2005.

—— (1989) *Phrenology in the British Isles: An Annotated Historical Bibliography and Index*, London: Scarecrow Press.

Davies, J.D. (1971) *Phrenology: Fad and Science. A Nineteenth-Century American Crusade*, Hamden, CT: Archon Books.

De Giustino, D. (1975) *Conquest of Mind: Phrenology and Victorian Social Thought*, Lanham, MD: Rowman and Littlefield.

Hollander, B. (1931) *Brain, Mind, and the External Signs of Intelligence*, London: Allen & Unwin.

Van Wyhe, J. (2004) *Phrenology and the Origins of Victorian Scientific Naturalism*, Aldershot: Ashgate.

Young, R.M. (1972) 'Franz Josef Gall', in C.C. Gillespie (ed.) *Dictionary of Scientific Biography*, New York: Scribner's.

PHYSIOGNOMY

The interpretation of personality or character from facial shape and appearance. Although going back to antiquity physiognomy enjoyed a great revival towards the end of the eighteenth century due to the work of the Swiss pastor J.K. Lavater (1741–1802). Lavater's copiously illustrated four-volume *Essays on Physiognomy*, originally published 1775–8, was translated into most European languages by 1800, including several English editions (one including a few illustrations by William Blake). Unlike previous physiognomists who simply identified specific features as signs of particular traits (such as thick lips denoting sensuality), Lavater's approach was underpinned by the notion that 'form' reflects 'essence', that there is some natural law at work resulting in the outward form of an organism reflecting its inner essential character. This was a typically 'Romantic' notion. The cultural impact of Lavater's work was enormous, being used as a sort of 'personnel selection' manual by those hiring servants, by artists wishing to ensure that the faces of famous historical figures conformed to their known personality and by novelists describing their characters' looks (Tytler, 1981). This persisted into the mid-nineteenth century and, in a residual fashion, is with us yet. As with *graphology* there are problems in condemning physiognomy outright as nonsense since we all naturally make judgements about people (not all erroneous) on the basis of their facial appearance, while Lavater's idea that form reflects essence is not entirely mistaken either – if we replace 'essence' with 'function', it is pretty accurate. Rendering it 'scientific', however, is quite another matter, especially as facial appearance is also determined by genetically governed bone structure and musculature. Physiognomy is not to be confused with its contemporary **phrenology** although many popular nineteenth-century texts on phrenology combined them. Phrenology has received much more attention from historians of Psychology due its more obviously 'scientific' aspirations and its place in the history of the study of brain functioning. The only English biography of Lavater seems to be one anonymously published in 1848 or 1849, while Hartley (2001) is the only substantial book-length study. Gilman (1996) on physiognomical depictions of the insane also merits at least a browse.

References

Anon (1848 or 1849) *The Life of John Kaspar Lavater, Minister of St. Peter's Church, Zurich*, London: Religious Tract Society.

Gilman, S.L. (1996) *Seeing the Insane*, Introduction by E.T. Carlson, Lincoln, NE: University of Nebraska Press.

Hartley, L. (2001) *Physiognomy and the Meaning of Expression in Nineteenth-Century Culture*, Cambridge: Cambridge University Press.

Lavater, J.-C. (1789–98) *Essays on Physiognomy, Designed to Promote the Love and the Knowledge of Mankind*, trans. H. Hunter, London: John Murray.

Tytler, G. (1981) *Physiognomy in the European Novel: Faces and Fortunes*, Ewing, NJ: Princeton University Press.

PHYSIOMORPHISM

A term introduced by the French anthropologist Claude Lévi-Strauss (Lévi-Strauss, (1966) to refer to the opposite of **anthropomorphism**.

The psychological assimilation of, identification with, or introjection of, properties found in the external world. Thus external phenomena such as coldness, hardness and slipperiness enable us to identify ourselves and others as cold, hard or slippery in a psychological sense. This was explored at length by the present author particularly in relation to the evidence provided by everyday psychological language and the nature of human psychological evolution (Richards, 1989).

References

Lévi-Strauss, C. (1966) *The Savage Mind*, London: Weidenfeld & Nicolson.
Richards, G. (1989) *On Psychological Language and the Physiomorphic Basis of Human Nature*, London: Routledge.

PIAGETIAN THEORY

From the 1920s till the 1970s, the Swiss psychologist Jean Piaget (1896–1980) (see **Schools of Psychology**: *Geneva School*) developed a complex and detailed 'stage theory' of child development, with a special interest in the growth of the child's knowledge and understanding of the world ('*genetic epistemology*'). His works in this field, often co-authored with close associates, covered a wide range of topics such as language, thinking and reasoning, morality (see also **moral development**) and the concept of causality. Many remain still to be translated into English. Piagetian theory has been contested on a number of grounds. First are those who have challenged the 'stage' approach generally, whether Piagetian, Psychoanalytic or any other (see also **development**). Second, its universality has been questioned on the basis of cross–cultural research. Third, it has been accused of neglecting the social nature of child development, particularly in contrast to Vygotsky's approach (see **zone of proximal development**). In the course of his work, Piaget introduced or deployed a number of technical concepts (see also **schema**). We should begin with the four 'stages' developmental themselves:

1 *Sensori-motor stage.* Period up to about 2 years of age during which the child acquires the basic 'schemata of action' – grasping, hand co-ordination, walking, etc. – and shifts from a simple reflex mode of behaving to having a structured or organised system of action. During this process it also comes to understand the permanent existence (*conservation*) of objects, though not of quantitative physical properties such as volume.

2 *Pre-operational stage*. The second developmental stage from c.2 years to c.7 years. sub-divided into 'pre-conceptual' (up to c.4 years) and 'intuitive thinking' stages. This sees the child's language maturing, and a gradual shift from an *egocentric* position to one which can take account of others and engage in social relationships. However, it still does not use logical operations, relying primarily on perception, especially during the pre-conceptual period. In the intuitive thinking phase, the child begins to form concepts and acquires some insight into *reversibility* and quantitative *conservation* in relation to specific situations as well as discovering more complex ways of combining schemata.

3 *Concrete operations*. Third stage of child development from c.7 years to 11 or 12 years. Its key feature is mastery of logical classification systems facilitating fully 'operational' modes of behaving. The child acquires the concepts of causality, conservation (as a general principle), spatial relationships and, of central importance, the general 'reversibility' of operations. Nevertheless its behaviour and understanding relates only to 'concrete' physical situations.

4 *Formal operations*. Final stage of child development from c.11 years onwards. Only at this stage does the child acquire fully abstract, formal and conceptual thought and the ability reflexively to perform 'operations on operations' and engage in hypothesis testing. It also acquires a formal understanding of logic and the use of linguistic propositions. How far full acquisition of formal operations is universally achieved is a matter of some dispute, and clearly some levels of abstract thinking (especially in mathematics and formal logic) elude the majority of people!

It cannot be too highly stressed that in Piaget's account this gradual transition from neonate reflex action to formal operations is a dynamic process in which the overall structure is constantly changing (at variable rates) as the insufficiencies or inadequacies of current schemata and operations manifest themselves and require further modification (see *accommodation, assimilation* below). It is the features and principles of this active process which most Piagetian research actually addresses:

- *accommodation*. Change in the existing structure of schemata and operations when this proves incongruent with experience.
- *assimilation*. The application of an existing schema to the construal of an experience. In other words, the object or event is treated as belonging to an existing category or can be appropriately dealt with using an operation already acquired.

- *décollage*. A phase of instability or loss of equilibrium in the structure of schemata and operations.
- *equilibration*. Re-establishment of stability in the structure of schemata and operations following *accommodation*. This cycle of assimilation, décollage, accommodation and equilibration constitutes the basic dynamic of cognitive development and change.
- *conservation/constancy/invariance*. The principle that quantities of matter, weight and volume remain the same despite changes in form (usually acquired in that order). The classic test for conservation of matter involves transferring a liquid between containers (e.g. glasses) of difference shapes or sizes, usually varying in height–breadth ratio. Children lacking understanding of conservation will judge quantity simply by height of the liquid's surface in the container.
- *egocentricity*. Inability to adopt the position or viewpoint of another person. Characteristic of children up to the *pre-operational stage* phase. Typically, the egocentric child will be unable to understand that, for example, someone in a different position cannot see something visible to itself due to an intervening object.
- *operations*. Logically structured schemata acquired during and after the *concrete operations stage*. Prior to this the child is reliant on a repertoire of specific behavioural schemata and concepts which, though becoming increasingly complex and integrated, is not used in a systematically logical fashion.

There is a huge literature on Piaget, but a number of useful basic introductions were published during the 1960s and 1970s, of which Boden (1979) and Flavell (1963) remain among the most accessible. A monumental examination of his mature theory in both its Psychological and philosophical aspects is Vuyk (1981), a further collection of evaluations and critiques is and Modgill and Modgill (1982). Of Piaget's own works (Piaget, [1926] 1962) remains a helpful introduction to the spirit of his approach while his mature theoretical position is most conveniently presented in Piaget (1971, 1972a, 1972b). Finally, it should be stressed that Piaget's aims extended beyond understanding child development as such to the much broader philosophical issue of the very nature of knowledge itself. He identified the tradition in which he was working as *structuralist*. In that respect his Psychological research was intended to provide an empirical scientific grounding for what was ultimately a philosophical theory.

References and further reading

Boden, M. (1979) *Piaget: Outline and Critique of his Theory*, London: Fontana
Flavell, J.H. (1963) *The Developmental Psychology of Jean Piaget*, Princeton, NJ: Van Nostrand.
Modgill, S. and Modgill, C. (eds) (1982) *Jean Piaget: Consensus and Controversy*, London: Routledge and Kegan Paul.
Piaget, J. ([1926] 1962) *The Language and Thought of the Child*, London: Routledge and Kegan Paul.
—— (1971) *Structuralism*, London: Routledge & Kegan Paul.
—— (1972a) *The Principles of Genetic Epistemology*, London: Routledge & Kegan Paul.
—— (1972b) *Psychology and Epistemology. Towards a Theory of Knowledge*, Harmondsworth: Penguin.
Siegel, L.S. and Brainerd, C.J. (eds) (1978) *Alternatives to Piaget: Critical Essays on the Theory*, New York: Academic Press.
Vuyk, R. (1981) *Overview and Critique of Piaget's Genetic Epistemology 1965–1980*, 2 vols, London: Academic Press.

POSITIVISM

Coined by the early nineteenth-century French philosopher Auguste Comte (1798–1857) to denote his own philosophical system which centred on a highly progressivist and pro-scientific vision (culminating in an ill-fated attempt at founding a new 'Religion of Humanity' with its own temples, etc.), the term has subsequently undergone a number of modifications and mutations. In late nineteenth-century philosophy of science, exemplified in the work of German physicist Ernst Mach, it was given a rigorous reformulation. Essentially, Mach argued, science is about data and their most parsimonious, preferably mathematical, description. Phenomena are knowable only by the sense-data they produce, hence Mach's positivism was opposed to *Realism* – the assumption that there is a real world independent of our efforts to know it – as entirely redundant for scientific purposes. This approach also entailed a version of **operationalism**; there is, for example, no such 'thing' as time in the abstract, only readings of clock measurements, a notion which played an important role in Albert Einstein's formulation of the Special Theory of Relativity (1905). By the 1920s, positivism was becoming the leading European philosophical movement under the title 'Logical Positivism', initially centred in Vienna. This sought systematic, formally logical, definitions and accounts of good scientific method, the nature of knowledge and linguistic meaning. Their main targets were what they saw as pseudo-sciences (such as Marxism) and old-style philosophical metaphysics (which they considered meaningless). Despite their efforts, certain issues defied the logical resolution they sought. In his 1934 *Logik der Forschung* (trans. 1954), Karl Popper challenged a central tenet known as 'the verification criterion of meaning' on the grounds that empirical propositions can never be definitively verified, only falsified. By the 1960s, classical logical positivism was under severe pressure on two main fronts. The 'linguistic turn' in English-speaking philosophy was undermining its account of language (even though this turn itself emerged from logical positivism) while philosophers and historians of science (such as T. Kuhn, P. Feyerabend, N. Hanson, S. Toulmin and others) were subverting its image of the nature of science. The upshot has been that although certain positivist doctrines and concepts have entered the philosophy of science repertoire, the term itself can no longer be said to denote a specific school. Rather, it has become a more rhetorical way of referring to ardent commitment to 'hard' scientific methods and modes of theorising. What has all this to do with Psychology? It actually has quite a close bearing on how Psychology developed during the twentieth century because, anxious to demonstrate its 'hard' scientific credentials, psychologists were especially prone to take notice of what philosophers of science were saying about what constituted good scientific methods and theorising. Central to this was an obsession with measurement, greatly reinforced by the Ernst Mach tradition. The discipline thus became widely infused with the general positivist ethos and attitude from the 1920s– 1960s and an awareness of this background factor is necessary if one is to fully understand what psychologists were then up to and why, both opponents of the approach as well as supporters. Perhaps ironically both positivists and realists are now in a loose alliance against **social constructionism**. For recent evaluations of logical positivism, see Friedman (1999) and Weinberg (2001).

References

Friedman, M. (1999) *Reconsidering Logical Positivism*, Cambridge: Cambridge University Press.
Weinberg, J.R. (2001) *An Examination of Logical Positivism*, London: Routledge.

POST-FREUDIAN/NEO-FREUDIAN

The difference between these is a little subtle. Usually post-Freudian refers to those who, while starting from Freud's **psychoanalysis**, then made radical departures from central doctrines. These were frequently American or US-based and typically rejected Freud's thesis that *all* behaviour was ultimately in the service of the *Id* or *pleasure principle* (see psychoanalysis sub-entries), introducing the term *ego-autonomy* for functioning they considered transcended this. E. H. Erikson also argued that there were eight developmental stages extending throughout life, and saw **adolescence** as a pivotal phase (Erikson, [1950] 1965). In various ways, the post-Freudians seem to have been offering more optimistic versions of Psychoanalysis consistent with US cultural values. Another group, such as K. Horney, began revising the Psychoanalytic account of women's psychology, a trend which by the early 1970s had become a major theme in feminist Psychology. This, however, spanned both categories. Neo-Freudian, by contrast, refers to those who were less heretical and continued to try and develop Psychoanalytic theory in its own terms. While this sometimes took radical forms (e.g. **object relations theory**), those in this camp saw, and see, themselves as firmly in the Freudian tradition. This category also includes the work of the French analyst Lacan. Brown ([1961] 1964) remains a handy introduction to the post-Freudians but see also Frosh (1999). There are no comparable surveys of the neo-Freudians as a group except Birnbach (1961). As well as the Object Relations School, H.S. Sullivan, Michael Balint and David Rapaport are among the most eminent. The term is sometimes also rather loosely used for Alfred Adler, C.G. Jung and even Anna Freud herself, Erich Fromm properly belongs in the post-Freudian camp in my opinion, though he too is sometimes so described.

References

Birnbach, M. (1961) *Neo-Freudian Social Philosophy*, Stanford, CA: Stanford University Press.

Brown, J.A.C. ([1961] 1964) *Freud and the Post-Freudians*, Harmondsworth: Penguin. There is also a 2004 reprint by Free Association Books (London)

Erikson, E.H. ([1950]1965) *Childhood and Society*, Harmondsworth: Penguin.

Frosh, S. (1999) *The Politics of Psychoanalysis: An Introduction to Freudian and Post-Freudian Theory*, New York: New York University Press.

POST-TRAUMATIC STRESS DISORDER (PTSD)

Although PTSD has only received wide public attention in the past few decades, it has an interesting history. Veterans of the Napoleonic Wars in the early 1800s suffered 'cannonball wind', in the late 1800s 'railway spine' was common among survivors of train crashes (which were then quite frequent) and during the First World War (1914–18) the best-known antecedent, 'shell shock', was identified. There was, however, a great deal of controversy about the latter two of these as to whether they were physiological or psychological conditions. Since insurance companies would only pay out for physical damage, the development of psychological understanding of 'railway spine' was greatly inhibited. The question then became the centre of heated debate regarding 'shell shock', with head-on confrontation between the two camps. (Incidentally, although the British side of the story is well known, German, Austrian and Italian doctors also diagnosed it.) After 1918, it rather fell from view, but interest revived in the Second World War under the term 'combat stress', before declining again after 1945. Only in the last quarter of the twentieth century did attention begin to be paid to effects of trauma among civilians, PTSD entering the **DSM** in the 1980 DSM III. PTSD is generally viewed as a normal response to external traumatic events, and can take a variety of forms such as **depression**, **panic attacks**, preoccupation with reliving the event and inability to function properly in work settings and social relationships. By the end of the last century PTSD **counselling** was becoming routinely offered to survivors of trauma in most 'first world' countries. The concept has undoubtedly played a role in combating the feelings of guilt and shame that trauma survivors have often felt. Nevertheless it remains in some regards problematic. There is widespread scepticism about the value of PTSD counselling. More seriously, its value has been questioned as being too broad a category since the effects of traumatic child abuse and torture, for example, are of quite a different order and character to those experienced by survivors of accidents or witnesses of very upsetting events. It is, however, acknowledged that not all effects of trauma can be included in the PTSD category, some indeed taking genuinely pathological forms. Bereavement, unless under unexpected or exceptionally unpleasant circumstances, is not usually considered a cause of PTSD, its consequences being the province of grief or bereavement counselling.

References and further reading

Brewin, C.R. (2003) *Post-Traumatic Stress Disorder: Malady or Myth?* New Haven, CT: Yale University Press.

Schiraldi, G.R. (2000) *Post-Traumatic Stress Disorder Sourcebook*, New York: McGraw-Hill.

Scott, M.J. and Palmer, S. (2000) *Trauma and Post-Traumatic Stress Disorder*, London: Cassell.

Scott, M.J. and Stradling, S.G. (2006) *Counselling for Post-Traumatic Stress Disorder*, London: Sage.

PRAGMATISM

An American school of philosophy initially formulated by C.S. Peirce then adopted by William James and John Dewey. The precise relationship between their different versions is complex and a matter of continued debate. While it is difficult to do justice to pragmatism in a succinct fashion, its central thrust is that the real-life consequences of an idea, theory or doctrine provide the criteria for accepting its truth. 'A distinction which makes no difference is no difference.' This principle had several targets. In the first place it was aimed at abstract metaphysical philosophical concepts and propositions such as 'The Absolute is Unknowable'. Second, in doing this, it sought to reformulate the notion of 'truth' itself, and the limits of applicability of the concept. Third, especially in William James's version, it left the door open for accepting that people could have a wide range of religious and philosophical beliefs, given the beneficial consequences of their doing so. The term 'pluralism' was widely used, not least by James himself, to describe this. The pragmatist vision greatly informed subsequent twentieth-century developments in both philosophy and Psychology, its influence being visible in **operationalism**, the philosophical movement logical positivism, later British linguistic philosophy and more recently **mutualism**. This brief list indicates how varied have been the conclusions which have been drawn from pragmatist insights. In the USA, the pragmatist philosophical tradition continues, particularly in the works of Richard Rorty and Hilary Putnam.

References and further reading

Gallie, W.B. (1952) *Peirce and Pragmatism*, Harmondsworth: Penguin, also rep. 1975 by Greenwood Press (Westport, CT).
Goodman, R.B. (2005) *Pragmatism: Critical Concepts in Philosophy*, London: Routledge.
Malachowski, A. (ed.) (2004) *Pragmatism*, 3 vols, London: Sage.
Shook, J.R. (ed.) (2006) *A Companion to Pragmatism*, Oxford: Blackwell.

PREJUDICE

A very general term referring to the, usually negative, 'prejudging' of unknown others on the basis of some visible (or aural) feature such as skin colour, dress, age, gender, facial hair, possession of tattoos, accent, or body build. Analogously to the term '**racism**', many of these forms of prejudice have over recent years been labelled with the suffix '-ism', such as 'sexism', 'ageism' and 'fattism'. In Psychology, the topic began to receive attention from social psychologists in the 1930s, as a facet of the study of **attitudes**, 'race prejudice' being in the forefront of their concerns. A large amount of work was published during the next few decades but the classic text from this period was Allport (1954). For a more recent work, see Nelson (2005).

References

Allport, G.W. (1954) *The Nature of Prejudice*, Reading, MA: Addison-Wesley.
Nelson, T.D. (2005) *The Psychology of Prejudice*, 2nd edn, Harlow: Pearson Education.

PREMENSTRUAL TENSION (PMT)

Irritability and anxiety often affecting women in the days preceding menstruation. Received widespread publicity and attention from feminist Psychologists during the 1970s and 1980s. Little heard before the 1970s (although some Psychological research on the menstrual cycle itself had been done in the 1930s), the term 'PMT' rapidly entered the popular vocabulary thereafter. This was not of course because it was in any way a new phenomenon but because, like all issues related to menstruation, public discussion of the topic had hitherto been largely taboo, albeit surrounded with much folk myth.

PRESENTISM

Uncritically viewing things from the perspective and values of the present-day, assuming the present represents 'normality'. Used by historians and critical psychologists. In history of science (including history of Psychology), this can lead to simplistic *progressivism* in which current knowledge is assumed to be the successful end result of all previous work. In fields such as Social Psychology and Child Psychology, it can result in a narrowing of understanding of the true range or scale of the phenomenon in question and unquestioned moral assumptions. More broadly, however, it can result in blind acceptance of the current culturally, or even politically, set priorities and agendas in setting research goals, rather than reflecting on these priorities and agendas themselves.

PRIMACY EFFECT

The superior recall of the first stimuli to which the organism is exposed. For example, the first words in a word-list in a memory experiment. It is though more general than this, manifesting itself in the tendency to better recall the first occasion on which we had a particular experience of almost any kind. In association with the **recency effect**, this means that in, say, learning a lengthy word-list, it is the first and last words which are most easily remembered.

PRIMAL THERAPY

One of the numerous 'alternative' approaches to **psychotherapy** which emerged in the late 1960s (John Lennon flirting with it at one point). Devised by Arthur Janov, primal therapy centred on the need for clients to regress to the point where they reactivated their first traumatic experience of loss or rejection, usually by a parent. This was marked by their emission of the 'primal scream', and this in turn was related to the birth trauma itself. Janov claimed that having undergone this, people shifted to a new 'post-primal' phase of psychological well-being. Over the years, primal therapy became increasingly cultish and Janov's ambitions and claims for it progressively more inflated.

Reference

Janov, A. (1970) *The Primal Scream, Primal Therapy: The Cure for Neurosis*, New York: Putnam's.
—— (1992) *New Primal Scream: Primal Therapy 20 Years on*, Wokingham, Berks: Kaplan.

PRIMING

Usually used as an experimental technique in **Cognitive Psychology** and to a lesser extent Social Psychology. This exploits the phenomenon in which processing of a stimulus is changed following presentation of another stimulus. Thus, in the study of language processing, semantic, phonological (sound) and repetition priming can be deployed. Presentation of the priming stimulus may be subliminal (**subliminal perception**). In Social Psychology, priming frequently takes the form of presentation of a **stereotype** or **attitude**-related stimulus.

PRISONER'S DILEMMA

Each isolated prisoner is told: 'Here's the deal. You confess and your partner in the other cell doesn't – you go free, he takes the full rap of 5 years. You both confess and you both get a reduced sentence of 4 years. You both refuse to confess and we have to convict you on a lesser charge for 2 years.' The dilemma here is obviously that if you do not confess, you risk doing the full sentence if the other prisoner confesses, but if you do confess, you still risk going to prison for a substantial time as well as sending your non-confessing partner down for the full stretch, or as one source succinctly puts it: 'The "dilemma" faced by the prisoners here is that, whatever the other does, each is better off confessing than remaining silent. But the outcome obtained when both confess is worse for each than the outcome they would have obtained had both remained silent' (*Stanford Encyclopedia of Philosophy* – this has an excellent review of the topic, available via www.prisoners-dilemma.com). A number of variants of this have been devised since it was originally thought up in the 1950s by people working on **Game Theory** for the Rand corporation, the name itself, and this specific form, being given by Albert Tucker. It has continued to fascinate psychologists ever since as it can be seen to have bearings on decision-making, tensions between individual and group interests, **altruism**, and in, some versions, evolutionary processes.

PROBLEM-SOLVING

Problem-solving tasks have figured prominently in **Gestalt** and **Cognitive Psychology**, as a research tool for studying practical reasoning and **cognitive style**. Although a research topic in its own right, it is now more commonly treated as an overt behavioural expression or manifestation of cognitive processes which lends itself to experimental manipulation in a way which can illuminate these.

PROJECTIVE TESTS

A collective term for all Psychological tests which require the taker to respond to the stimulus material in an open-ended imaginative or creative fashion, typically by describing a visual image, telling a story, completing a sentence, creating a picture or arranging models to create a scene. The assumption is that in doing so they will reveal their own needs, anxieties, modes of thinking, etc. In some cases the administrator will be more active, asking specific questions regarding characters depicted. This is more usual with tests designed for children. Methods of scoring and underlying theoretical assumptions vary considerably. The most famous projective test is the **Rorschach test** in which symmetrical ink-blots are presented, also widely known and used is Henry Murray's original **thematic apperception test (TAT)**. An early (1926) 'Draw-a-Man Test' devised by US psychologist Florence Goodenough was originally intended to measure child **intelligence** but also later given a projective spin (Machover, 1949). Although dating much back earlier, e.g. to C.G. Jung's word association method, first reported in 1905, projective tests enjoyed a great vogue from the late 1930s into the 1960s and continue to be used for some purposes, however, the creation of new tests significantly declined after about 1970. The use of projective tests has been two-fold. Initially, they were seen primarily as a way of assessing personality and for psychiatric diagnosis, quite quickly, however, they came to be used as therapeutic techniques in their own right, and some were designed for this purpose. Methodologically the main problem with the former use was that of reliable scoring, which played a major part in their decline as a research tool. As well as the Rorschach and TAT, the following may be noted as among the most widely used projective tests, although there are numerous others.

- *Blacky test*. A set of pictures depicting a cartoon dog, Blacky, in a variety of situations. These were designed for use with children and are based on Psychoanalytic principles (**psychoanalysis**) to tap into the child's feelings about sexuality, siblings, parental anger, etc. Invented by Blum (1950).
- *Child Thematic Apperception Test*. Introduced by Bellak (1954). The child is presented with pictures which it has to describe. Two versions were devised, one with animal figures, the other with humans, although the situations depicted were the same.
- *Make a Picture Story Test (MAPS)*. Devised by Shneidman (1947, 1952), this consists of a set of backgrounds (a street, a bedroom, a bridge, a raft adrift at sea, etc.) and a large set of cut-out figures depicting people of

various ages, types and dress (or lack of it), plus the odd animal, a ghost, a 'Superman' type, and so forth. The person taking the test is asked to place these on a succession of backgrounds and describe what is going on. Shneidman claimed that certain kinds of response were especially significant, such as having any figure other than the ghost off the ground, including large numbers of figures in the same picture and placing the prone injured man figure in any background other than the street scene. Great fun but now curiously dated, strongly evoking 1950s America. One boggles at what a contemporary version might look like with a rock guitarist, an astronaut (presumably also permissible off the ground!), a hoody and a woman church minister, etc. etc.!

- *Mosaic test*. Following the *World test*, Margaret Lowenfeld (1954) devised a more convenient test, usable with adults as well as children, which consists of a large number of small tiles of various bright colours and shapes, the client being required to make a design out of these. This has proved one of the more enduring tests and lends itself to diagnostic uses.

- *Symonds Picture Story Tests*. Symonds (1949) designed several TAT type tests for use with adolescents and children. These differed from Murray's TAT pictures in showing quite ordinary scenes from everyday life, particularly as it pertained to teenagers.

- *World test*. Introduced in her child therapy practice by British-based psychotherapist Margaret Lowenfeld in 1929, and first published in Lowenfeld (1939). A large number of small model figures of people, buildings and numerous other objects enable the client (usually a child) to create a 'world' in a sand-pit. Primarily a therapeutic technique. Related to other 'play therapy' methods used with children. Also sometimes called *sand-play*, especially in the USA.

While projective tests have a continued place in Psychology and psychotherapy, they have proved difficult to use in a rigorously **psychometric** fashion primarily because they are so rich in the responses they elicit and so hard to render quantifiable in a reliable way. Interpretation of responses is also rendered problematic by the fact that it is often unclear which 'level', as it were, they are tapping. They do, however, perhaps represent psychologists giving free rein to their more creative and imaginative side.

References and further reading

Anderson, H.H. and Anderson, G.L. (1951) *An Introduction to Projective Techniques*, New York: Prentice-Hall.

Bellak, L. (1954) *The Thematic Apperception Test and the Children's Apperception Test in Clinical Use*. New York: Grune & Stratton.

Blum, G.S. (1950) *The Blacky Pictures: A Technique for the Exploration of Personality Dynamics*. New York: Psychological Corporation.

Lowenfeld, M. (1939) 'The World Pictures of Children: A Method of Recording and Studying Them', *British Journal of Medical Psychology*, 18(1): 65–101. See also: www.sandplay.org/index.htm

—— (1954) *The Lowenfeld Mosaic Test*, London: Newman Neame.

Machover, K. (1949) *Personality Projection in the Drawing of the Human Figure*. Springfield, IL: Charles C. Thomas.

Shneidman, E.S. (1947) 'The Make-a-Picture-Story (MAPS) Projective Personality Test: A Preliminary Report', *Journal of Consulting Psychology*, 11: 315–25.

—— (1951) *Thematic Test Analysis*. New York: Grune & Stratton.

Symonds, P.M. ([1949] 1965) *Adolescent Fantasy: An Investigation of the Picture-Story Method of Personality Study*, New York: Columbia University Press.

Useful website

www.cohendelara.com/publicaties/history.htm is a handy on-line history of projective testing.

PRO-SOCIAL BEHAVIOUR

Rather a jargon-like term used in Social Psychology for all helpful and supportive social behaviour. Related to **altruism**, but without any motivational connotations.

PSYCHEDELIC

This term was widely popularised in the 1960s by the ex-Harvard psychologist Timothy Leary in his promotion of the use of LSD-25 (lysergic acid) and other drugs to induce altered states of consciousness variously described as heightened, expanded or deepened. It rapidly spread from being used of the states themselves to art, music and writing produced under their influence or inspired by them. Soon any art which was very colourful, complicated, weird and whirling came to be called 'psychedelic'. It has now rather fallen into disuse and, in psychopharmacology, the term **psychotropic** is generally used.

PSYCHOANALYSIS

Forever associated with the name of its founder, the Viennese psychiatrist/neurologist Sigmund Freud (1856–1939), psychoanalysis became the single most culturally influential school of twentieth-century Psychological thought. Having said that, psychoanalysis is virtually a separate discipline its own right, never taken seriously by many academic, experimental and applied psychologists. The literature on it is vast and the references are thus highly selective. For the main Psychoanalytic concepts, see next entry.

The theory of psychoanalysis

Although Freud's theorising went through several stages, some involving fairly radical revisions, its key features may be summarised as follows. (1) All human behaviour is rooted in a single source – variously called the sex-instinct, libido or 'pleasure principle', during the 1920s, however, he added an opposing 'death' instinct ('Thanatos') and the term 'Eros' often became used for the sex-instinct. (2) These instincts, the energy source for all psychological phenomena, are **unconscious** and thus inaccessible in principle to full direct awareness, the 'wishes' they generate are also totally amoral and irrationally contradictory. (3) Opposing the 'pleasure principle' (and also the 'death instinct') is the 'reality principle', the real-life conditions in which gratification has to be achieved. It is in this encounter between unconscious instincts and the reality principle that human consciousness is generated. (4) From this scenario it follows that the very early stages of life are crucially important and the detail of psychoanalytic theory is concerned with tracing and analysing both the developmental stages by which infants become adults and the numerous strategies and mechanisms which are adopted and used in negotiating this path. (5) While access to the unconscious is necessarily indirect, it can be achieved by decoding the meanings of dreams, parapraxes (or 'Freudian slips'), irrational habits and neurotic symptoms, etc. This, however, requires psychoanalytic training.

Origins of psychoanalysis

Freud's theory arose in Vienna in the context of treating psychiatric patients and was part of a broader shift towards **psychotherapy** occurring in the late nineteenth and early twentieth centuries. Among other things such an approach enabled the psychologically distressed to seek professional medical help without the stigma of 'madness' or degeneration (**degenerationism**), this naturally being especially important for the middle and upper classes. There is, however, a huge hinterland of both 'pre-history' and similar contemporary ideas, regarding the concept of the unconscious, the role of sexuality, and use of psychotherapeutic methods. (The French psychiatrist Pierre Janet (1859–1947) was especially significant, and has been rather unfairly overshadowed by Freud.) The classic work on this historical background is Henri F. Ellenberger's *The Discovery of the Unconscious* (Ellenberger, 1970), but see also Schwartz (1999). While it soon became a general Psychological theory, psychoanalysis thus began as a medical theory concerning treatment of neuroses and other psychopathologies. The traditional medical 'case history' approach also continued to underpin its methodology. The non-experimental character of psychoanalysis was thus not in itself 'unscientific', but due to its source in a branch of medical science not, at that time, of an experimental kind. Although preceded by several crucial journal papers, Freud's first book was *The Interpretation of Dreams* (Freud, 1954) (first German edition 1900 as *Die Traumdeutung*). For the flavour of Freud's writing and early views of Psychoanalysis, the 'Five Lectures on Psycho-Analysis' of 1910 is most accessible (these are included in Freud, 1962).

Related schools

Several of Freud's early associates and disciples, along with numerous, variously sympathetic or rebellious, later psychotherapists developed alternative or variant theories. The most famous is Carl Gustav Jung (1875–1961). The extent to which he was ever an uncritical disciple of Freud has been exaggerated in the past. His own ideas began to develop prior to his relationship with Freud and their association lasted barely a decade. Jung's **Analytical Psychology** is a distinct theory in its own right and should not be considered simply as a variant of psychoanalysis. Analytical psychology became more marginalised in academic Psychology than even psychoanalysis during the late twentieth century, but for a recent, well-received, re-evaluation of Jung's place in modern Psychology, relocating him more centrally, see Shamdasani (2003). Alfred Adler (1870–1937) called his theory **Individual Psychology** and this again departed widely from Psychoanalysis. By the mid-twentieth century the list of related approaches had become quite lengthy, ranging from Wilhelm Reich's bizarre 'orgone' theory to Melanie Klein's **object relations** school in Britain, Jacques Lacan in France and several major US-based figures such as Erik Erikson,

Karen Horney and Erich Fromm. These are usually sub-classified as **neo-Freudians** and **post-Freudians** depending on how far they remained within the Freudian theoretical framework. During the 1970s and 1980s, several feminist writers, therapists and psychologists (e.g. Juliet Mitchell and Susan Miller) revisited psychoanalytic ideas and sought to recast the theory in a less male-centred or patriarchal fashion.

Cultural impact

Although originating in Vienna, and clearly having a considerable, if patchy, impact in Central Europe, by the 1920s it was in the English-speaking world that psychoanalysis was receiving most attention. To simplify very schematically, this impact was in three directions: (1) within psychiatry, psychotherapy and Psychology themselves; (2) among intellectuals, artists, dramatists and film-makers; and (3) on religion. In Britain, the most intense period of popular interest was during the 1920s, even *The Times* inveighing against its sinister influence, after which its presence became stabilised. A further phase of mainstream British Psychological influence came in the 1930s when three major female figures, Melanie Klein, Anna Freud and Susan Isaacs, were promoting its value in the contexts of child development, education and child psychotherapy. In the 1950s, its place in British culture faded considerably and after the 1960s it has remained but one strand in the wider psychotherapy and counselling world. In the United States, there was also a brief, but less intense, period of early interest from around 1910 to the 1920s but its main heyday came in the immediate post-Second World War period, when it grew to dominate psychiatry in a way never matched elsewhere. Only towards the end of the 1960s did this slowly decline with the advent of new psychopharmacological methods of treatment and rising competition from the home-grown psychotherapeutic approaches often generically referred to as the **growth movement**. The major impact of psychoanalysis, however, surely lies at the linguistic level, for terms and expressions such as *ego, repression, Oedipus Complex, projecting one's anger, super ego, the unconscious, fixation, Freudian slip* and many more have become part of our everyday language for thinking about ourselves. See also the entry on **psychology of religion** for its influence on religious thought.

Criticism of psychoanalysis

Controversial from the outset, psychoanalysis as a theory and Freud himself have attracted perennial criticism, with popular best-sellers such as Eysenck's *Decline and Fall of the Freudian Empire* (Eysenck, 1985) and Richard Webster's *Why Freud was Wrong* (Webster, 1995) periodically declaring psychoanalysis dead and buried. The criticisms of psychoanalysis are of three main types. First are technical and theoretical criticisms of its merits as a scientific theory. Second are criticisms of Freud's personal character and honesty. Third are basically ethical attacks on its pernicious cultural influence and the image of human nature it offers. These cannot be evaluated here, but one important observation is that the first at least may be countered by arguing that we (including Freud himself) have perhaps been mistaken about the kind of creation psychoanalysis is. If failing in a number of respects as an orthodox scientific theory, the very fact that its image of human nature *has* elicited such a profound range of responses and permeated culture so widely is in itself a psychological fact, requiring that it be taken seriously on those grounds alone. Perhaps indeed it is more akin to an ideology or a religion in providing a framework of meanings for human experience rather than a scientific explanation for it. And maybe it had to *look* scientific in order to achieve this in the twentieth century. Finally, Freud's late and icily stoical *Civilization and Its Discontents* (Freud, 1930) is, in my personal opinion, one of the greatest and bravest works of the last century and should be read by everybody.

References and further reading

Appignanesi, L. and Forrester, J. (1992) *Freud's Women*, London: Weidenfeld & Nicolson.

Bouveresse, J. (1996) *Wittgenstein Reads Freud: The Myth of the Unconscious*, Ewing, NJ: Princeton University Press.

Ellenberger, H.F. (1970) *The Discovery of the Unconscious: The History and Evolution of Dynamic Psychiatry*, London: Allen Lane.

Eysenck, H.J. (1985) *The Decline and Fall of the Freudian Empire*, Harmondsworth: Penguin.

Forrester, J. (1997) *Dispatches from the Freud Wars: Psychoanalysis and its Passions*, Cumberland, RI: Harvard University Press.

Freud, S. ([1900] 1954) *The Interpretation of Dreams*, trans. of 8th German edn by J. Strachey, London: Allen & Unwin. (This is superior to the earlier A. A. Brill translation.)

—— (1930) *Civilization and its Discontents*, London: Hogarth Press.

—— (1962) *Two Short Accounts of Psychoanalysis*, Harmondsworth: Pelican.

—— (1986) *The Essentials of Psychoanalysis*, Introduction and Commentaries by Anna Freud. Harmondsworth: Penguin. (An anthology of basic writings.)

—— (1999) *The Interpretation of Dreams*, trans. J. Crick, Oxford: Oxford University Press.

Jones, E. (1955) *The Life and Work of Sigmund Freud*, 3 vols, London: Hogarth Press.

Mitchell, J. (1975) *Psychoanalysis and Feminism*, Harmondsworth: Penguin.

Schwartz, J. (1999) *Cassandra's Daughter: A History of Psychoanalysis*, New York: Viking.

Shamdasani, S. (2003) *Jung and the Making of Modern Psychology: The Dream of a Science*, Cambridge: Cambridge University Press.

Webster, R. (1995) *Why Freud Was Wrong: Sin, Science and Psychoanalysis*, London: HarperCollins.

PSYCHOANALYTIC CONCEPTS

The definition of psychoanalytic concepts can sometimes become problematic since their precise technical meanings often depend on their role within the wider version of psychoanalytic theory in which they occur. This varies both across time within Freud's own work and between different neo-Freudian and post-Freudian theorists. The following is intended as an initial guide only. Cross-referencing within this list is frequently necessary and not always indicated. For distinctively Jungian concepts and variant senses see **Analytical Psychology.** For what is still a most handy and intelligent dictionary of Psychoanalysis, see Rycroft (1972). While this coverage may seem extensive for what is now widely regarded as a failed theory, the Psychoanalytic vocabulary has so pervaded general popular and Psychological discourse that it remains extremely important.

- *abreaction.* Sudden eruption into consciousness of emotionally laden unconscious feelings in response to a particular situation or comment by someone else (notably the psychoanalyst). Abreactive responses are crucial as they compel the analysand to confront hitherto unconscious emotions.
- *ambivalence.* Having opposing or mixed emotions towards a person or object, most typically referring to 'love–hate relationships'. In psychoanalytic theory the infant's ambivalent feelings towards its parent or parents are a major factor driving psychological development, emergence of the *ego* resulting in part from its efforts at consciously resolving this tension.
- *anal phase.* The second of phase of infantile development during which libidinal pleasure centres on bowel functioning, typically expressed by fascination with faeces. Fixation at this level is held to have various consequences for future character traits depending on the form it takes. Severe toilet training, for example, may, it is

argued, result in an *anal retentive* character given to meanness, hoarding and secretiveness. (The personality effects of the various infantile fixations were explored by Freud's early follower Karl Abrahams.)

- *analysand.* A person undergoing psychoanalysis
- *catharsis.* An instance of *cathexis.*
- *cathexis.* General term for the process of gratifying emotionally intense wishes or desires ('cathecting' being the verb form).
- *censor.* The mechanism by which the ego prevents emotionally unacceptable unconscious wishes becoming fully conscious during dreams, typically converting them into disguised symbolic forms.
- *complex.* An unconscious system of unresolved emotional conflict and ambivalence centred on a specific issue. Thus the *Oedipus complex* revolves around an unresolved mixture of feelings of hate, love, fear, envy, etc. for a male's father.
- *condensation.* Compression of a multiplicity of meanings into a single dream symbol.
- *counter-transference.* The feelings which a psychoanalyst develops towards an analysand, typically in response to the analysand's 'transference'. For Freud himself this was a factor disrupting the analyst's objectivity, subsequently, however 'working with the counter-transference' became central to the psychoanalytic process since it was believed it could provide insights into the analysand and facilitated the analyst's own self-understanding. This assumed a major role in the analyst's own psychoanalysis or supervision sessions.
- *defence mechanisms.* General term for the various means, such as *repression* and *reaction-formation*, by which the ego prevents unwelcome unconscious material from becoming conscious
- *ego.* In Freud's final 'topological' model the ego is one of the three basic psychological structures, along with the *Id* and the *super ego*. It is the central integrating system which produces our identity or conscious personality, and is largely, if not entirely, conscious. It is the ego which strives to defend itself against and come to terms with the demands of the other systems and is in direct contact with reality (see *reality principle*). Both over- and under-defensiveness of the ego can have psychopathological consequences. The term *ego ideal* is often used to refer to the kind of person one would most like to be (see *super ego*).
- *Eros.* Synonym for the *pleasure principle*, used by Freud in his later writing as the opposite of *Thanatos*.
- *fixation.* Fixation occurs as a result of a developmental failure to move beyond a particular phase of psychosexual development. Thus fixation

at the anal phase might result in an enduring erotic fascination with issues related to excretion, and male fixation at the Oedipal phase with an enduring attraction to older women. Fixations may sometimes be more specific, e.g. an early erotic experience involving a particular item of clothing resulting in a life-long fetish.

• *Id*. The Id is the core unconscious instinctual energy-source driving all psychological functioning. The term was introduced by Freud in the later 'topological' version of his theory as one of the three basic psychological systems (the others being *the ego* and *super ego*), it is thus more or less synonymous with the *unconscious*. The goal of the Id is, for Freud, solely the attainment of erotic gratification or pleasure, hence the primacy of the *pleasure principle*.

• *identification* (see also *introjection* below and **identification**). Identification is particularly important in Psychoanalytic theory since it is held to be central to the resolution of the child's *complexes* regarding its parents. Typically a boy comes to identify primarily with his father and a girl with her mother, although the reverse also occurs to some extent.

• *introjection*. The internalisation of, and identification with, the emotions and attitudes of others, particularly those they express towards oneself. This is a central mechanism in the development of the *superego*, for example. The related term *identification* also generally refers to introjection of some else's perceived personality and interests as a whole. See also **object relations theory**

• *Jocasta complex*. Female equivalent of the *Oedipus complex*. Less clear-cut in its nature, however, and less elaborated theoretically. A central factor is the *castration complex*, much disputed by feminists, involving a belief by the infant female that she has been castrated and thus suffers from *penis envy*.

• *latency phase*. The developmental period between the age of about 7 years and puberty during which the wish for sexual gratification is in abeyance. Its onset is marked by the individual's resolution of the *Oedipus complex* (in the male case) or *Jocasta complex* (the female case).

• *libido*. Instinctive sexual energy. Someone who has apparently lost interest in sex may be described as suffering a 'loss of libido'. Strictly speaking, however, since this is, for Psychoanalysis, the root of all our motivational energies, albeit transformed in the course of development by *sublimation* and *defence mechanisms*, any loss of energy, such as that accompanying **depression** may be ascribed to a loss or weakening of libido. Used prior to introduction of the Id concept.

- *moratorium*. Used by some psychoanalysts and post-Freudians such as Erik Erikson to refer to any developmental phase in which creativity or ambitions, etc. lie fallow and invisible. Held to be due to an unconscious 'working through' of relevant issues or other developmental tasks of higher priority and considered quite normal.
- ***object–relations theory*** (see separate entry).
- *Oedipus complex*. Perhaps the most famous of Freud's concepts, this refers to the theory that infant males wish sexually to possess their mothers and kill their fathers. The anxieties produced by this generate the Oedipus complex, resolution of which it is a major developmental task, this occurring roughly during the fourth–eighth years. Oedipal anxieties are, however, rarely entirely allayed, their enduring character determining life-long attitudes towards, and relationships with, older men and women. The expression derives from the Greek story of Oedipus who, unwittingly, slew his father King Laius and married his mother Jocasta, becoming King of Thebes, the most famous version being Sophocles's play *Oedipus Rex*.
- *oral phase*. The earliest developmental phase in which the *libido* is centred on the mouth. During this phase the baby's primary mode of responding to external objects is to explore them orally. How this phase is experienced allegedly has profound effects on later personality development. Its importance is testified in numerous popular phrases such as 'its hard to swallow', 'being a sucker', 'tight-lipped' and 'tongue in cheek' as well as the etymology of 'gullible' (roughly meaning 'will swallow anything'). Interestingly many of these pertain in some way to trust and attitudes towards knowledge. More technically it has generated expressions such as *oral aggression* and *oral dependency* for personality traits traceable to this phase.
- *parapraxis* (pl. *parapraxes*). General term for what are commonly called 'Freudian slips'. An action which appears to go 'accidentally' awry, but which, on closer scrutiny, proves to express an unconscious, repressed, wish. Slips of the tongue and typing or writing errors are common forms of parapraxis – e.g. typing 'fiend' instead of 'friend' or calling a current partner by the name of a previous one in a fit of 'absent-mindedness'. The main theme of one of Freud's earliest and most popular works, *The Psychopathology of Everyday Life* (Freud, 1914). (Not all such errors are parapraxes. e. g. typing errors increase in later life simply due to poorer motor co-ordination.) The 1960s British film star Diana Fluck, better

known as Diana Dors, was once revisiting Swindon, her home town. The mayor, understandably anxious about saying her real name, nervously announced his great pleasure in welcoming Diana Clunt. The source of this particular parapraxis is hardly mysterious.

- *phallic symbol.* Any symbol occurring in a dream or work of art, etc. which is seen as representing a male penis or phallus.

- *pleasure principle.* The central psychoanalytic principle that all behaviour is ultimately aimed at obtaining pleasurable gratification. Synonymous with *Eros.* In his 1920 *Beyond the Pleasure Principle* (Freud, 1922) Freud proposed a major qualification to this, introducing the notion of the 'death instinct' or *Thanatos.*

- *pre-conscious.* In his earlier work, Freud used this to refer to the region below consciousness in which unrepressed memories were stored and remained accessible. Later replaced by 'subconscious'.

- *primary process thinking.* Thinking dominated by fundamental, infantile, instinctive wishes and goals. Fantasising about slaughtering people you dislike or giving full rein to your basic emotions is primary process thinking, as also is much sexual fantasy. When primary process thinking gives way to action, the consequences can be disastrous, especially if this occurs collectively as in mass panic, massacres and, at the individual level, rape, sexual abuse or murder. However, we all engage in it to some degree and doing so can, if monitored, keep us in touch with what is really going on in our unconscious.

- *projection.* (1) A defence mechanism which operates by 'projecting' repressed unconscious wishes and feelings onto others. (This is a common form of *primary process thinking.*) An individual might 'know' at some level that there is a wish to kill her mother, but cannot admit this wish to be hers, thus she might ascribe it to someone else, such as a brother or doctor. More typically we often 'project' our anger onto others, seeing them as hostile to us when in fact it is we who are angry with them. (2) At a more collective level the concept is used in psychoanalytic analyses of **prejudice** and **stereotyping,** where it is argued that social, ethnic, national or religious groups can come to project their own anxieties and repressed wishes onto other, usually minority, groups. In the case of Nazi anti-Semitism, for example, it was proposed that certain features of typical German child-rearing, combined with the historical trauma of defeat during the First World War, produced a high prevalence of repressed Oedipal fears and fantasies which were projected onto the Jews. The crucial twist is that this then facilitated the literal enactment of these violent 'primary process' fantasies against the Jews, resulting in their gratification. (3) Non-pathologically it is also held that when faced with ambiguous information or situations we all tend to perceive or interpret them in terms of our own unconscious emotions, values, interests, etc. This is the premise underlying many **projective tests**. These various senses are really different levels at which projection manifests itself, and should be understood as a continuum rather than distinct meanings.

- *reaction formation.* Defence mechanism in which the individual consciously adopts the opposite attitude towards another to the one they unconsciously feel. This might typically manifest itself in excessive expressions of love and affection towards a parent, and horrified denials of suggestions that they might feel otherwise. In Shakespeare's phrase, 'Methinks he doth protest too much.'

- *regression.* Returning to an earlier phase or stage of psychological development, e.g. 'infantile regression' may be said to occur when an adult throws tantrums and sulking fits. Such behaviour is not a necessary accompaniment for regression, however, which refers primarily to a psychological rather than a behavioural state. Regressive episodes are necessary for *repressed* material to become accessible during psychoanalysis.

- *repression.* A key psychoanalytical concept, repression denotes the mechanism whereby unwelcome experiences are expelled from consciousness into the unconscious. This differs from *suppression* crucially in that repression is itself unconscious. Repressed contents of the unconscious are central in causing neuroses. Examples would be the aggressively homophobic man whose homophobia results from repression of his own homosexual feelings, or the obsessionally clean individual who might, on a psychoanalytic reading, have repressed pleasurable feelings felt during the anal phase.

- *screen memory.* A memory which is actually symbolic of what actually happened, most often used to refer to apparently trivial early memories which as it were 'mask' witnessing parental sexual activity. Such memories can be analysed in the same way as dream symbols.

- *subconscious.* May be conceived of as a layer intervening between consciousness and the *unconscious*. The contents of the subconscious are not *repressed*, though may be *suppressed*. Basically, however, its contents are simply all those things to which we are not consciously attending. In that sense, it may be thought of as a long-term **memory** store.

- *sublimation.* The satisfactory resolution of unconscious desires by finding a healthy and socially acceptable outlet for them. Thus becoming a surgeon may represent a sublimation of deep sadistic impulses, or anal obsessiveness may be sublimated in a successful career in accountancy.

- *super ego*. Often loosely equated with the conscience, the super ego is a basic psychological system, along with the *ego* and *Id*. In Freudian theory, it emerges from the resolution of the *Oedipus complex* (or *Jocasta complex* in females) with the internalisation or *introjection* of the father's and/or mother's authority, or that of the figure who fulfils their role in the child's life. The super ego is not fully conscious and it is possible to be, as it were, victimised by an over-punitive super ego operating unconsciously. This may result in irrational guilt feelings. The super ego is double-faceted, on the one hand supplying positive moral principles and ideals, on the other, producing guilt and feelings of inadequacy for failing to live up to its demands. In addition to parental models, the super ego can have other sources in figures held up to the child as social ideals, such as religious leaders, folk heroes, esteemed acquaintances and figures from fiction. Particularly important figures of this kind can become *ego ideals*, persons one strives to emulate and be like or who encapsulate everything one admires.

- *suppression*. Unlike *repression*, this is not itself an unconscious process but the result of a more or less conscious decision 'not to think about it'. Suppression may be quite short-lived and occur for quite functional reasons such as in emergency situations and crises when the priority is dealing with immediate practical matters. If sustained for longer periods, however, suppression of emotions and memories for unpleasant incidents may cause psychological problems. These are, however, more easily resolved than those arising from *repression*.

- *Thanatos*. Introduced by Freud in *Beyond the Pleasure Principle* (Freud, 1922), Thanatos is also called the *death instinct*. It is the polar opposite of *Eros*. Freud developed a detailed theory that all living things had a deep instinct towards self-annihilation as an ultimate goal. The concept remained controversial and was in part a response to the slaughter of the First World War, which seemed to many psychoanalytic thinkers to be inexplicable in terms of the 'pleasure principle' or 'Eros' alone.

- *transference*. At some point during psychoanalysis the analysand invariably begins to cast the analyst in the same role as one of their parents (depending on the analyst's gender), thus replicating their emotional relationship to that parent. This is known as the 'transference' since it involves transferring their emotions from parent to analyst. See also *counter-transference*.

- *transitional object.* An object, typically adopted by the young child, which serves as a medium via which they can play out their psychological fantasies and unconscious feelings. It is an 'object' because it is clearly external to them, but serves an essentially psychological function as it is treated not as it 'really' is but as the target for *projection* and fantasy behaviour. Typical transitional objects include 'comfort blankets', teddy bears and particular dolls to which the child is extremely attached, and the loss or absence of which can cause great distress. Transitional objects are often not entirely abandoned even in adult life, sometimes being 'sentimentally' held onto throughout adulthood, even if no longer serving their original function. (My teddy bear is in a basket in the corner as I write. How sad is that?) An important concept in object relations theory.

- *unconscious* (see also **unconscious**). Really *the* fundamental concept in Psychoanalysis. Unlike the *subconscious*, the unconscious is in principle inaccessible to consciousness its contents only being manifested in symbolic, often disguised, forms. Dreams are the primary arena in which this happens and their psychoanalytic interpretation is aimed at decoding their meaning in terms of the unconscious wishes which they express. In Psychoanalysis, the unconscious is conceived of as being pre-logical, atemporal, amoral and, generally speaking, the repository of all our *repressed* fantasies and desires. It is thus essentially negative in character, unlike the Jungian and other conceptions (see **Analytical Psychology**: *collective unconscious*).

References and further reading

Freud, S. (1914) *The Psychopathology of Everyday Life*, London: T. Fisher Unwin.
—— (1950) *Beyond the Pleasure Principle*, London: Hogarth Press.
Rycroft, C. (1972) *A Critical Dictionary of Psychoanalysis*, London: Penguin Books.

Note: A 24-volume *Standard Edition of the Complete Psychological Works of Sigmund Freud* was issued 1953–74 by Hogarth Press. Much academic writing cites this rather than the individual editions of works being cited.

PSYCHOHISTORY

A sub-discipline that emerged in the 1950s, building on a number of earlier works by Sigmund Freud and others. Psychohistory sought to use psychoanalytic concepts and theories to analyse historical events and, most commonly, famous historical figures. While this yielded a number of interesting works of enduring value, P. Manuel's biography of Newton (1968) and E. Erikson's *Young Man Luther* (Erikson, 1959) being among the most highly esteemed, Psychohistory failed to become a major academic genre. This was for two main reasons, most obviously its identification with **psychoanalysis** counted against it as the academic status of Psychoanalysis declined during the post-1950 period. Second, it was a little at odds new developments within History, which were moving away from the 'Great Man' approach and, especially in history of science, towards socially contextualised accounts. Among the non-biographical works which may be classed as psychohistory E.E. Hagen's *On the Theory of Social Change* (Hagen, 1964) and the works of Barbu (1960) should be noted. Psychohistory has not, however, disappeared, its cause being kept alive by Bruce Mazlish at the Massachusetts Institute of Technology.

References and further reading

Barbu, Z. (1960) *Problems of Historical Psychology*, London: Routledge & Kegan Paul.

Erikson, E.H. (1959) *Young Man Luther: A Study in Psychoanalysis and History*, London: Faber & Faber.

Hagen, E.E. (1964) *On the Theory of Social Change: How Economic Growth Begins*, London: Tavistock.

Manuel, P. (1968) *A Portrait of Isaac Newton*, Cambridge, MA: Harvard University Press.

Mazlish, B. (1990) *The Leader, the Led and the Psyche: Essays in Psychohistory*, Middletown, CT: Wesleyan University Press.

PSYCHOMETRICS

Umbrella term for the use of mathematical, usually statistical, methods for measuring psychological phenomena. It thus covers, primarily, **intelligence** testing, many **personality** assessment techniques and **attitude** measurement. The goal of most psychometrics is the production of measuring instruments such as questionnaires. Rao and Sandhip (2006) should tell you all you need to know, but Bacharach and Furr (2007) is a better first step.

References.

Bacharach, V. and Furr, R.M. (2007) *Psychometrics: An Introduction*, London: Sage.

Rao, C.R. and Sandhip, S. (eds) (2006) *Handbook of Statistics, Psychometrics*, New York: Elsevier.

PSYCHOPATH

A person apparently lacking genuinely internalised moral standards and who typically infringes these in an opportunistic and guilt-free fashion. Psychopaths may be very socially skilled and/or intelligent, but show no **empathy** with their victims, are indifferent to punishment, and concerned only with immediate gratification of their desires by whatever means, including violence. This **stereotype** of the psychopath has, however, been frequently challenged as little more than a catchall phrase for incorrigible criminals, and its value as a psychiatric diagnostic category called into question. It is also claimed that psychopaths do not respond to psychotherapy, but therapists who have persisted report this to be far from the case. The term is recorded in English as early as 1885 (in the *Pall Mall Gazette* of all places), but became widely used in its full current sense after its use in Cleckley (1941) (which listed 16 characteristics from 'superficial charm' to 'suicide rarely carried out'), largely replacing the earlier expressions *moral imbecility* and *moral insanity*. The term *sociopath* is virtually synonymous with psychopath and **DSM** III in 1980 replaced it with 'antisocial personality disorder'. Blair *et al.* (2006) is the most accessible recent critical overview.

References and further reading

Blair, J., Mitchell, D. and Blair, K. (2006) *The Psychopath*, Oxford: Blackwell.
Cleckley, H. (1941) *The Mask of Sanity: An Attempt to Reinterpret the So-Called Psychopathic Personality*, St Louis, MO: C.V. Mosby.
Meloy, J.R. (1988) *The Psychopathic Mind: Origins, Dynamics, and Treatment*. Northvale, NJ: Jason Aronson Inc.

PSYCHOPATHOLOGY

A general term for all types of psychological disorder or malfunctioning except those with a clear organic basis. It also tends not be used for certain functional disabilities such as **dyslexia** or **learning difficulties**.

PSYCHOPHYSICS

Branch of Psychology concerned with quantitative research on basic sensory phenomena such as size and weight estimation and discrimination, perception, hearing and the like, also including **reaction time**. The earliest field in which experimental methods were adopted in

Psychology, particularly in Germany in the work of Weber (on senses of touch and taste) (Weber, [1834] 1977) and Fechner (1859). Initially considered a branch of physiology, this research came, in Fechner's work, to provide the basic formats of experimental method in Psychology, extending beyond psychophysics itself. Although basic research on topics such as RTs has largely been exhausted, psychophysics remains an important topic in Psychology as such psychophysical phenomena lend themselves well to the testing of theoretical hypotheses of a very wide variety of kinds.

References and further reading

Fechner, G. (1859) *Elements of Psychophysics*, trans. 1966, New York: Holt, Rinehart & Winston (vol. 1 of original only).

Gescheider, G.A. (1997) *Psychophysics: The Fundamentals*, Mahwah, NJ: Lawrence Erlbaum.

Weber, E.H. ([1834] 1977) *The Sense of Touch: De Tactu-Der Tastsinn*, trans. H.E. Ross and D.J. Murray, London: Academic Press.

PSYCHOSIS

In the nineteenth century this word was sometimes used simply to mean a 'state of mind', without any other connotations. This usage soon disappeared and it now refers to forms of mental illness marked by delusional states and beliefs, ranging from irrational **paranoia** to believing one is Jesus Christ. This may be accompanied by behaviour reflecting the nature of the delusion. When resulting from alcohol or narcotic use, psychoses are generally transient, although may leave the individual susceptible to subsequent psychotic episodes. In fact, the term is almost synonymous with 'madness' in the full-blown classic usage of the word. For a recent overview, see Fujii and Ahmed (2007).

Reference

Fujii, D. and Ahmed, I. (eds) (2007) *The Spectrum of Psychotic Disorder: Neurobiology, Etiology and Pathogenesis*, New York: Cambridge University Press.

PSYCHOSOMATIC

Used to describe physical symptoms caused, or believed to be caused, by psychological rather than physical factors, hence the expression 'psychosomatic illness'. In some contexts, the expression *conversion symptom* is used, meaning that psychological distress has been 'converted' into a physical form. The term has quite a wide range of applicability and theoretical explanations for the phenomena vary with broader theoretical allegiances. There is an extensive technical literature on psychosomatic medicine and psychotherapy. The references below are intended only to provide a broader background to the topic.

References and further reading

Furst, L.R. (2002) *Idioms of Distress: Psychosomatic Disorders in Medical and Imaginative Literature*, Ithaca, NY: State University of New York Press.

Shorter, M. (1993) *From Paralysis to Fatigue: A History of Psychosomatic Illness in the Modern Era*, New York: Free Press.

PSYCHOTHERAPY

The term 'psychotherapy' was introduced in the late nineteenth century, particularly by Swiss psychiatrist Paul Dubois (1848–1918). Now used in a very general fashion to refer to all methods of treating mental distress involving some kind of extended discussion between the therapist and their client or patient. **Group therapy** may also, in some of its forms, be considered a form of psychotherapy. Since the late 1960s onwards, the borderline between **counselling** and psychotherapy has, in practice, virtually disappeared, although those practising **psychoanalysis** and similar older theoretically elaborated and medically rooted approaches would reject being called counsellors.

PSYCHOTROPIC

Having the effect of altering the state of consciousness. Usually used to describe drugs such as LSD and cannabis. It is not, however, used for drugs inducing sleep or antidepressants although may be used for some tranquillisers. Psychotropic effects may also be achieved by other means such as visual stimuli and meditation. Closely related to **psychedelic** but more strictly medical and lacking that term's positive connotations.

Q-SORT

A **psychometric** method initially devised by British psychologist W. Stephenson (1935) but which only began to be widely explored and developed by others in the 1960s, with a more widespread resurgence since the 1980s. The central aim is to access the individual's subjective evaluation and mode of construing a target stimulus (which may be anything from another person to a painting). It involves sorting cards containing terms or phrases possibly descriptive of the target into a fixed number of piles ranging from most to least descriptive, the number to be placed in each pile being fixed (often in a quasi 'normal distribution' fashion). The key distinction from most other methods is that whereas, taking 'honest' as an example of a personality descriptive term, these would require a rating of how honest the target was compared to the population as a whole, the Q-sort would indicate how important 'honest' was compared with other descriptors in the test-taker's subjective evaluation or perception of the target individual. An additional advantage is that it overcomes some technical problems such as *response bias* affecting conventional rating scales. This approach has been called '*ipsative*' as opposed to 'normative'. It has proved to be an extremely versatile and flexible technique with uses ranging from general personality assessment (e.g. the California Adult Q-set) to highly specific targets. It enables in-depth exploration of a single individual's understanding of a target-stimulus, comparison of a large number of individual's ways of understanding it, and identification of commonalities between these. The method is popular among some **Humanistic Psychology** and **social constructionist** researchers, but it is also now well established in more orthodox **personality** research, **psychometrics**, Child Psychology and Social Psychology. The statistical analysis of Q-sort data can become quite complex and there remain a number of differences between Q-sort users regarding methods of interpretation. In focusing on subjectivity, there are some affinities between Q-sort and the *repertory grid*, although they are quite different in form. To some extent, the revolutionary aspirations originally motivating Stephenson's innovation (and his own broader theoretical position) have been lost among its mainstream users.

References

Block, J. (1961) *The Q-Sort Method in Personality Assessment and Psychiatric Research*, Springfield IL: C.C. Thomas.

Stephenson, W. (1935) 'Correlating Persons Instead of Tests', *Character and Personality*, 6: 17–24.

QUALIA

A philosophical term which became widely used from the 1930s onwards to refer to raw sensations as experienced prior to any interpretation. Occasionally met with in Psychological writing, particularly in relation to the nature of consciousness.

QUALITATIVE METHODS

A broad term referring to all research methods that do not involve measurement or quantification, or involve them only minimally for descriptive purposes rather than statistical analysis. These include the **idiographic** 'case-history' approach, **projective tests** and, to some degree, **discourse analysis.** Qualitative methods are often used in preliminary stages of research as well as representing an independent alternative to *quantitative* methods. Qualitative research has received much attention in recent years particularly in Social Psychology. It is widely felt that such methods provide a better way of capturing the complex totality of the phenomena being studied than can be achieved by quantitative methods involving, for example, standardised questionnaires.

References and further reading

Fischer, C. (ed.) (2005) *Qualitative Research Methods for Psychologists. Introduction through Empirical Studies*, New York: Elsevier.

Smith, J.A. (2003) *Qualitative Psychology: A Practical Guide to Research Methods*, London: Sage.

Todd, Z. (2004) *Mixing Methods in Psychology: The Integration of Qualitative and Quantitative Methods in Theory and Practice*, London: Taylor & Francis.

RACISM

Expressing hostility to people, or otherwise discriminating against them or treating them negatively, on the ground solely of their perceived 'racial' identity. A central component of this is the belief that people may indeed be objectively classified in racial terms. The latter belief in itself, unaccompanied by negative behaviour, may perhaps better be termed 'racialism'. In reality, the concept of 'racism' has become extremely complicated since individuals may suffer negative treatment without those responsible consciously admitting to being racist, hence, for example, the term 'institutional racism' for situations where it is clear from statistical evidence that some kind of 'racism' is taking place within an organisation, but cannot be pinned down to any individual source.

See also: **prejudice**.

References and further reading

Heldke, L. and O'Connor, P. (eds) (2003) *Oppression, Privilege and Resistance: Theoretical Readings on Racism, Sexism and Heterosexism*, New York: McGraw-Hill.
Kovel, J. ([1970] 1988) *White Racism: A Psychohistory*, London: Free Association Books.
Richards, G. (1997) *'Race', Racism and Psychology: Towards a Reflexive History*, London: Routledge.
Willis-Esqueda, C. (ed.) (2007) *Motivational Aspects of Prejudice and Racism*, New York: Springer-Verlag.
Winston, A.S. (ed.) (2003) *Defining Difference: Race and Racism in the History of Psychology*, Washington, DC: American Psychological Association.

REACTION TIME (RT)

The time between the presentation of a stimulus and behavioural response to this. RTs were among the earliest phenomena studied by **psychophysics** in the mid-nineteenth century. They retain a central role in experimental Psychology as they can be deployed in a variety of different kinds of research.

RECENCY EFFECT

In **learning** and **memory** research, the recency effect refers to the superior recall of stimuli and/or behaviour to which the organism was most recently exposed.

See also: **primacy effect**.

REDINTEGRATION

Now scarce but once fairly widely used, 'redintegration' literally means 'to make whole again'. In Psychological contexts, it typically referred to the bringing together again of fragmented elements of a memory or pattern of behaviour. Thus if you have not ridden a bicycle for many years and then remount one, there will be a brief phase in which you struggle to balance and steer but then 'it all comes back' – the pattern of motor co-ordinations has 'redintegrated'. Redintegration is typically triggered by (1) recurrence of part of the original memory, image, behaviour pattern or other mental state – a memory of a face pops into your mind and almost immediately you recall where and when you saw that person before; (2) exposure to part of a complex stimulus – you hear a few notes of a tune and immediately remember it in its entirety. A potentially useful term but somewhat awkward to say and hence, I suspect, destined for oblivion.

REDUCTIONISM

In the physical sciences, reductionism is the explanation of phenomena occurring at one level (e.g. chemistry) in terms of the phenomena occurring at a 'lower' or 'more basic' level (e.g. physics). This assumes a hierarchy from subatomic physics at the bottom to animal physiology at the top. The reductionist aim of explaining 'higher' phenomena in terms of 'lower' ones was long central in the physical sciences. 'Higher' phenomena are produced by the mass occurrence of 'lower' ones, resulting in apparently new kinds of events or objects, but scientifically explaining these does not, it is argued, involve invoking new kinds of law or principle. Even in the physical sciences there are certain problems with this. Most notably it is not entirely clear how this hierarchy of 'levels' is to be defined – it is not size as such since Astronomy is not considered 'above' Biology; complexity is a better candidate, but even so, the global weather systems studied by Meteorology are not self-evidently 'simpler' than many botanical phenomena. Without disputing that the 'Laws of Physics' are in some sense fundamental, or that they directly determine chemical phenomena, there is clearly increasing ambiguity as one ascends the hierarchy and some disciplines appear to cross-cut it, such as Geology or Ecology. When we turn to the human sciences, the situation acquires added difficulties. These should, we assume, be at the top of the hierarchy, but it is hard to explain how Sociology is more complex than sub-atomic physics, certainly students would on the whole find the former far easier!

In Psychology, there has thus been a perennial problem in relation to reductionism. There are those who believe all psychological phenomena can be 'reduced' to physiological ones, but it has always proved difficult to see how this can cope with the social and inter-personal aspects of psychology. Somewhat paradoxically, there are also those who claim that psychological phenomena can all be explained sociologically, which is again considered 'reductionist' even though logically Sociology should be a 'higher' discipline. Within Psychology, both **behaviourism** and **psychoanalysis** have aspired to provide comprehensive explanations of all or most psychological phenomena within their own theoretical terms, 'reducing' everything to *S-R* con-nections or unconscious infantile wishes respectively (to over-simplify a little). Opposing this, there have always been those such as *Gestalt psychologists*, *humanistic psychologists* and many **personality** theorists who have argued passionately for 'holistic', anti-reductionist, approaches.

There are thus two underlying issues. The first is the conceptual coherence of reductionism in general, the second is the justifiability of reductionist approaches within Psychology. Perhaps the core of the problem is the implicit assumption that reductionism leads to 'The Explanation' in some absolute sense, when in fact it is the nature of the specific problem we face which determines which kind of expla-nation is appropriate or relevant. For a philosophical critique of the concept, see Midgley (2001). The topic is frequently discussed in older general works on theories and systems in Psychology, the references below are a selection of more recent texts.

References and further reading

Agazzi, E. (1991) *The Problem of Reductionism in Science*, Amsterdam: Kluwer.

Austen, C. (1980) *Psychological Models and Neural Mechanisms: An Examination of Reductionism in Psychology*, Oxford: Oxford University Press.

Brown, T. and Smith, L. (eds) (2007) *Reductionism and the Development of Knowledge*, London: Taylor and Francis.

Midgley, M. (2001) *Science and Poetry*, London: Routledge.

Sarkar, S. (1998) *Genetics and Reductionism*, Cambridge: Cambridge University Press.

REFLEXIVITY

A somewhat fashionable term in several areas of Psychology, but often used simply to mean 'being reflective' or 'reflecting on how one's practice affects oneself'. This is a little misleading, since reflex-ivity technically means 'self-referring'. Logicians have, for example, had great fun analysing reflexive propositions such as 'This sentence has five words'. More broadly, we can perhaps define it as occurring when the referent of an activity and the activity itself belong in the same class. To bring this down to earth, and indicate how it is important for Psychology, it is obvious that doing Psychology is itself a psychological activity – Psychology is about the very thing that is doing it. There are a number of reflexive loops in play in Psychology – a comprehensive Psychological theory should be able to explain its own production, it is both a product of its own subject matter (as just noted) and in some respects produces and/or changes this subject matter in the very process of investigating it. What is unclear is how importantly we should take these loops, and until the late twentieth century few psychologists took them seriously even if wryly acknowledging them. The reflexivity issue has, however, begun to receive more serious attention from *social constructionists* and *critical psychologists*, as well as within *philosophical Psychology* and history of Psychology. In particular, it appears to signify that the scientific status of Psychology is necessarily somewhat anomalous (which need not mean that it is actually 'unscientific'). There are no book-length works on the topic as yet but see the introduction to Richards (2002a), and journal papers Morawski (1992, 2005), and Richards (2002b).

References

Morawski, J.G. (1992) 'Self Regard and Other Regard: Reflexive Practices in American Psychology, 1890–1940', *Science in Context*, 5: 281–308.
—— (2005) 'Reflexivity and the Psychologist', *History of the Human Sciences*, 18: 77–105.
Richards, G. (2002a) *Putting Psychology in its Place: A Critical Historical Overview*, Hove: Psychology Press/Routledge.
—— (2002b) 'The Psychology of Psychology: A Historically Grounded Sketch', *Theory and Psychology*, 12(1): 7–36.

REIFICATION

A technical philosophical term referring to the tendency to ascribe concrete thing-like status to abstract concepts or properties. In Psychology, this is quite an important issue because probably the majority of psychological concepts have a somewhat slippery status in this regard. We easily move from using terms like **intelligence**, **motivation**, or **introversion** to refer descriptively to behaviour of a particular kind to using them as if they denoted real entities or distinct physically embodied faculties (see also **category mistake**, **faculty**). The problem is endemic in English because it is so easy to turn words into nouns, verbs or adjectives. This does not mean such shifts are unjustified in principle, indeed, they are one factor in the dynamic ever-changing nature of language. But one should not, as Gilbert Ryle observed, confuse the grammatical and the ontological (see **category mistake**).

RELIABILITY

In statistics, 'reliability' refers variously to: (1) how well a statistically generated test yields the same results across time (*test–retest reliability*); (2) the level of agreement between different test scorers (e.g. of **projective tests**) or different observers in a field study (*inter-rater reliability*); and (3) the internal consistency of items on a psychometrically designed test, usually assessed by comparing scores on one half of the items with scores on the other, known as *split-half reliability*. Not to be confused with **validity**.

RELIGION, PSYCHOLOGY OF

Contrary to what is widely assumed, the relationship between Psychology and religion (primarily Christianity) has rarely been directly confrontational, and frequently almost collaborative (especially regarding **psychotherapy**). This is an important and as yet relatively unexplored historical topic, extending far beyond the topic here – the Psychology *of* Religion. This sub-discipline originated in the USA during the 1890s (Starbuck, 1899), receiving considerable impetus from James's enduring classic *The Varieties of Religious Experience* (James, 1902) and Hall's various efforts on its behalf (Hall, 1917). By the mid-1920s, Psychology of Religion was a familiar genre in the USA, but while drawing on extensive anthropological information and evolutionary speculation, the authors' goals tended to be towards vindicating Christian belief (Leuba 1925 being a major exception). Criticism came mainly from some sections of **psychoanalysis** and radical **behaviourism**. Psychology of Religion also acquired a considerable mainland European presence during these years and British work began appearing during the post-Great War period, but by around 1930 the project had largely run of steam and, while the religious continued to engage with Psychology – often enthusiastically – the sub-discipline itself almost disappeared. A more modest revival, of rather different character, took place during the 1950s. Avoiding any claims to evaluate the truth or falsity of religious beliefs, attention turned to its psychometric assessment as a personality trait, the classification of 'types' of religious belief, and correlations between belief and psychological well-being. A leading British figure in this was the social psychologist Michael Argyle (himself a practising Christian). (In the meantime a few explicit attacks on religion had appeared within Psychology, notably Vetter, 1958.) While this type of research never died out, the sub-discipline long remained a very minor strand within Psychology, usually ignored entirely in textbooks and secular undergraduate teaching. Since 2000, the cultural climate has ensured that the fortunes of Psychology of Religion are on the rise again, but it is as yet unclear which direction it is taking. The best starting point for anyone wishing to explore the field is Wulff (1997).

References and further reading

Argyle, M. (1958) *Religious Behaviour*, London: Routledge & Kegan Paul.

Hall, G.S. (1917) *Jesus, the Christ, in the Light of Psychology*, 2 vols, New York: Doubleday, Page & Company.

James, W. (1902) *The Varieties of Religious Experience*, London and New York: Longmans, Green.

Leuba, J.H. (1925) *The Psychology of Religious Mysticism*, London: Kegan Paul, Trench & Trubner.

Vetter, G.B. (1958) *Magic and Religion: Their Psychological Nature, Origin and Function*, New York: Philosophical Library.

Wulff, D.M. (1997) *Psychology and Religion: Classic and Contemporary Views*, Chichester; Wiley.

REM

Acronym for Rapid Eye Movement. Generally used in the context of discussions of sleep, in which the presence of REM signifies that the sleeper is dreaming. This is referred to as 'REM sleep'. It is associated with highly active alpha rhythmns (see **EEG**) as opposed to deep sleep in which delta rhythms predominate.

See also: **hypnogogia**.

REPETITION COMPULSION

A common symptom or manifestation of *obsessional compulsion disorder* (see **obsessional**) in which a behaviour such as hand-washing is constantly repeated to a pathological degree.

REPRESENTATIONALISM

The doctrine that our knowledge of the external world exists in the form of picture or analogue 'representations' of that world. The topic primarily arises in relation to visual perception, where it is held that we cannot see the world 'directly' but experience only its representations. The '*direct versus indirect*' perception debate goes back as far as the 1700s at least and persists down to the present. It is, however, a conceptually confused distinction in the present author's view, since it is impossible for either camp to specify what kind of empirical evidence would settle the matter and rather revolves around what one means by 'direct' in this context (and also to some extent 'representation'). **Visual illusions** are often considered to demonstrate that what we see is not what is actually there, but this conflates the notion of 'directness' with 'accuracy' (and often with 'completeness'). The doctrine is, however, a general one applying to language and cognitive processes as well as sensory ones. One deep problem is that representationalism appears to lead to an infinite regress – 'seeing' the representation implying surely that we must then have a 'representation of the representation'. It was thus traditionally castigated as an example of a '*homunculus theory*', that is to say, it simply proposes that there is a 'little man' in our heads who deals with our representations in the same way we do with the outside world – which clearly solves nothing. Modern versions of the doctrine are not as naïve as this, and our perceptions, ideas, thoughts, etc. must exist in *some* form or other. One suspects the idea of representationalism is not so much wrong as obsolete and that what is required is an approach which can integrate the merits of both camps and be consistent with psycho-neurological knowledge. This seems to be the direction current debates are actually taking, although the term 'representationalism' is being retained, its meaning is clearly undergoing considerable mutation (see 'The Representationalism Website'). The issue is intimately bound up with debates about the nature of consciousness, **AI,** and the **mind–body problem**. Smythies (1994) has some original thoughts on this, but the on-line Stanford Encyclopedia entry 'Epistemological problems of perception' is probably the easiest starting point and has an excellent bibliography.

References

Smythies, J. (1994) *The Walls of Plato's Cave: The Science and Philosophy of Brain, Consciousness and Perception*, Aldershot: Ashgate.

RESTRICTED VS ELABORATED CODE

In the 1960s, British sociologist Basil Bernstein (1924–2000), when
studying reasons for the differences between middle-class and working-
class children's educational performance, proposed that one factor was
a difference in the way they tended to use language (Bernstein, 1971).
Working-class children were more prone to using what he called
'restricted code', characterised by reliance on the hearer's implicit
knowledge to understand what was being said and usually grammatically
simple. This worked to enhance in-group membership and exclude
outsiders. Middle-class 'elaborated code' use, as the name implies, fully
articulated what was being spoken about and was more grammatically
complex. All of us employ both modes depending on circumstances, but
the bias towards restricted code use of working-class children put them,
Bernstein argued, at a disadvantage in learning situations and made them
less skilled in being able to express themselves in a generally compre-
hensible way. This idea proved controversial at the time, especially as it
was widely misunderstood as denigrating the working class and Black
English dialect (which was not actually on his agenda at all). In fact,
he was aiming to help diagnose the roots of underachievement and
suggest ways of addressing this. Restricted code was not, in itself, 'inferior', but simply unsuited for certain uses and contexts (e.g. letter-writing
or dealing with those exercising social power). In some contexts, the
working class was quite able to use elaborated code as well as any-
body, but these did not fully extend to situations such as the classroom
where they were dealing with members of another (socially 'superior') social class or others from outside their normal social group. For
an overview of Bernstein's work, see Sadovnik (1995), and his 2002
Obituary available on line via link from Wikipedia entry on him.
Littlejohn and Foss (2007) also include discussion of this topic.

References

Bernstein, B. (1971) *Class, Codes and Social Control*, vol. 1, London: Paladin
(a further three volumes were published by Routledge & Kegan Paul/
Routledge, the last in 1990).

—— (2000) *Pedagogy, Symbolic Control and Identity: Theory, Research, Critique*, rev. edn, Lanham, MD: Rowman & Littlefield.

Littlejohn, S.W. and Foss, K.A. (2007) *Theories of Human Communication*, Belmont, CA: Wadsworth.

Sadovnik, A.R. (1995) *Knowledge and Pedagogy: The Sociology of Basil Bernstein*, Norwood, NJ: Ablex Publishing.

RETICULAR ACTIVATING SYSTEM (RAS)

Net-like and rather diffuse component of the brain-stem of significance to Psychology as controlling arousal, motivation and alertness (in its 'ascending' functions) and body posture, reflexes and muscle-tone (in its 'descending' ones). Eysenck invoked individual differences in ascending RAS (ARAS) functioning in his **personality** theory, arguing that introverts had naturally high levels of arousal and thus sought a quiet life, while extraverts had low levels of arousal and thus sought exciting stimuli. The aim in both cases is to maintain an optimum level of ARAS activity.

REVERSAL THEORY

Theory developed by British psychologist Michael Apter from the late 1970s onwards. He had become interested in the relationship between **arousal** and **hedonic state** and saw this as requiring an integration between **behaviourist** and **phenomenological** approaches. His key insight was that whether arousal was felt as pleasurable or not depended on what he came to call 'metamotivational state'. While other such states have since been added, at the outset he identified two types which he called *telic* (goal-directed, purposeful) and *paratelic* (doing something for its own sake). These crudely equate to work and play respectively. High arousal in a *telic* state causes **anxiety** with consequent negative effects on performance, while low arousal gives a pleasant feeling of relaxation and laid-back confidence. In a *paratelic* state high arousal is experienced as exciting and pleasurable but low arousal is boring, leading to lowered performance. The first obvious strategy is to try and alter one's state of arousal in the desired direction, but this is often not possible and always difficult. The second strategy is to *reverse* one's metamotivational state. Start treating the 'work' task as a game or the boring 'play' task as a serious job of work and the level of arousal becomes satisfactory again. It soon became apparent that there were individual differences regarding which metamotivational state people were inclined to adopt, the theory thus linked up with **personality** issues and a 'Telic Dominance Scale' was produced. Further bipolar metamotivational states also came to light. In interpersonal relations, for example, Apter identifies 'Mastery' versus 'Sympathy'. Although the success of Reversal Theory has perhaps not been as great as Apter and his followers hoped, it has established a significant niche for itself and has become widely used in Sport Psychology as well as, to some degree, in **psychotherapy**. In its early days it undoubtedly suffered by being between two camps. Phenomenologists saw it as too conventionally experimental, while the more behaviourally inclined considered it too phenomenological. Apter's most recent accounts of his theory are given in (Apter, 2005, 2007). Further references are listed on www. reversaltheory.org/Bibliography.htm

References

Apter, M.J. (2005) *Personality Dynamics: Key Concepts in Reversal Theory*, Loughborough: Apter International.
—— (2007) *Reversal Theory: The Dynamics of Motivation, Emotion and Personality*, 2nd edn, Oxford: Oneworld Press.

RHETORIC

Popularly understood as referring to emotionally powerful and colourful speech which aims to persuade listeners by force of the speaker's eloquence and passion alone, and thus incompatible with reasoned argument. Technically though, rhetoric is merely 'the art of persuasion' and, non-evaluatively, refers to all ways of achieving this. Originally it referred primarily to spoken oratory and until the end of the Renaissance received much attention from all those exercising social power, from priests to princes, figured on university courses and was the subject of numerous books going back to antiquity (Quintillian's being perhaps the most popular). It became the target of renewed attention in the 1970s, notably from historians of science interested in how early scientific writers persuaded others of the truth of their findings, Shapin and Shaffer (1985) being a classic text. This shifted attention from the spoken word to printed prose and images. Illustrating a report on your latest brain-research with coloured high-tech MRI images is thus, from this perspective, as much a rhetorical device as shouting and prodding the air with your forefinger (and certainly likely to be more successful). This does not mean the images are dishonest, unnecessary or not what they appear to be, they simply reinforce the impression that you are a good scientist who has done the research you claim to have done and can present what seems to be good evidence for your case. The social psychologist Michael Billig (Billig, 1987) has argued that *all* advances in knowledge boil down, at the end of the day, to successful rhetoric in this sense, and that our on-going arguments, debates and discussions, centring on trying to persuade other people of the truth or value of what we have to say, can best be understood as rhetorical in this sense – and rhetoric is, moreover, the very life-blood of social life from science to politics. This entails establishing criteria for what are to count as sound arguments and valid evidence, and is not therefore 'irrational'. On the contrary, it is the rhetorical task of persuasion which itself ultimately drives our efforts to be rigorously rational. What it does suggest, however, is that we should remain wary of the possible use of high-flown technical jargon, mathematical equations, etc. in a way which is rhetorical in the popular sense – serving not to actually communicate anything concrete but simply to give us the impression that the user is an expert we are unqualified to criticise.

References

Billig, M. (1987) *Arguing and Thinking: A Rhetorical Approach to Social Psychology*, Cambridge: Cambridge University Press.
—— (1990) 'Rhetoric of Social Psychology', in I. Parker and J. Shotter (eds), *Deconstructing Social Psychology*, London: Routledge, pp. 47–60.
Shapin, S. and Schaffer, S. (1985) *Leviathan and the Air-Pump: Hobbes, Boyle and the Experimental Life*, Princeton, NJ: Princeton University Press.

ROLE/ROLE THEORY

As the word suggests, a role may be understood as akin to an actor's part in a play. It is a specific way of behaving (and appearing) considered socially appropriate for an individual in a specific situation. As such, it has a very wide range of application, from parental roles to those appropriate to someone's age, gender, occupation, status, etc. During the 1950s, those working on the borderline between Sociology and Social Psychology embarked on a complex analysis of the topic, their efforts usually being called 'Role Theory'. They identified numerous facets of the issue such as '*role-conflict*' – a person being required to play roles which were in some respect incompatible, '*role expectations*' – the behaviour expected of someone in a particular role, '*role confusion*' – when it is unclear exactly which of several possible roles a situation requires one to play, and '*role models*' – people who are seen as enacting the role in an ideal way (this phrase is perhaps role theory's most enduring legacy). They also studied how roles were learned or acquired, and the various kinds of role which emerge in social groups (such as *task leader* and *socio-emotive leader*). Beneath all this lay a concern regarding how far an individual could be considered to exist as a separate personality or self apart from the totality of roles they played. Some kinds of role are especially comprehensive and the individual enacting them may display *role-identification*, they *are* a rock star, ship's captain, comedian or Hollywood diva, living almost their entire lives 'in role', behaving as someone in that role is (in their view) supposed to behave whether it be in a restaurant, at a party, in personal relationships or on a chat show. On occasion, an individual enacting a particular role may enact it in a way which dramatically redefines it, or establishes a new role model. Instances would include Elvis Presley, Admiral Nelson, Florence Nightingale, Lord Byron and Martin Luther King who provided quite new role models for popular singer, admiral, nurse, poet and political leader respectively. With the rise of feminism, sex roles came to attract much attention during the 1970s, e.g. (Frieze, 1978). In many respects, role theory anticipated aspects of what later came to be called **social constructionism**, particularly the claims which this makes regarding the fickle nature of personal identity and the elusiveness of an enduring 'self' existing apart from the individual's social life. Even being a hermit is a social role. For the most comprehensive exposition of 1960s role theory, see Biddle and Thomas (1966). Harré (1979) also explored the theatrical analogy of roles in depth, extending this to 'stages' and 'scripts'.

References and further reading

Banton, M. (1965) *Roles: An Introduction to the Study of Social Relations*, London: Tavistock.

Biddle, B. and Thomas, E.J. (eds) (1966) *Role Theory: Concepts and Research*, New York: Wiley.

Frieze, I.H. (1978) *Women and Sex Roles: A Social Psychological Perspective*, New York: Norton.

Harré, R. (1979) *Social Being: A Theory for Social Psychology*, Oxford: Blackwell.

Rommetveit, R. (1955) *Social Norms and Roles: Explorations in the Psychology of Enduring Social Pressures*, Minneapolis, MN: University of Minnesota Press.

Zurcher, L.A. (1983) *Social Roles. Conformity, Conflict and Creativity*, Beverly Hills, CA: Sage.

RORSCHACH TEST

Introduced by Hermann Rorschach in 1921, the 'Rorschach Test' soon became the most widely known of all **projective tests**, often known as the 'ink-blot' test (Rorschach, 1921). (An American edition appeared in the same year as the Swiss first edition.) It comprises a set of ten cards, each with a symmetrical 'ink-blot' image. The individual taking the test is required to say what they see in this image. Contrary to popular belief, the specific content of responses, while significant, is considered less important than how the ink-blot is used – whether someone picks out lots of fine detail or responds in generalised terms to the whole image, whether they use the white spaces and margins, when they report movement, how many things are seen in the blot, response times, and so on. A highly detailed scoring method was developed for analysing responses. During the 1960s, its reputation nose-dived following research which showed lower inter-rater **reliability** between supposed 'experts' in the test's use. Its fortunes then revived in the 1980s with the work of Exner (Exner, 2002) and his associate Weiner. This included revisions of the scoring system. The resulting 'Exner system' is now widely used and regularly updated.

References

Exner, J.E. (2002, 2005) *The Rorschach: A Comprehensive System*, 2 vols, New York: John Wiley.

Rorschach, H. (1921) *Psychodiagnostik*, Berne: E. Bircher.

SCALING

Term used in **psychometrics** for the statistical process of creating a parametric measurement scale for the phenomenon in question on which test scores are normally distributed (thus being amenable to parametric inferential analysis) and of equal interval. The latter may not always be achievable and testers may have to settle for an 'ordinal' scale (i.e. one in which, although 10 is 'bigger' than 9, the actual difference is not necessarily the same as between 8 and 9 or 10 and 11).

SCHEMA

A general basic term referring to specific behaviours (such as 'grasping'), and all the ideas or concepts employed in understanding and engaging with the world. The key feature of a schema is that it has a clear structure of some sort. (Strictly speaking the plural of 'schema' is 'schemata' but 'schemas' seems to be becoming acceptable.) The term was widely used by Piaget (see **Piagetian theory**), but has also become fairly common in **Cognitive Psychology** as well as being used in other contexts, such as the phrase '*body schema*' used by the early twentieth-century British neurologist Sir Henry Head to refer to a hypothesised internal representation of our current bodily posture and position.

SCHIZOGENIC

Causing schizophrenia, hence phrases such as 'a schizogenic family' for a family with interpersonal dynamics which, it is claimed, lead to one or more members becoming **schizophrenic**, but can be used of drugs or any other factor leading to schizophrenia.

SCHIZOPHRENIA

Since its introduction by Swiss psychiatrist E. Bleuler in 1911 as a replacement for **dementia praecox** (which simply meant early or premature dementia, as opposed to *senile dementia*), this has become one of the most problematic terms in psychiatry and the target of much critical analysis. The popular image of it implying 'two minds' or a 'split personality' has long been recognised as misleading (this is more suggestive of **multiple personality disorder/dissociative identity disorder**) but continues to be inadvertently promoted in the popular media. Due to changes over time in its alleged symptomatology and wide variations between sites and among psychiatrists in its use, it is, however, hard to specify precisely what it does refer to. Certain symptoms such as hearing voices, **paranoia**, inert detachment, *ideas of reference* (experiencing events as somehow referring directly to oneself), inappropriate laughter and emotional disorder have all figured as diagnostic of the condition but they are far from representing a coherent syndrome and none are universal to all 'schizophrenics' or exclusive to them. (Hearing voices, for example, is surprisingly common, it is the meanings ascribed to them and whether they are located externally or internally that create the problems.) Controversy is no less regarding its causes, explanations ranging from the neurological and genetic to family dynamics, with compromise 'interaction' positions now being most common. There is also doubt as to whether the conditions diagnosed as schizophrenia prior to the 1920s (E. Kraepelin being the leading figure at this time) correspond at all to those for which the term is now used. Boyle (1990) argued that many of the symptoms originally identified, and now virtually never encountered, were identical with those of post-encephalitic Parkinsonism, there having been an encephalitis epidemic during the second decade of the twentieth century. The family origins of schizophrenia were very strongly proposed by the **anti-psychiatry** movement in the 1960s and early 1970s (see also **double-bind**). One cannot help suspecting that the term is an umbrella label for a variety of types of mental distress which fall between the neurotic disorders (see **neurosis**) and fully-blown **psychosis**.

Reference

Boyle, M. (1990) *Schizophrenia: A Scientific Delusion?* London: Routledge.
McDonald, C., Schulze, C., Murray, K. and Wright, R.M. (2004) *Schizophrenia, Challenging the Orthodox*, London: Taylor & Francis.

SCHIZOTHYMIC

A **personality** type with a tendency for mental illness to take the form of **schizophrenia**, introduced by the German psychiatrist Emil Kraepelin (1856–1926). The schizothymic personality was contrasted to the **cyclothymic** personality, prone to what now would be called **bipolar disorder**.

SCHOOLS OF PSYCHOLOGY

A variety of 'schools' of Psychology have been identified over the years, largely as a pragmatic way of differentiating various theoretical and research traditions. However, while reference is commonly often made to 'functionalist', 'behaviourist', 'psychoanalytic', etc. schools, the term can be used more narrowly to refer to geographical locations rather than theories as such. In these cases the term 'school' is still frequently used in the looser sense of a 'school of thought' rather than a specific institution, although in some instances this distinction virtually disappears.

- *Cambridge School*. Usually used to refer to the main group of psychologists based in Cambridge University during the 1900–40 period. These included C.S. Myers, W.H.R. Rivers and F. Bartlett. The major difference from the *London School* (see below) is seen as being less interest in psychometrics and statistics, as well as a greater concern with social and applied issues. The Cambridge School is routinely juxtaposed with the London School as representing the poles of early twentieth-century English academic Psychological thought, although this grossly distorts the picture since Manchester, Liverpool, Reading, and possibly Bristol, schools could also be identified. The Scottish universities were also pursuing their own agendas to some extent but are rarely referred to as 'schools'. Oxford, however, was out of the picture for most of this period.

- *Chicago School of Functionalism* (see also **functionalism**). Effectively founded around 1900 by pragmatist philosopher-cum-psychologist J. Dewey and psychologist J.R. Angell, the Chicago functionalist school initially appeared to be continuing and developing a broadly evolutionary approach to Psychology seeking explanations in adaptive terms. Angell famously differentiated functionalism from E.B. Titchener's **structuralism** (see Angell, 1907). Fairly rapidly, however, it assumed a more distinctly **behaviourist** character, and was where J.B. Watson did his doctorate. The more philosophical Dewey tradition was, however, maintained by G.H. Mead (who called himself a social behaviourist) and in a rather complex fashion fed into the Chicago-based sociological school known as *symbolic interactionism*. In the 1940s and 1950s, this in turn influenced some leading figures on the social psychology-sociology boundary such as E. Goffman via whom a thread may be traced to **social constructionism**. The Chicago variant of functionalism differed in a number of respects from the *Columbia* version (see sub-entry below), which in the long run played a more influential role in mid-twentieth-century American Psychology.

- *Columbia 'Culture and Personality School'*. This developed, initially under anthropologist Franz Boas, from the late 1920s onwards, fading out by around 1960 as a distinct movement. Its most famous representative was Margaret Mead whose *Coming of Age in Samoa* (Mead, 1928) and *Growing up in New Guinea* (Mead, 1930) in effect launched it. Subsequently numerous figures, not all Columbia-based, became associated with it including Ruth Benedict, Abram Kardiner, Eleanor Maccoby, Wayne Dennis, and Erik H. Erikson. Although theoretically fairly eclectic, most were nevertheless heavily influenced by **psychoanalysis**. Their main aim was to explore how the diversity of cultural practices and customs related to child-rearing and gender-roles translated into differences in personality type. Initially concentrating on traditional societies such as those of Pacific islanders and American Indians, in the late 1940s they also turned their attention to German and Japanese societies, hoping, by doing so, to shed light on the rise of Nazism and the specific nature of Japanese militarism. In that respect there was a linkage with Psychoanalytic analyses of the roots of **authoritarianism**. Their work on gender roles played a major role in laying the grounds for feminist theory.

- *Columbia School of Functionalism*. Originating, like the *Chicago School* (see above) in the first decade of the twentieth century, the Columbia functionalists were from the outset less concerned with purely theoretical questions and more with Psychology as a practical discipline. While committed to rigorous scientific methods, they were always more eclectic than **behaviourism**, hence this version of functionalism was a very broad affair, from E.L. Thorndike's early pioneering work in educational Psychology onwards. The long-lived R.S. Woodworth (1869–1962) is perhaps its most typical representative, author of the almost universally used mid-century Psychology textbook, *Experimental Psychology* (Woodworth, 1938) which went through numerous later editions, and editor for several crucial decades of the *Psychological Monograph* series in which many highly important works were published. His *Dynamic Psychology* (Woodworth, 1918), is the nearest to a full theoretical position statement produced by the school during its early years. This was fairly synthetic in character, endeavouring to integrate a wide variety of approaches in a single framework. (Although J. McK. Cattell (1860–1944) was involved as Professor of Psychology from 1892, his own early Psychological research was marginal as far as functionalism was concerned and he soon turned to other things.) Other figures associated with the school include J.F. Dashiell (1888–1975) and Leta Hollingworth (1886–1939), child psychologist and one of the leading women psychologists of the period. The links between Columbia functionalism and the *Columbia 'Culture and Personality School'* (see previous) are difficult to tease out, but the latter was closely related to functionalism in the anthropological sense (see **functionalism**), and Columbia sociologist R.K. Merton is also classified as a functionalist. Although naturally having long-term effects on the ethos of Columbia's Psychology department, the label 'functionalist' rather ceases to mean very much after about 1950.
- *Frankfurt School*. This flourished from the early 1920s into the early 1930s, when its main representatives emigrated to the United

States with the advent of Nazism, constituting what was in effect a 'Frankfurt School in Exile'. Broadly Marxist in sympathies, but not dogmatically so, they were particularly concerned with using Psychology and its methods to explore the nature of social issues, pioneering the use of questionnaires, for example. They were also receptive to many of the ideas introduced by psychoanalysis. Following their exile, they had to downplay their socialist leanings to some degree, especially in the post-1945 period, but had a major impact on social psychology and **personality** theory, introducing the idea of authoritarianism, for example. Major figures identified with this school include Theodor Adorno, Erich Fromm, Else Frenkl-Brunswik and Herbert Marcuse. Classifying this simply as a school of Psychology would be misleading since its concerns spanned sociology and philosophy as well.

- *Geneva School.* Although, strictly speaking, one should consider E. Claparède as the founder of the Geneva School prior to the First World War, from the 1920s onwards the term is used exclusively to refer to his successor, Jean Piaget (1896–1980), and Piaget's numerous associates at the Institut Rousseau in Geneva. Piaget's central concern was with child development, his theoretical account of which, elaborated over many years, became the most widely influential in the field, although its US impact only came in the 1950s. Behind this interest, however, lay a deeper philosophical agenda, which he called *genetic epistemology*, regarding the nature of knowledge itself, this coming to the fore in several of his later works. While dominated by Piaget, the term 'school' is justified in the light of the roles played by numerous associates such as Barbel Innhelder, Alina Szeminska, and E.W. Beth (see **Piagetian theory**).

- *Gestalt School.* See **Gestalt Psychology** This, although commonly called a 'School', was not associated with any specific university.

- *Harvard School.* As a major centre for academic Psychology from the time of William James in the 1880s, Harvard has always figured prominently. To talk of a 'Harvard School' is somewhat misleading as the hallmark of Harvard Psychology has been creative diversity rather than promotion of a specific theoretical orientation. It played a major role in the origins of **Cognitive Psychology**, G.A. Miller being based there, but Harvard psychologists also include the experimental psychophysicist S.S. Stevens, social psychologist G.W. Allport, arch-behaviourist B.F. Skinner, Jung-influenced personality theorist Henry Murray and historian of psychology E.G. Boring.

- *Leipzig School.* Academic experimental Psychology largely originated with the work of German psychologist and philosopher Wilhelm Wundt (1832–1920) at Leipzig University. In his experimental work, Wundt sought to identify the basic structure of consciousness using **introspection** and **psychophysical** methods, famously founding a laboratory there in 1879. From the 1870s to 1890s Leipzig University remained Psychology's leading European institution, although with mounting competition from the *Würzburg School* (see below) and elsewhere. A large number of the first generation of US and British psychologists either obtained their PhDs under Wundt or spent time in Leipzig. The term 'Leipzig School' thus refers to the work of Wundt and his numerous associates during the late nineteenth century. It is perhaps worth noting that at this time Psychology was taught under the auspices of Philosophy in German universities (and often elsewhere, Britain, for example), remaining in this position until the late 1930s.
- *London School.* Usually used to refer to the main group of University of London-based psychologists of the 1890s–1940 period, centred at University College London, its major representatives being James Sully (who founded the first UK Psychology laboratory there in 1897) and his successors Charles Spearman and Cyril Burt. These are viewed, a little simplistically, as having been primarily concerned with psychometric approaches, continuing the tradition established by Francis Galton and Karl Pearson (also at UCL). London-based psychologists adopting different approaches, such as the psychoanalytically oriented J.C. Flügel (also at University College) are not usually included in the category. Others, such as experimentally oriented Beatrice Edgell at Bedford College, probably should be.
- *Nancy School.* Nancy is the French town where T. Liébault and his younger associate H. Bernheim successfully revived the practice of **hypnotism** in the 1860s, eventually creating what they called the Nancy School. Bernheim rejected the 'animal magnetism' theories of earlier *Mesmerism*, explaining hypnotism in terms of **suggestion**. In the early twentieth century, several French therapists such as Charles Baudouin and Emile Coué revived Bernheim's approach, referring to themselves as the *New Nancy School.*
- *Russian School.* The term Russian School is generally used for Soviet era psychologists, primarily I. Pavlov, his immediate pre-revolutionary predecessors V.M. Bekhterev and I.M. Sechenov, and his colleagues such as B.M. Teplov, Y.P. Frolov, S.L. Rubinstein and A.G. Ivanov-Smolensky. Their approaches generally closely resembled to those of American behaviourism, which incorporated

Pavlovian concepts of *conditioning*. They were, however, more physiologically oriented than the behaviourists and became more interested in the higher mental processes in addition to **learning**. L. Vygotsky and, a little later, A.R. Luria do not fit quite so easily into the category, and the currently popular M. Bakhtin certainly doesn't (his work having more affinities with the philosophy of L. Wittgenstein and that of present-day social and critical psychologists like M. Billig and J. Shotter).

- *Vienna School.* The term 'Vienna School' is often found in works of the 1910–30 period to refer to Sigmund Freud and his associates, it is thus virtually synonymous with psychoanalysis. The main connotation of its use was to differentiate this from C. G. Jung's so-called *Zurich School* (see below).

- *Würzburg School.* Flourished from the 1890s till the First World War. The leading figures associated with the school were O. Külpe, N. Ach and K. Marbe. Having studied under W. Wundt at the *Leipzig School* (see above), Külpe reacted against his structuralist, introspection-based, approach. Extending research to higher mental processes Würzburg psychologists challenged the notion that all psychological processes were amenable to introspection (famously introducing the notion of 'imageless thought') and also showed that introspective reports could not be considered objective anyway, since they were affected by the person's 'set' or 'orientation' (*Vorstellungen*) to the task. The German psychologist K. Bühler began his career in the school, though his later interests diverged from theirs into language, perception and Child Psychology, having close contact with **Gestalt Psychology**. The Würzburg School may be viewed as the final phase of the nineteenth-century German introspectionist tradition. Historian M. Kusch (Kusch, 1995) has unravelled some interesting relationships between the Leipzig versus Würzburg controversy and underlying religious and cultural factors, seeing Leipzig as 'Protestant' and Würzburg as 'Catholic' (but see A. Mülberger's balanced on-line critique).

- *Zurich School.* Most often found in works of the 1910–30 period to refer to C.G. Jung and his associates, thus virtually synonymous with Jung's **Analytical Psychology** as distinct from Freud's so-called *Vienna School* (see above).

References

Angell, J.R. (1907) 'The Province of Functional Psychology', *Psychological Review*, 14: 61–91.

Jay, M. ([1973] 1976) *The Dialectical Imagination: A History of the Frankfurt School and the Institute of Social Research*, London: Heinemann.

Kusch, M. (1999) *Psychological Knowledge*, London: Routledge.

Mead, M. ([1928] 2001) *Coming of Age in Samoa*, New York: Harper.

—— ([1930] 2001) *Growing up in New Guinea*, New York: Harper.

Mülberger, A. (n.d.) http://psychology.dur.ac.uk/eshhs/review/kusch.htm

Woodworth, R.S. (1918) *Dynamic Psychology*, New York: Columbia University Press.

—— (1938) *Experimental Psychology*, New York: Henry Holt.

Wiggerhaus, R. (1994) *The Frankfurt School: Its History, Theories and Political Significance*, trans. M. Robertson, Cambridge, MA: MIT Press.

SELF

One of Psychology's most central and perennially problematic concepts. Although it may loosely be defined as denoting the central unifying, or unified, core of one's personal identity – who one really *is*, there is little consensus beyond that, even regarding whether it actually exists or is only a narrative (see **narrativism**) fiction we tell ourselves. William James's chapter on 'The Self' (James, 1890) is a classic overview, and in many respects, preview, of the issues. For James, we possess a multitude of social 'selves' corresponding to the various people who know us, while our 'self' extends to everything we identify with and feel for, including our country, favourite football team or a cherished possession. He, in fact, denied that there was any single 'Transcendental Ego' as he called it. In Jung's **Analytical Psychology**, the Self only emerges fully at the end of the *individuation* process (see Analytical Psychology sub-entries) and is as much unconscious as conscious. More recently, numerous post-modernist writers have challenged the reality of the Self as an enduring unitary entity, viewing it as constantly changing and redefined throughout our lives. **Social constructionist** writers such as K. J. Gergen (1991, 1993, 2001) have been in the forefront of this. In **psychotherapy**, many approaches in the 1970s and 1980s claimed to be helping people discover their 'true self', although many sceptics view this as an endless chimerical quest. Obviously there is a major tension here between the everyday sense of a core *me* with a unique character and the problems which arise when this is subjected to rigorous analysis and Psychological theorising. In everyday life, people also regularly talk about poor 'self-images' and the notion that our self, or at least our sense of what it is, can be changed is not entirely consistent with the idea of it as an enduring unitary core of our identity. Much of the recent critique of the concept has come from feminist psychologists (e.g. Henriques *et al.*, 1998) and it has also been related to 'race' issues (e.g. Mama, 1995). (There are in fact connections with **existentialism**, in that 'Self' may be equated to 'essence' in Existentialist thought, where again it is something we have to actively create rather than an unchanging core, and is in a constant dynamically changing state.) It is therefore a rather slippery term of which students should be wary, close attending to the theoretical context in which it is appearing before assuming they know what it supposed to mean.

References and further reading

Gergen, K.J. (1991) *The Saturated Self: Dilemmas of Identity in Conemporary Life*, New York: Basic Books.
—— (ed.) (1993) *Refiguring Self and Psychology*, Aldershot: Ashgate.
—— (2001) *Social Construction in Context*, London: Sage.
Henriques, J. *et al* (1998) *Changing the Subject: Psychology, Social Regulation and Subjectivity*, London: Routledge.
James, W. (1890) *Principles of Psychology*, New York: Henry Holt.
Mama, A. (1995) *Beyond the Masks: Race, Gender and Subjectivity*, London: Routledge.

SEMANTICS

Branch of linguistics concerned with the study of word meaning. More broadly 'semantic' means pertaining to language meaning and is used in everyday contexts such as debates about the precise 'semantics' of political statements. The topic is a little complicated by the fact that two kinds of meaning are usually recognised: *denotative* and *connotative*. A word's 'denotation' is equivalent to its dictionary definition, the precise species to which the word 'tiger' refers, for example, its 'connotations' are the penumbra of associations which a word acquires, so in the case of 'tiger' it has connotative meanings of fierceness and stealth. We might also 'decode' a phrase like 'a frank exchange of views' as connoting an almighty argument.

See also: *semantic memory* under **memory.**

SENSORY DEPRIVATION

To a large degree self-explanatory – the removal of sensory stimulation from someone who is awake. This may be achieved to varying degrees and in various ways, by immersion in a flotation tank blind-folded and with ear-muffs, for example. It achieved widespread pub-licity in the 1960s following a series of experiments in 1958 by D.O. Hebb at McGill University in Canada (discussed in Hebb, 1958). Since then, sensory deprivation has proved extremely controversial, much early work being funded by the military in connection with developing interrogation techniques and understanding **brainwash-ing** (McCoy, 2006). However, psychotherapeutic applications of the phenomenon were later pioneered by John Lilly (best known for his work with dolphins) (Lilly, 1977), after which a great popular demand for flotation-tank sensory deprivation as a therapeutic tech-nique for meditation and relaxation developed and continues. Prolonged sensory deprivation can, however, have serious and enduring psychological consequences. An early and accessible review of the topic was Vernon (1963), more recently, however, most cov-erage is to be found in more general works on sleep and physiological psychology or in historical works such as McCoy's. Book-length texts on it now tend to be of non-Psychological 'New Age' and literary kinds.

References and further reading

Biderman, A.D. and Zimmer, H. (1961) *The Manipulation of Human Behavior*, New York: Wiley.
Hebb, D.O. (1958) *Textbook of Psychology*, Philadelphia, PA: W.B. Saunders.
Lilly, J. (1977) *The Deep Self: Profound Relaxation and the Flotation Tank Technique*, New York: Simon & Schuster.
McCoy, A. (2006) *A Question of Torture: CIA Interrogation from the Cold War to the War on Terror*, New York: Metropolitan Books.
Solomon, P. *et al.* (eds.) (1961) *Sensory Deprivation: A Symposium Held at Harvard Medical School*, Cambridge, MA: Harvard University Press.
Vernon, J. (1965) *Inside the Black Room*, London: Souvenir Press.

SEXUALITY AND GENDER

It is now fairly standard practice to differentiate between these. Sexuality refers to an individual's sexual orientation and preferences, while gender refers to biological identity as male, female or her-maphrodite. The distinction began to make headway during the 1970s and more rapidly in the 1980s. It was felt necessary in the context of feminist thinking, the gay rights movement and broader **social constructionism** within Psychology to challenge the notion that there was a necessary, clear and universal linkage between biological sex and 'psychological' sexuality, sex-roles or other behaviours considered 'natural' in their gender-appropriateness. Usage does, however, remain fuzzy on occasion. In particular, 'gender identity' can be the opposite of a person's biological gender, i.e. they may 'feel' as if they are thoroughly female while being biologically male. This goes beyond psychological sexual orientation as hetero-, homo- or bi-sexual and may be considered as 'psychological gender'. While not excluding the existence of linkages between the two levels, the distinction enables these to be discussed and analysed on a case-by-case basis rather than treated as straightforwardly obvious, as had usually happened in the past. For an overview of the issue from a radical standpoint, see Stainton Rogers (2001).

References and further reading

Lips, H.M. (1996) *Sex and Gender: An Introduction*, New York: Mayfield.

Paul, E.L. (ed.) (2000) *Taking Sides: Clashing Views on Controversial Issues in Sex and Gender*, New York: McGraw-Hill.

Smith, B (2006) *The Psychology of Sex and Gender*, London: Pearson Education.

Stainton Rogers, W.R. (2001) *The Psychology of Gender and Sexuality: An Introduction*, Milton Keynes: Open University Press.

Turner, P.J. (1995) *Psychology: Sex, Gender and Identity*, Leicester: BPS Books.

SIBLING RIVALRY

Competitive rivalry typically exhibited towards each other by children in the same family. While Alfred Adler's *Individual Psychology* played a major initial role in introducing the topic, the general use of the phrase now lacks any theoretical significance.

SIGNAL DETECTION THEORY (SDT)

Developed by J.A. Swets and W.P. Tanner Jr during the 1950s and early 1960s, SDT adopted information theory concepts to study and interpret perceptual and auditory processes and, crucially, decision-making based on these. The central notion was that these processes involved detecting information ('signals') against the background of 'noise' (in the technical sense of irrelevant information), which includes 'internal' as well as 'external' noise. There are obviously four options: (1) signal present and detected: (2) signal present and unde-tected (or rejected); (3) signal absent but wrongly detected; and (4) signal absent and undetected. On this relatively simple basis it became possible to explore and mathematically model sensation-based decision-making in a wide variety of conditions. Clearly the consequences of failing to detect a signal and erroneously detecting one – (1) and (3) – differ enormously, resulting in greater or lesser willingness to detect or reject in different circumstances. Individuals will also have biases in this regard. SDT thus marked a meeting point between **psychophysics** (which it largely revolutionised) and **Cognitive Psychology**. One interesting consequence of the SDT approach was the aban-donment of the idea of clear-cut sensory thresholds and their repla-cement by the notion of a declining curve of probability. SDT continues to play a role as a powerful mathematically rigorous tech-nique. Contextually it is no accident that SDT originated at a time when radar and diagnostic use of X-rays were rapidly developing.

References and further reading

Swets, J.A. (ed.) (1964) *Signal Detection and Recognition by Human Observers*. New York: Wiley.
Tanner, W.P., Jr. and Swets, J.A. (1954) 'A Decision-making Theory of Visual Detection', *Psychological Review*, 61: 401–9.

SITUATIONISM

Broad term referring to the role of situational factors in determining behaviour as opposed to internal psychological ones. As well as cri-tiques of conventional **personality theory** of the 'trait' or 'type' kind, situationist approaches have been very prominent in social Psychology. The **obedience** experiments of S. Milgram and P. Zimbardo's Stanford Prison Experiment could both be cited as famous examples. While the term can be used descriptively of any approach which explains the psychological in situational terms, there is a self-identified 'Situationist' group within US Psychology (see the website www.thesituationist.wordpress.com) which advocates the situationist perspective in a more evangelical fashion. While this movement appears to have a fairly radical agenda, it seems to have little explicit connection with **social constructionism** as such. Current 'situationism' and 'situationists' in Psychology should not be confused with the revolutionary 1960s movement of the same name which was prominent in the mayhem of 1968, especially in mainland Europe.

SLEEPER EFFECT

An effect identified by American social psychologist C. Hovland (see Hovland *et al*, 1949). In researching **attitude** change and persuasion it was found that the effects of someone's giving a speech advocating a position unpopular with the audience were minimal when their opinion was assessed immediately after the speech. When re-assessed some days or weeks later, however, it seemed that they had, in the meantime, shifted towards the speaker's position. In the initial research the focus was on the credibility of the message's origin and related to the delayed effect of information from a discreditable source. This was called the 'sleeper effect'. The robustness of the effect has been much disputed since, and for a recent overview, see Kumkale and Albarracín (2004).

Reference

Hovland, C., Lumsdaine, A. and Sheffield, F. (1949) *Experiments on Mass Communication*, Princeton, NJ: Princeton University Press.
Kumkale, G. T. and Albarracín, D. (2004) 'The Sleeper Effect in Persuasion: A Meta-analytic Review', *Psychological Bulletin*, 130 (1): 143–72.

SOCIAL COGNITION

A rather broad term referring both to the social nature of cognition itself and the ways in which people think about, explain and conceive the social world (and how to behave within it). In the first sense, it covers the study of **social representations** and some aspects of **social constructionism**. In the latter sense, however, it represents the anti-constructionist tradition within social Psychology and includes **attribution theory**, **cognitive dissonance theory**, and **just world hypothesis** research, plus various facets of **attitude** research. Regarding the individual as a 'social cognizer', a person thinking about the social world, five main approaches have been identified (Leyens and Dardenne, 1996). These they call 'the consistent or rationalizing person', 'the naïve scientist', 'the data-processing trainee', 'the cognitive miser' and 'the motivated tactician or social agent'. It is unclear to what extent we should consider these as rival theoretical models or complementary in addressing rather different aspects of social life.

References and further reading

Augustinos, M., Walker, I. and Donaghue, N. (2006) *Social Cognition: An Integrated Introduction*, London: Sage.
Leyens, J.-P. and Dardenne, B. (1996) 'La Perception et Connaissance d'Autrui', in M. Ruchelle, J. Requin and M. Roberts (eds) *Traité de psychologie expérimentale*, Paris: Presses Universitaires de France.
Moskowitz, G.B. (2004) *Social Congition: Understanding Self and Others*, New York: Guilford.

SOCIAL CONSTRUCTIONISM

Historically, social constructionism has a variety of quite different roots including the Marxist view of consciousness as mirroring social relations, British linguistic philosophy, the 'Historical Psychology' position of the German philosopher-historian Wilhelm Dilthey (1833–1911) and post-1950 developments in the philosophy and sociology of knowledge (Berger and Luckman, [1966] 1976). Billig (2008) has recently traced its lineage even as far back as Anthony Ashley Cooper, Lord Shaftesbury (1671–1713). In Psychology, its modern re-emergence took place within social Psychology and was signalled by a 1973 paper by US social psychologist Kenneth Gergen, who remains its leading proponent. The European intellectual climate has, however, proved more receptive than the North American.

Essentially 'social constructionism' proposes that knowledge is the product of social (including social psychological) processes. It therefore follows that the ways we experience both the world and ourselves, the phenomena we identify, and the meanings they have, can never be known to correspond 'objectively' to reality: reality is 'socially constructed'. Even so, there are numerous interpretations of what this really means, reflecting the doctrine's complex origins. One central ambiguity is whether it is understood as applying to all knowledge as a matter of logical necessity or whether it should be taken as an empirical hypothesis with regard to only some kinds of knowledge. A second issue is whether it is only the 'knowledge' which is socially constructed or the phenomena, the objects of knowledge, themselves. For Psychology, therefore, the question is whether *all* Psychological knowledge and/or psychological phenomena are socially constructed or only specific empirically identifiable instances. On the second interpretation, psychological phenomena may be considered as actually differing in this respect from those studied by the physical sciences. One might concede that the objects of physical scientific knowledge have an objective existence beyond our understanding of them, but for Psychology the very objects of knowledge themselves might well only exist as 'social constructions'. It is easy to identify a whole range of psychological concepts and phenomena produced by specific social circumstances in this second sense – 'feeling in a state of grace', for example, can only occur in the context of Christian religious belief while 'race prejudice' requires a concept of 'race', contact between people classified as belonging to different such 'races' and hostility towards at least one of these other than one's own. It is also perhaps anachronistic to apply some twentieth-century Psychological terms, to earlier periods and non-western cultures – 'authoritarianism', 'high IQ', and 'conformity', for example – at least with their full Psychological meanings. On the other hand, we might reasonably assume that certain basic emotions and personality traits are universal 'natural' psychological phenomena – being happy or sad, being lazy or hard-working – our terms for them presumably having their synonyms in all societies. Yet surprisingly, even such a basic category as 'emotion' has no obvious equivalent in some societies (see **emotion**).

Why this is an important theoretical issue is because the natural sciences in general assume the phenomena they study to be constant, for example, that the laws of physics and chemistry apply throughout the universe and always have done. But to the extent that psychological phenomena are socially constructed, they cannot be assumed to be constant in this way, on the contrary, they are in continuous flux. This has obvious bearings on the scientific status of Psychology itself, for it may be argued that far from simply discovering 'objective' 'scientific truths' about its subject matter, it is itself a factor in bringing about psychological change. On this view, the very language which Psychology introduces reflects and initiates changes in how we understand and experience ourselves, i.e. changes us psychologically. Beyond social Psychology, social constructionist approaches have been widely used by feminist psychologists and historians of Psychology as well as applied to more traditionally orthodox topics such as **memory** (Middleton and Edwards, 1990) and intellectual disability (Rapley, 2004). Often identified by its critics with what they see as nihilistic post-modernism, this is an over-simplification. It has in fact generated much valuable and insightful work, drawing attention to features of both Psychology and its subject matter that were long ignored, casting the discipline's history in new lights, and focusing attention on some central, if still unresolved, theoretical issues of crucial importance. These include the scientific status of Psychology, the role of language in 'constructing' psychological reality, and the fixity or not of 'human nature'. See also **reflexivity**.

References and further reading

Berger, P. and Luckman, T. ([1966] 1976) *The Social Construction of Reality: A Treatise in the Sociology of Knowledge*, Harmondsworth: Penguin.
Billig, M. (2008) *The Hidden Roots of Psychology*, London: Sage.
Gergen, K.J. (2001) *Social Construction in Context*, London: Sage.
Harré, R. (ed.) (1988) *The Social Construction of Emotions*, Oxford: Blackwell.
Middleton, D. and Edwards, D. (1990) *Collective Remembering*, London: Sage.
Parker, I. (ed.) *Social Construction, Discourse and Realism*, London: Sage.
Potter, J. (1996) *Representing Reality: Discourse, Rhetoric and Social Construction*, London: Sage.
Rapley, M. (2004) *The Social Construction of Intellectual Disability*, Cambridge: Cambridge University Press.
Searle, J.R. (1997) *The Construction of Social Reality*, New York: Free Press.

SOCIAL DARWINISM

The application of Darwinian evolutionary theory, particularly the 'survival of the fittest' concept (a phrase actually coined by Herbert Spencer), to human affairs. Generally used for the late nineteenth–early twentieth-century period when this approach became very influential (see also **eugenics**). In retrospect, this is seen as exploiting evolutionary theory to justify, and view as natural, extreme competitive capitalism and international rivalry up to and including war itself. These were simply 'natural selection' operating in human affairs and were necessary for continued 'progress'. Ideologically this was often used to counter the rising left-wing socialist and communist movements. One aspect of this was what is now called *scientific racism* – the explanation of race differences in evolutionary terms, and perception of the relationships between 'races' as either competitive or naturally hierarchical. Events between 1914 and 1945 effectively killed off the appeal of Social Darwinism, while scientifically it also lost its credibility. In different forms, it has subsequently seemed to resurface from time to time, notably in some aspects of **sociobiology** during the 1980s.

References and further reading

Crook, P. (2007) *Darwin's Coat-Tails: Essays on Social Darwinism*, Bern: Peter Lang.

Dickens, P. (2000) *Social Darwinism*, Milton Keynes: Open University Press.

Hawkins, M. (1997) *Social Darwinism in European and American Thought, 1860–1945: Nature as Model and Nature as Threat*, Cambridge: Cambridge University Press.

Hofstadter, R. (1955) *Social Darwinism in American Thought*, Boston: Beacon Press.

Jones, G. (1980) *Social Darwinism and English Thought: The Interaction between Biological and Social Theory*, Brighton: Harvester.

SOCIAL FACILITATION

The enhancement of performance in the presence of others. A long-standing topic in social Psychology – the topic indeed of what some claim to be the very first social Psychology experiment (Triplett, 1898). It is of course well known to actors, stage entertainers and sports people that audiences can raise one's performance to levels unobtainable in rehearsal or solitary practice. The effect can, however, be demonstrated to occur more widely, but is dependent on how well the task has already been mastered.

References and further reading

Triplett, N.D. (1898) 'The Dynamogenic Factor in Pacemaking and Competition', *American Journal of Psychology*, 9: 507–33.

Zajonc, R.B. (1965) 'Social Facilitation', *Science*, 149: 169–74.

SOCIAL IDENTITY THEORY

Theoretical account developed, initially by British-based social psychologist H. Tajfel, to explain inter-group conflict and the role of group membership in creating and sustaining self-esteem. Much work has now been done in attempting to unravel the relationship between self-esteem and discriminatory behaviour or attitudes towards out-group members. The causal dynamics remain confused, however. Although social identity theory itself is very much associated with Tajfel and his followers, the study of inter-group relations in social Psychology goes back to the early post-Second World War years. What is distinctive about social identity theory is the theoretical integration of self-esteem and 'identity' issues with inter-group dynamics as a whole, earlier work tending to look only at the latter.

References and further reading

Brown, R. (1996) 'Intergroup relations', in M. Hewstone, W. Stroebe and G.M. Stephenson (eds) *Introduction to Social Psychology*, Oxford: Blackwell.

Tajfel, H. (ed.) (1978) *Differentiation between Social Groups: Studies in the Social Psychology of Intergroup Relations*, London: Academic Press.

—— (1981) *Human Groups and Social Categories: Studies in Social Psychology*, Cambridge: Cambridge University Press.

SOCIAL REPRESENTATIONS

Related to the early twentieth-century notion of *collective representations* introduced by the French sociologist Émile Durkheim, this concept was promoted by the French-based, Romanian-born, social psychologist Serge Moscovici in the 1960s (although English translations only became available much later, see especially Moscovici, 2000). The argument is that we rarely see the world (especially the social world) objectively 'as it really is', but rather through the filter of a socially learned repertoire of collectively established assumptions and ideas. In doing so, we impose a prior set of meanings upon it. There are thus 'social representations' of all kinds of things, but particularly of types of people – the 'single mother', the politician, the Muslim youth, the vicar ... the list is endless. But we also have them of situations ('the football match'), settings ('the operating theatre'), institutions (the Church of England) and individuals (Jimi Hendrix, Queen Victoria, Albert Einstein ... in fact almost anyone who has become famous). In relation to abstract ideas, social representation renders them concrete and objectifiable – think, for example, of how we understand 'justice' in terms of social representations of police, courtrooms, prisons, etc. Social representations are in fact necessary for communication to occur at all. One task of social Psychology then is to understand how social representations are formed and operate, sometimes in a negative fashion. There are clear connections with **stereotyping**, and **roles**, but these may considered as specific kinds of social representation.

References and further reading

Duveen, G. and Lloyd, B. (eds) (1990) *Social Representations and the Development of Knowledge*, Cambridge: Cambridge University Press.

Markova, I. (2003) *Dialogicality and Social Representations: The Dynamics of Mind*, Cambridge: Cambridge University Press.

Moscovici, S. (1985) *The Age of the Crowd: A Historical Treatise on Mass Psychology*, Cambridge: Cambridge University Press.

—— (2000) *Social Representations: Essays in Social Psychology*, Oxford: Blackwell.

SOCIOBIOLOGY

A sub-discipline effectively founded by the American natural historian, evolutionary theorist and ethologist E.O. Wilson in 1975. At their most ambitious sociobiologists claimed that virtually all human behaviour could, potentially at least, be explained in genetic evolutionary terms. Central to this was the idea of *inclusive fitness*, the principle that behaviour was ultimately aimed at enhancing the survival of, in the first instance, one's own genes, and then those of one's closest relatives. This concept proved extremely versatile in relation to much enigmatic animal behaviour (such as apparent altruism in vampire bats, lesbianism in sea-gulls and male homosexuality in a wide range of species). The extension of this analysis to human behaviour was rapid and in 1981 C.J. Lumsden and Wilson introduced the notion of the 'culturgen' as a cultural equivalent of the 'gene' – an artefact, custom, idea or behaviour, the historical fate of which was analysable in terms of its 'survival' value for those adopting it. This anticipated Richard Dawkins's later concept of the 'meme'. During its 1980s heyday, sociobiology was very fervently promoted and seen by many as raising the spectre of **social Darwinism** at a time when the ideological climate in the USA and Britain was especially congenial to this interpretation. Other evolutionary theorists such as Stephen J. Gould and R.C. Lewontin also opposed sociobiology's ambitions on theoretical grounds, as did many psychologists, since it appeared to be challenging the discipline itself. Its popular image was not helped by the adoption of its ideas by psychologists such as the Canadian J.-P. Rushton who supported the idea of innate race-differences in intelligence and other psychological traits. It took some time for the wheat to be sifted from the chaff, but by the early 1990s much of the furore had died down, and within Psychology the sub-discipline of **Evolutionary Psychology** emerged, based to a considerable degree on sociobiological principles. Whatever its merits when applied to human behaviour (and there are some), there is little doubt that as far as animal behaviour is concerned, sociobiology greatly enhanced our understanding. (I am referencing this only minimally as Psychologically relevant texts are given under Evolutionary Psychology.)

See also: **altruism, ethology**.

References and further reading

Lumsden, C.J. and Wilson, E.O. (1981) *Genes, Mind and Culture. The Coevolutionary Press*, Cambridge, MA: Harvard University Press.

Wilson, E.O. (1975) *Sociobiology: The New Synthesis*, Cambridge, MA: Harvard University Press.

SOMATISATION

The expression of mental distress via physical symptoms. This is similar in meaning to, but distinct from, **psychosomatic**. The difference is that somatisation is a general tendency or style of manifesting mental distress rather than the appearance of specific physical symptoms having a psychological cause. In recent decades those working with, for example, torture victims, from a wide range of African, Asian and South American countries have come to appreciate that there are substantial cultural differences in the level of somatisation.

SOMATOTYPES

Term introduced by American personality theorist W.H. Sheldon for the three basic types, or more accurately, dimensions, of body-build, which he believed were intimately bound up with **personality**. These were: *ectomorphs* (thin and lean, to put it crudely), *mesomorphs* (muscular) and *endomorphs* (fat). He developed a technique for measuring the relative presence of these in the individual case (each being rateable on a 1–7 scale). The major outcome was the amazing *Atlas of Man* (1954) with photos of examples of the entire range (faces and genitals masked), each being jocularly given an animal label (some extreme endomorphs being 'Dugongs and Manatees'). A comparable project for an *Atlas of Woman* collapsed in scandal, and the application of the typology to females was in any case more problematic. The German psychiatrist E. Kretschmer had also related personality to body-build in the 1920s, and the notion of such a connection goes back to antiquity and **physiognomy**, as well being common in **Folk Psychology**. Fun, but little developed subsequently, and some conclusions from early applications of the theory were staggeringly obvious, e.g. that mesomorphy was more likely to be associated with juvenile delinquency than either of the two (Glueck *et al.*, 1956).

References and further reading

Glueck, S., Sheldon, E.H. and Glueck, E. (1956) *Physique and Delinquency*, New York: Harper.

Sheldon, E.H. (1954) *Atlas of Man: A Guide for Somatotyping the Adult Male at All Ages*, New York: Harper.

STEREOTYPING

Introduced as a Psychological term (as opposed to referring to a printing technique) by US journalist Walter Lippman in 1922 (Lippman, 1922), this rapidly entered everyday language. Stereotyping is perceiving and treating others as representative of some group to which, on the basis of superficial appearance alone, one assumes they belong, and in the belief that they possess the psychological traits which one believes to characterise members of that group. 'Racial', religious and national stereotypes are numerous and often quite detailed. If some level of stereotyping is unavoidable in everyday encounters, the danger lies in accepting predominantly negative stereotypes and using them to justify one's behaviour and beliefs. The greater the social or cultural distance between two people, the more likely they are to perceive and treat the other stereotypically on first encounter. In some circumstances this may amount to no more than light-heartedly playing a familiar national stereotype role when in another country as the first move in establishing a closer acquaintance with the other. In others, it may be offensive, provocative, patronising and verging on delusional. There is something a little paradoxical about condemning all stereotyping outright, since we are all torn between visually signalling the way we wish to be treated, or **role** we see ourselves as playing, in any given context and wanting to be treated as an individual without others making prior assumptions about us. Professional roles, from police-person and doctor to night-club bouncer or waitress all rely on eliciting a form of stereotyped response, typically signalled by dress and posture. Most Psychological work, however, has addressed negative stereotyping in the contexts of inter-group relations, **racism** and various other forms of **prejudice** involving uncontrollable physical traits, gender or sexual orientation. Many such stereotypes can be considered as forms of **social representation**.

Reference

Lippman, W. (1922) *Public Opinion*, New York: Harcourt, Brace.

STRESS

There can be few popular Psychological terms which have become so hazy as 'stress'. Essentially, of course, it refers to a state caused by being subject to excessive demands on one's emotions and/or time which render it difficult to function effectively in all areas of life. This can result in a host of symptoms such as depression, chronic tiredness, bad temper, anxiety, impotency and lowered quality of work-performance. It is, however, accepted in Psychology that it is a very vague term for a broad sweep of real-life situations. The first move to bring order to the scene is, as so often, to differentiate between stress caused by external 'stressors' (e.g. an impending work interview or exam) and by internal factors (such as conflicted emotional feelings towards a partner or having to reconcile work and domestic life or conflicting **roles**). The different responses to stress have also been studied intensely in recent years, especially in health Psychology, since these can be as diverse as heavy drinking and **psychosomatic** illness. Disentangling physiological and hormonal aspects of stress from purely psychological ones is another important issue. Stress is not therefore a distinct unitary phenomenon but something of a catch-all term. But while psychologists now mostly understand this, in the world at large it has come to function as a sort for universal explanation for psychological discontents and malaise of almost every kind. Stress is real enough, but the word itself often masks as much as it reveals about what is actually going on. For the linguistically minded, the *New Oxford English Dictionary* takes over seven columns to cover the noun form of 'stress', the Psychological/biological sense we are concerned with being definition I 3g. While I 1a, dating back to the Middle Ages, is very similar, referring to affliction (and closely related to 'distress'), sense I 3g dates only to 1942, and most other senses are in one way or another physical. There is a large related literature, much of it either medical or of the popular 'self-help' and 'coping' kind.

References and further reading

Cooper, C.L. (ed.) (2004) *Handbook of Stress Medicine and Health*, 2nd edn, London: Taylor & Francis.

Hobfoll, S.E. (2004) *Stress, Culture and Community: The Psychology and Philosophy of Stress*, Amsterdam: Kluwer.

Oxington, K.V. (ed.) (2005) *Psychology of Stress*, London: Nova Science.

Perrewé, P.L. and Ganster, D.C. (eds) (2002) *Historical and Current Perspectives on Stress and Health*, New York: Elsevier.

STROOP EFFECT

The **reaction time** taken to name the ink-colour of a printed colour name is longer if the colour of the ink is different from the colour name (e.g. if the word 'red' is printed in green). Named after its discoverer J.R. Stroop (Stroop, 1935). This interference effect has proved to be enormously useful as an experimental variable (generally known as the 'Stroop task') in a multitude of contexts, particularly those related to attention and brain functioning. It is particularly robust and resists practice effects. A few variants have been developed for other sense modalities, including an 'emotional Stroop' in which colour-naming of negative emotional words is slower in depressed patients, while colour-naming of emotion-related words is also slower to some degree among 'normals'. The literature on the Stroop effect is almost all in journal paper form, but the Wikipedia entry is a useful starting point.

Reference

Stroop, J.R. (1935) 'Studies of Interference in Serial Verbal Reactions', *Journal of Experimental Psychology*, 18, 643–62.

STRUCTURALISM

A more than usually difficult term as it has at least five meanings within Psychology and other human sciences. The first was its use by the English, US-based, pioneer psychologist E.B. Titchener, a follower of the German W. Wundt. He used the word as a name for his theoretical approach in opposition to **functionalism**. The goal of Titchener's Structuralism was to identify the basic 'structures' of consciousness, by analogy with anatomy in the study of physiology. This he argued was the discipline's necessary foundational task (see also **introspection)**. Almost simultaneously, the French linguist F. de Saussure adopted the term for his 'Structural Linguistics', which was concerned with the structure of how language socially operated and marked a departure from the previous historical focus on etymology and how languages change over time. Shortly after this (during the second decade of the twentieth century), a similar shift in concern occurred in British anthropology, identified with figures such as A. Radcliffe Brown, attention again turning from an evolutionary approach to one focused on how societies operated in the present.

Somewhat confusingly, in the light of the Titchnerian meaning, this was called 'Structural Functionalism' since it addressed the present functions served by the various social 'structures' it was concerned with. Also within anthropology, French anthropologist C. Lévi-Strauss used the term (without 'functionalism') to describe his own theoretical position, which was centrally concerned with so-called 'primitive' thinking and how it was structured by frameworks of symbolic meaning. And finally, Jean Piaget re-introduced the concept into Psychology to describe his own theoretical approach (Piaget, 1971) and that of those, like the Gestalt school, whom he saw as having close affinities with it (see **Piagetian theory**). It is therefore essential to be aware of the context in which it is being used in order to understand its meaning. Finally, the term 'Post-structuralism' was introduced in France in the 1960s by those rejecting C. Lévi-Strauss's tradition, which had greatly influenced French literary criticism and philosophy. Their reaction hinged on a rejection of the reality of the **Self** and, more specifically in relation to writing, the primacy of the author's intentions was also rejected, to be replaced by the notion that all texts are in a sense autonomous and open to a multitude of readings. There are numerous apparent paradoxes and infinite regresses with all this, most obviously that it then becomes a contradiction to try to understand what these post-structuralists meant, if this is what it was! This move is associated with J. Derrida and R. Barthes, while M. Foucault is also often included in the post-structuralist camp. Referencing this topic is clearly problematic, but the following may help.

Reference

Piaget, J. (1971) *Structuralism*, London: Routledge & Kegan Paul.

SUBLIMINAL PERCEPTION

Unconscious awareness of, and usually response to, a visual or auditory stimulus of which one was not conscious. The extent to which this actually occurs remains uncertain but it has periodically received widespread media attention and concern. When first proposed in the 1950s, there was an immediate outcry about the possibility of subliminal advertising – as comedian Lenny Bruce quipped 'I don't know about subliminal advertising but I just bought six tractors'. During the 1970s and intermittently thereafter worries arose, especially in the United States, about subliminal messages being hidden in pop music –

to the extent of people imagining that even reverse messages (only audible when the recording was played backwards) could have an effect. This received wide publicity in the United States in the so-called 'Judas Priest Trial' in Nevada when it was claimed by their parents that 'subliminal messages' embedded in an album by British group Judas Priest had made two boys attempt to commit suicide, one dying immediately, the other three years later. It is, however, difficult to reconcile with **signal detection theory** which denies the existence of fixed sensory thresholds, let alone fixed collective thresholds. While perceptual defence mechanisms may arguably result in repression of perception of unwelcome stimuli which are patently *above* any threshold, subliminal perception involves the reverse and so is less plausible from a 'perceptual defence' perspective. (The phenomenon of **blindsight** is well attested, but this arises in a rather different, physiological, context.) The classic critical study of subliminal perception was Dixon (1971). Although it is possible that something like subliminal perception may occur in the context of certain experimental tasks (such as dichotic listening), little serious Psychological research has been reported since Dixon's book to justify fears of potential covert persuasion and 'brainwashing' being achievable by this means (let alone understanding an inaudible reverse message!).

Reference

Dixon, N.F. (1971) *Subliminal Perception: The Nature of a Controversy*, London: McGraw-Hill.

SUGGESTION, SUGGESTIBILITY

The term 'suggestion' has a long and chequered history in Psychology. In essence, it is the notion that individuals may come to experience or believe things, or even behave in a certain way, as result of being exposed to stimuli which often unconsciously or subliminally (see **subliminal perception**) 'suggest' these experiences, beliefs or behaviours. 'Suggestibility' refers to an individual's susceptibility to this effect. One of the earliest contexts in which the concept was used was **hypnosis**, which came to be seen as a paradigm example of suggestion – not only the induction of the hypnotic state itself ('you are feeling sleepy ... your eyelids are heavy ... ') but the subsequent amenability of the hypnotic subject to behaving and experiencing as the hypnotist instructed them exemplified 'suggestion' in operation. By the end of the nineteenth century, the term was quite ubiquitous, especially in psychotherapeutic discourse. High suggestibility was held to be symptomatic of **hysteria**, many of the psychological symptoms patients reported were supposedly the result of suggestion, and suggestion could also be used to cure them. This culminated in the idea of *auto-suggestion* as promoted by the 'New Nancy' school (see *Nancy School* under **Schools of Psychology**), in which desirable feelings etc. could, it was claimed, be 'implanted' by patients themselves. Crowd behaviour and mass hysteria were also ascribed to 'mass suggestion' while it figured prominently in the earliest works on the psychology of advertising before the First World War. While it gradually lost its central place in Psychological theorising during the 1920s and 1930s, the phenomenon of suggestibility as a **personality** trait has remained widely accepted. (A simple, standard – if unquantifiable – test is to ask someone to stand with their eyes closed and arms outstretched and softly say 'You are falling forward' several times. If the individual quickly begins to lean forward, they are highly suggestible, if they stay vertical, they are not, and if they begin to lean slightly after a couple of repetitions, they are in between. Do not try this at home.) The main difficulty with the concept of suggestion as some kind of fundamental psychological principle was its rather fuzzy generality. Everything, it seemed, could be explained by 'suggestion', but it was hard to delve any deeper into exactly what psycho-physiological and perceptual processes were involved, or how and why it actually operated. In short, 'suggestion' lost most of its explanatory value and came to mask as much as it revealed. This does not mean, however, that expressions like 'she's a very suggestible person' or 'he's highly suggestible' have to be abandoned, only that there is no need to invoke 'suggestion' as a sort of unitary and concrete causal principle. Ellenberger (1970) provides good historical coverage in the broader context of the history of the 'unconscious'. The other references below are a small sample of typical early twentieth-century texts.

References and further reading

Baudouin, C. (1920) *Suggestion and Autosuggestion*, London: Allen & Unwin.
Coué, E. (1922) *Self-Mastery through Conscious Autosuggestion*, London: Allen & Unwin.
Ellenberger, H.F. (1970) *The Discovery of the Unconscious: The History and Evolution of Dynamic Psychiatry*, London: Allen Lane.
Forel, A. (1907) *Hypnotism or Suggestion and Psychotherapy*, New York: Rebman
Jacoby, G.W. (1912) *Suggestion and Psychotherapy*, New York: Charles Scribner's.

SYNAESTHESIA

Strongly associating or even experiencing stimuli in one sense modality with, or as being in, another – seeing sounds, hearing colours, and being able to associate abstract terms and names (like the days of the week) with specific colours. Strictly speaking, the term should only refer to circumstances in which this literally occurs beyond the individual's control. Synaesthesia can occur particularly powerfully during mescalin and LSD intoxication, and is often given mystical significance. It is, however, more mysterious subjectively than neurologically, requiring only some linkage between the neural pathways conveying sensory information. Such linkages occur to some extent quite normally, has anyone ever *not* thought red was a 'warm' colour? In the looser sense, most people are able to make synaesthetic connections, saying the sound of a trumpet is bright red, or that blue reminds them of a muted saxophone. Francis Galton, the Victorian British pioneer psychologist, had great fun with this, distributing questionnaires to acquaintances about the colours of the days of the week (see his *Inquiries into Human Faculty*, 1883). Virtually all the work on synaesthesia focuses on the sound-visual perception case, but taste and smell instances can also occur, although rarely, touch.

References and further reading

Baron-Cohen, S. and Harrison, J.E. (eds) (2000) *Synaesthesia: Classic and Contemporary Readings*, Oxford: Blackwell.

Brougher, K. and Strick, J. (eds) (2005) *Visual Music: Synaesthesia in Art and Music since 1900*, New York: Thames & Hudson.

Dann, K.T. (1998) *Bright Colors Falsely Seen. Synaesthesia and the Search for Transcendent Knowledge*, New Haven, CT: Yale University Press.

Galton, F. (1883) *Inquiries into Human Faculty and Its Development*, London: Macmillan. This was frequently reprinted in a J.M. Dent 'Everyman series' edition.

Harrison, J.E. (2001) *Synaesthesia: The Strangest Thing*, Oxford: Oxford University Press.

SYNAPSE

The junction between nerve endings via which neural activation is transmitted. The adjective is *synaptic*.

TACHISTOSCOPE

A mechanical perceptual research instrument enabling visual stimuli to be exposed for varying lengths of time. Several different versions of this were developed in the late nineteenth century, but its use declined fairly quickly after about 1970 as computer-based versions became available. The latter remain widely used in research on visual perception and **attention**.

TELEKINESIS

The movement of physical objects by the power of thought alone. One of the most doubtful of supposed **paranormal** phenomena. There is some faint evidence that the distribution of small balls falling through a pyramidal arrangement of spikes – which should statistically result in a *normal distribution curve* – can be very slightly affected by a highly concentrating observer, but this finding is very elusive. Discussed in more general parapsychology books, but the following give opposing positions.

References and further reading

Charpak, G. and Broch, H. (2005) *Debunked! ESP, Telekinesis and Other Pseudoscience*, Baltimore, MD: Johns Hopkins University Press

Holt, H. (2005) *Telekinesis*, Whitefish, MT: Kissinger (reprinted from Holt's 1914 book *On the Cosmic Relations*).

TEMPERAMENT

Along with *character*, the term 'temperament' was long used in contexts where psychologists now use **personality**. Its origins go back to antiquity and the notion that the basic elements identified by classical philosophers – earth, air, fire and water – were embodiments of the four permutations of the cold *vs* hot and wet *vs* dry principles. After a long and convoluted evolution, taking in the physician Galen's 'humoural' theory, this yielded the popular notion of four basic temperaments (the term being related to 'temperature', revealing its source, like that of 'temper' in the 'cold *vs* hot' polarity) generally called sanguine, choleric, melancholic and phlegmatic. These lay at the core of the personality *type* concept. By the late nineteenth century the term had lost its earlier theoretical connotations as signifying which of the four traditionally identified bodily humours of, respectively, blood, choler, black bile and yellow bile was dominant and had become a term usually simply describing an individual's general style of relating and reacting to the world. It differed from *character* primarily in that the latter had a moral dimension to it, as evident in the phrase 'strength of character'. The reasons for the replacement of these terms by personality are well discussed in Danziger (1997).

Reference

Danziger, K. (1997) *Naming the Mind: How Psychology Found Its Language*, London: Sage.

THEMATIC APPERCEPTION TEST (TAT)

Devised by US **personality** theorist Henry Murray and an associate Christiana D. Morgan in 1935, the TAT is a **projective test** comprising a set of 31 pictures (see Murray, 1938). The scoring method underwent a subsequent period of development and the final version of the test appeared in 1943. The person taking the test is required to describe what each presented picture shows, their responses are recorded and then scored according to the **needs** expressed. (Only a sample of the full set are used.) Murray's original TAT was soon followed up by others, notably P.M. Symonds, E.S. Schneidman and the '*Blacky Test*'. Scoring methods varied, including forms of **content analysis**.

References and further reading

Murray, H.A. (ed.) (1938) *Explorations in Personality: A Clinical and Experimental Study of Fifty Men of College Age*. New York: Oxford University Press.
—— (1943) *Thematic Apperception Test*, Cambridge, MA: Harvard University Press.

THEORY OF MIND (TOM)

In addition to straightforward philosophical and Psychological senses – theorising about the nature of mind – the expression is now widely used in developmental Psychology to refer to the individual's understanding of how their own and other people's minds work, including their emotions and feelings. The term 'theory' here is being used somewhat loosely, being intended to signify the existence of some kind of model or image or set of working assumptions. The topic, if not identified as such, has long been present in studies of child development and maturation but is currently receiving intense attention. This sense of the phrase elides fairly imperceptibly into its use in the **Folk Psychology** debate, in which a central bone of contention is how far 'Folk Psychology' can be considered to contain an implicit 'theory of mind'.

References and further reading

Astington, J.W. and Baird, J.A. (2005) *Why Language Matters for Theory of Mind*, New York: Oxford University Press.

Baird, J.A. and Sokol, B.W. (2004) *Connections between Theory of Mind and Sociomoral Development*, Indianapolis, IN: Jossey-Bass.

Doherty, M. (2008) *Theory of Mind: How Children Understand Others' Thoughts and Feelings*, London: Psychology Press.

Repacholi, B. and Slaughter, V. (2003) *Individual Differences in Theory of Mind: Implications for Typical and Atypical Development*, Hove: Psychology Press.

Saxe, R. and Baron-Cohen, R.S. (eds) (2007) *Theory of Mind* (Special Issue of *Neuroscience*), Hove: Psychology Press.

THERIOMORPHISM

An uncommon, primarily anthropological, concept occasionally used by C.G. Jung and others to refer to the notion of humans acquiring or internalising animal 'souls'. Related to **physiomorphism** but narrower in range of use and used primarily of religious beliefs. It also does not, of course, imply acceptance that such humans really can possess animal souls whereas physiomorphism refers to an actual, if hypothetical, psychological process. In some respects, theriomorphism may be related to 'possession' phenomena in which humans appear to become 'possessed' by animal spirits (e.g. the 'werewolf' or 'lycanthrope' beloved of horror movie makers). This is ritually undertaken in some cultures. The term *zoomorphism* is virtually synonymous.

TOP-DOWN AND BOTTOM-UP

Academic colloquialisms differentiating between theoretical approaches. Top-down theories are those which take the whole situation or phenomenon as their starting point and analyse it into its components or component processes. Conversely, bottom-up approaches start from a single elementary process or phenomenon and see how far this can be used to explain more complex processes or phenomena. Examples of each would be **Gestalt Psychology** as a 'top-down' approach and **behaviourist learning theory** as a 'bottom-up' one (building upwards from the (stimulus-response) S-R connection as a basic unit). The connection with **reductionism** is not straightforward as both may be used in either a reductionist or anti-reductionist spirit. There is some ambiguity in how these terms are used in that they may refer both to styles of theorising and to the nature of a theory itself. In the latter sense, top-down theories ascribe a major role to prior knowledge in how we process currently experienced stimuli, while bottom-up theories minimise this role. A Psychological theory in which 'higher' cognitive processes are seen as primary determinants of behaviour is thus a 'top-down' theory, but this does not in principle mean that the theorist has a broader philosophical commitment to 'holistic' approaches as Gestalt psychologists did. Conversely, an 'instinct' theory prioritising genetic determination of behaviour would be 'bottom-up', but not necessarily imply commitment to explanation in terms of some quasi-atomic basic units (even 'genes').

TOPOLOGICAL PSYCHOLOGY

Term usually used to refer to Kurt Lewin's (1890–1947) work (Lewin, 1936 being the classic text). Lewin, an associate of the *Gestalt* school and their fellow German exiles in the USA, developed an elaborate theoretical model using the concept of the 'life space', its various regions, and how these were interrelated, including relations between two or more people's 'life spaces'. He devised a technique for graphically representing these. The summary by Hall and Lindzey (1957) remains the most accessible account. While Lewin's Topological Psychology had disappeared by the 1960s, its covert influence within Social Psychology and **personality** should not be underestimated and he remains very highly regarded. Although virtually defunct as a self-identified school in North America and Western Europe, there is a Kurt Lewin Center for Psychological Research at Kazimierz Wielki University in Bydgoszcz, Poland, founded in 2004, dedicated to promoting his theory.

References

Hall, C.S. and Lindzey, G. (1957) *Theories of Personality*, London & New York: Wiley.

Lewin, K. (1936) *Principles of Topological Psychology*, New York: McGraw-Hill.

Useful website

Kurt Lewin Center website: www.lewincenter.ukw.edu.pl/index.php

TRAIT

Used in **personality theory** to refer to discrete behaviours, or behavioural tendencies, commonly displayed by an individual. The term was effectively introduced by F.H. and G.W. Allport (Allport and Allport, 1921) (see also Allport, 1937). Traits may be understood to signify broader underlying factors such as position on a particular personality dimension, and can thus be used as a basis for **psychometric** personality tests. If asked to describe someone who is **obsessional**, extraverted or, in Freudian terms, *orally aggressive*, we would typically list a number of traits we believe typify this, in the case of the obsessional: tidiness, being extremely prompt, preoccupation with neatness, attentiveness to detail, etc. Whether all such traits actually do correlate as signifiers of obsessionality would be a matter for empirical enquiry, but some almost amount to defining characteristics. Commonly contrasted to the 'type' approach in personality theory texts.

References

Allport, F.H. and Allport, G.W. (1931) 'Personality Traits: Their Classification and Measurement', *Journal of Abnormal and Social Psychology*, 16: 6–10.

Allport, G.W. (1937) *Personality. A Psychological Interpretation*, New York: Holt.

UNCONSCIOUS

One should observe at the outset that this term is grammatically versatile and slightly ambiguous. In everyday usage, it can mean: (1) completely unaware of the external world as in sleep, when comatose or in a fainting fit; and (2) not consciously aware of a specific action or external object, as in 'Despite their shuffling, he remained quite unconscious of the fact that the audience found his remarks highly offensive'. In the first sense it also, as a noun, yields unconsciousness. Traditionally it was used in these two descriptive senses. Although the concept has a long and complex history, the Psychological notions of 'the unconscious' and 'unconscious psychological processes' only clearly emerged in the mid-nineteenth century when British physiologist Carpenter (1852) initially proposed the idea that there were 'unconscious cerebrations' (a term he borrowed from his contemporary Thomas Laycock). During the late nineteenth century the notion of an active unconscious psychological realm gained rapid circulation, the classic philosophical treatment being German philosopher E. von Hartmann's three-volume *Philosophie des Unbewussten* (1869), translated into English in 1884 as *Philosophy of the Unconscious*. By the time Sigmund Freud was making the concept central to **psychoanalysis**, it was thus already in circulation. The 'unconscious' was widely popular in psychiatry and evolutionary thought had reinforced the plausibility of 'lower' levels of the mind operating instinctively or 'beneath' conscious awareness. In mainstream academic Psychology, the idea of 'unconscious awareness' is generally accepted in relation to phenomena such as **blindsight** and, far more controversially, **subliminal perception**, which appear to indicate that people can respond to stimuli of which they are consciously unaware. The classic historical study of the topic is Ellenberger (1970), a landmark work in the history of Psychology.

See also: *collective unconscious* under **Analytical Psychology**; **psychoanalytic concepts**.

References and further reading

Carpenter, W.B. (1852) *Principles of Human Physiology*, 4th edn, London: John Churchill.

Ellenberger, H.F. (1970) *The Discovery of the Unconscious: The History and Evolution of Dynamic Psychiatry*, London: Allen Lane.

Hartmann, E. von (1884) *The Philosophy of the Unconscious*, 3 vols, London: Trübner (a single volume edition was issued in 1931 by Kegan Paul, Trench and Trübner, London).

VALIDITY

In **psychometrics**, validity, to put it crudely, refers either to how far a measuring instrument measures what it is supposed to, or to the appropriateness of research designs to the research topic. Do not confuse with **reliability**. There are several kinds of validity:

- *concurrent validity*. How far the measures obtained by a measuring instrument correlate with those obtained using other instruments which measure the same phenomenon.
- *construct validity*. Whether the 'construct' – that which an instrument is aimed at measuring – is itself theoretically valid in the first place. A critic of **psychoanalysis**, for instance, might challenge the construct validity of a questionnaire for measuring 'anal aggressivity' on the grounds that no such thing existed.
- *ecological validity*. Whether performance on the instrument in question corresponds to performance in the real world, or whether the way a phenomenon is understood or defined for measurement purposes corresponds to its meaning as generally understood. Thus, a purported intelligence test comprised solely of mathematical items would lack ecological validity.
- *external validity*. Whether the conclusions drawn from a piece of research can be generalised as holding beyond the sample used.
- *face validity*. A rather loose term simply referring to whether or not the items on a questionnaire, for example, do appear to be relevant to what it is trying to measure. A question on colour preferences in an intelligence test would therefore lack face validity.
- *internal validity*. Whether a piece of research is designed in such a way that conclusions about causal relationships between variables logically follow from the procedures adopted.

Face validity and internal validity receive most attention but the others are really no less important. Other types include *convergent, predictive, representational*, and *discriminant* validity.

In everyday use, 'valid' is usually a synonym for either 'true' or 'logical' or 'applicable'. The technical senses of the term each, in their various ways, represent more rigorous formulations of the criteria for being valid in one or other of these senses.

VIGILANCE

Sustained **attention**, generally studied by psychologists in Applied Psychology contexts where individuals are required to retain alertness, in monitoring radar screens for example. It thus became the topic of much research on the 'man–machine interface' from the 1940s onwards, especially in military Psychology contexts. In everyday use, it often has moral connotations in official exhortations to the public to be 'vigilant' about terrorism, hospital infections, signs of foot and mouth disease, etc. In Psychological contexts, however, it is quite neutral in this respect. Vigilance tasks are, or have been, frequently used in research on **fatigue**, **attention**, **signal detection theory**, **arousal** and **reversal theory**.

VISUAL ILLUSIONS

Sometimes called optical illusions. Collective term for all those perceptual phenomena characterised by lack of correspondence between what is seen and what is actually there, or in which what is realistically depicted pictorially is impossible. It is usually extended to cases where stable perception is unsustainable, as in the case of ambiguous figures. The exploration of visual illusions has long fascinated psychologists and, before them, physiologists and physicists studying the nature of light. As in other areas, it is often felt that the abnormal can illuminate the normal. The illusion earliest to receive attention was the 'Moon illusion', the fact that the Moon looks larger on the horizon than when higher in the sky. There are now hundreds of examples liberally displayed in Psychology textbooks on perception as well as in art galleries and advertisements. Visual illusions can be generated in many ways, and analysing these provided a major route for advances in the understanding of the visual system from the mid-nineteenth century onwards. The following lists a few of these:

- *Contrast effects.* A light square on a dark background looks lighter than an adjacent square of the same lightness on a lighter background.
- *Cue ambiguity.* Best known from the Necker cube and face/vase examples. In these cases, insufficient cues are available to stabilise the image, either in terms of perspective (which is front, which back) or figure–ground distinction.
- *Cue distortion.* The 'Ames Room' is a very well-known example. An appropriately distorted room is constructed which, when seen from one viewing point, looks to be conventionally rectangular with an even-heighted ceiling, the illusion can then be created that a person standing in one far corner is gigantic alongside someone of normal height.
- *Processing effects.* A number of illusions such as the Müller-Lyer, vertical-horizontal and Moon illusions, appear to originate at the

level of neurological processing of visual data. It is impossible to over-ride them, even with intense practice, and they appear to be culturally universal (though that has been contested in the case of the Müller-Lyer).

- *Radiation effects.* Caused purely physiologically due to some kind of 'radiation' of neural responses in the retina, e.g. the appearance of grey fuzzy spots at the intersections of a grid of black squares on a white background.

In general, visual cues which are read as signifying distance, size and object structure can be juggled in numerous ways to create 'impossible figures', illusions of size difference and the like. Experimentally, visual illusions have always played a central part in research into the psychology and physiology of perception, and the list of standard illusions is now very lengthy. They have also been considered relevant in the context of the **representationalism** debate.

References and further reading

Coren, S. and Girgus, J.S. (1978) *Seeing is Deceiving: The Psychology of Visual Illusions*, Hillsdale, NJ: Lawrence Erlbaum.

Robinson, J.O. (1972) *The Psychology of Visual Illusion*, London: Hutchinson.

Ross, H. and Plug, C. (2002) *The Moon Illusion: Exploring Size Perception*, Oxford: Oxford University Press.

Wade, N. (1982) *The Art and Science of Visual Illusions*, London: Routledge and Kegan Paul.

VISUAL SEARCH

Experimental procedure in which the participant has to identify a specific visual stimulus embedded in a set of distracting stimuli. In practice, this usually involves manipulating the relationship between a target stimulus and distracting stimuli. Commonly used in **Cognitive Psychology**, particularly in relation to the cognitive processes involved in **attention**. The two prevailing theories which have emerged are Feature Integration Theory, the leading advocate of which is Treisman (Treisman and Gelade, 1980), and Guided Search Theory proposed by Wolfe (Wolfe, 1994). The former involves a two-stage process, beginning with **parallel distributed processing** and then moving to serial processing. The latter, basically a further development of this, holds that neither predominates but that the initial phase creates an 'activation map' with varied levels of activation for different features.

References

Treisman, A., and Gelade, G. (1980) 'A Feature-integration Theory of Attention', *Cognitive Psychology*, 12: 97–136.
Wolfe, J. M. (1994) 'Guided Search 2.0: A Revised Model of Visual Search', *Psychonomic Bulletin Review*, 1: 202–38.

WHORFIAN HYPOTHESIS

Also known as the *linguistic relativity hypothesis*. Proposed by American linguist Benjamin Lee Whorf in the 1930s and endorsed by the anthropologist Sapir (hence sometimes called the *Sapir–Whorf hypothesis*), but only became more widely known with the publication of Whorf's writings in 1956. Whorf argued that language has a profound effect on how we think. Such an idea has a long history but for Whorf this was not just a matter of vocabulary (the famous example of the Inuit having a vast number of words for snow is now discredited, by the way, see Pullum, 1991) but, more radically, the nature of grammar or syntax. Using evidence from Native American languages, particularly that of the Zuñi, Whorf showed that languages vary considerably at a grammatical level in how they ascribe agency, how they classify and prioritise phenomena into things as opposed to processes and in numerous other respects. Even in European languages, there are subtle differences in how agency is ascribed, for example, where in English we might say 'He was hit by a car', in German the usual phrase is translatable as 'He got himself hit by a car'. Despite a general consensus that there is at least a grain of truth in the Whorfian hypothesis, its importance has been highly controversial. There is also a paradox in that for the hypothesis itself to be articulated and the evidence presented, at least one language (English obviously) must be able to transcend it. While it was largely disregarded during much of the 1970s and 1980s, it is now being taken seriously again (see Lucy, 1992). Clearly the issue at stake is highly relevant to the tangled topic of the relationship between thought and language.

References and further reading

Lucy, J.A.(1992) *Language Diversity and Thought: A Reformulation of the Linguistic Relativity Hypothesis*. Cambridge: Cambridge University Press.
Pullum, G.K. (1991) *The Great Eskimo Vocabulary Hoax and Other Irreverent Essays on the Study of Language*, Chicago, IL: The University of Chicago Press.
Sapir, E. (1949) *Culture, Language and Personality*, Berkeley, CA: University of California Press.

Whorf, B.L. (1956) *Language, Thought and Reality*, ed. J.B. Carroll, Cambridge, MA: MIT Press.

WILL

Prior to the early twentieth century, the term 'will' was standard in Psychology and Philosophy, often referring to one of the basic human 'faculties'. It was the will which drove us to achieve our aims, to resist distraction, to persist against all odds and so forth, the psychological manifestation almost of our autonomous life-force itself. Alexander Bain entitled one of his two mid-nineteenth-century founding texts *The Emotions and the Will* (Bain, 1859) (the other being *The Senses and the Intellect*), and chapters devoted to it remained routine up to and including William James's great *The Principles of Psychology* (James, 1890). Although remaining in everyday use in expressions such as 'will power' it then oddly began to disappear from scientific Psychological texts. As Danziger (1997) explains, its role was then taken over by **motivation** and **drive**. The detailed reasons for this are too complex to enter into here but centre on Psychology's shift of focus from the internal structure and processes of the mind to our behavioural engagements with the environment (e.g. in **behaviourism**) and how these might be managed. It thus became necessary to try and analyse people's 'motives' for behaving as they did and in Applied Psychology the requirement was to then identify the factors which 'motivated' them. The idea of 'the will' as a unitary internal agency could not serve this purpose.

References

Bain, A. (1859) *The Emotions and the Will*, London: Longmans, Green.
Danziger, K. (1997) *Naming the Mind: How Psychology Found Its Language*, London: Sage.
James, W. (1890) *The Principles of Psychology*, New York: Holt.

WORD ASSOCIATION

The first important experimental work on word association was published by C.G. Jung in a German-language journal in 1905. In the word association technique, individuals are presented with a series of words, to each of which they must respond as quickly as possible with another word (or, less usually, phrase). The two variables in play are thus: (1) the actual response; and (2) the time taken to respond. Jung believed this provided a quick procedure for identifying unconscious *complexes* (see under **Analytical Psychology**), these being indicated by words for which the response time was unusually long and/or the response itself was unusual. The *Word Association Test* was further developed and standardised by G.H. Kent and A.J. Rosanoff in 1910 (Kent and Rosanoff, 1910), and found widespread applications beyond Jung's own theories. Norms of association were established, thus 'Black–White' would be very frequent, but 'Black–Carrot' would be somewhat bizarre. Versions are still widely used for diagnostic purposes but also in the study of creativity and personality. Jung's original work in English translation is included as 'Studies in Word Association' in Volume 2 of *The Collected Works of C.G. Jung* published by Routledge and Kegan Paul.

Reference and further reading

Jung, C.G. (1973) *The Collected Works of C.G. Jung*, Vol. 2, London: Routledge & Kegan Paul.
Kent, G.H. and Rosanoff, A.J. (1910) 'A Study of Association', *American Journal of Insanity*, 6: 37–96, 317–90.

ZEIGARNIK EFFECT

Unfinished tasks are better remembered than those completed. An unsolved crossword clue, for example, may linger in the mind for days, while the rest of the answers are quite forgotten. Named after Zeigarnik, psychologist who discovered it in 1927 (Zeigarnik 1927). Usually discussed in the context of the *Gestalt theory* concept of 'closure'.

Reference

Zeigarnik, B.V. (1967) 'On Finished and Unfinished Tasks', in W.D. Ellis (ed.) *A Sourcebook of Gestalt Psychology*, New York: Humanities Press.

ZONE OF PROXIMAL DEVELOPMENT (ZPD)

Russian psychologist Vygotsky (1896–1934) understood child development as a sociocultural process as well as an individual one, and is widely seen as contrasting in this respect with Piaget (see **Piagetian theory**). His work only became available in English during the 1960s.

One aspect of his position is that he saw there as being a region between what a child can do unaided and what it can do with help from others. This region he called the Zone of Proximal Development (ZPD). Successful education involves working within the ZPD. Educators (whether teachers or simply the child's companions) provide *scaffolding* in various forms, from arousing the child's interest and simplifying the task to giving them feedback on how they are doing, which enables them to progress from their current state of knowledge, skill or understanding. Scaffolding nevertheless has to remain linked to this existing state. The full range of Vygotsky's rich and original writings yet awaits translation into English, a 'Collected Works' still being in progress.

References and further reading

Vygotsky, L.S. (1978) *Mind in Society: The Development of Higher Psychological Processes*, Cambridge, MA: Harvard University Press.

Wertsch, J.V. (1985) *Vygotsky and the Social Formation of Mind*, Cambridge, MA: Harvard University Press.

Index

The Index does not include main entries.